THE Qi OF THE Scalpel

Vignettes: Recollections: Ruminations: Discussion
A Surgical Career

FRANK SEINSHEIMER III, M.D.

ACKNOWLEDGEMENTS

I wish to thank my wife and family for their love, strength and support these many years. Thanks are also due to the many teachers and mentors who helped, supported and guided me throughout my training. I need not mention them individually here. They are named and lauded within this book. To the extent that I learned and became a competent physician and surgeon I assign to them most of the credit. To the extent I failed to reach my potential, I shoulder all of the blame. A further call out to my wife, Lynne. Our 50+ years of living and loving together and our 37 ½-year partnership providing hand surgery and hand therapy have been special and precious. Few are as lucky as I have been. Thanks also to Steve Leighton, an old Yale friend, Robin Khan, a fellow classmate in a memoir writing class at the Writing Center in Bethesda, Maryland and again to my wife for their thoughtful criticism and suggestions.

Personal Mottos

- Learn from everyone
- Question everything
- Decide for yourself
- Become your own teacher

- If you practice the impossible, the difficult becomes easier

THE AUTHOR

Frank Seinsheimer III, M.D., is a graduate of Walnut Hills High School, Yale University and Harvard Medical School. He trained in General Surgery at Peter Bent Brigham Hospital, in Orthopedic Surgery at the Harvard Combined Orthopedic Residency Program at Massachusetts General Hospital, and in Hand Surgery at Thomas Jefferson University Hospital. He spent 37 ½ years in the private practice of orthopedic surgery and hand surgery in Montgomery County, Maryland. For those 37 ½ years he and his wife, Lynne, worked in partnership caring for hand surgery patients. Frank Seinsheimer III has trained for many years in martial arts and holds black belts in Tae Kwon Do, Aikido and Jujitsu. He has written three books; one, *Unarmed Defense Against Weapons*, is a real-world approach to defense against weapon attacks and multiple person attacks. With approximately 150 pages of text and over 600 photographs, this book offers comprehensive coverage of the subject.

His second book, *Poetical Commentary*, contains his commentary on life, the universe and everything. He considers himself more a commentator and less a poet. It seems just chance that his commentary is poetical. This book, *The Qi of the Scalpel*, details his medical and surgical career with commentary, insights and discussion.

TABLE OF CONTENTS

PART ONE
Introduction to The Qi of the Scalpel

CHAPTER ONE

PART TWO
Chronology: My Medical, General Surgical,
Orthopedic and Hand Surgical Training

CHAPTER TWO

CHAPTER THREE

CHAPTER FOUR

PART THREE
A Cornucopia of Vignettes

CHAPTER ELEVEN
The Art, The Science, The Thrill, The Confusion of the Practice of

PART FOUR
Beyond the Memoir

A Discussion of Some Common and Rare Diagnoses

AUTHOR'S NOTE

Who am I writing this book for? I have attempted to write this book for the non-medical public. I have tried to discuss and describe everything in language intelligible to all. I attempt to explain medical jargon when it creeps into my accounts. Although at times I may get too technical, I have endeavored to write so that a layperson can fully understand what I am discussing. Certainly, I expect this book to be interesting to pre-medical students, medical students, interns, residents and practicing physicians. As the result of my training much of my discussion centers on general surgery, orthopedic surgery and hand surgery. I expect this book to speak clearly to them. The practice of medicine and surgery is filled with innumerable traps and pitfalls. I have endeavored to highlight and discuss the many traps and pitfalls I found in my years of training and practice. A discussion of these alone should make this book worth reading for physicians, physicians in training and premedical students.

PREFACE

You are on your way to an appointment with a doctor for either a routine checkup or for the diagnosis and treatment of some symptoms you are having. What do you know about this doctor? How old is she? What training did he have? Does she have a pleasant personality? Is he any good? Usually, we pick a doctor through a recommendation from another doctor, a recommendation from a friend, through an internet search or because the physician works at a reputable hospital or institution. The doctor you have been referred to may just be a golfing buddy of the first doctor. Your friend may have been lucky with treatment from her doctor or may not have good judgement. Information obtained from the internet may be false and manipulated. Top-rated medical centers employ the occasional really mediocre doctor. Unfortunately, you are having symptoms. You have no choice. You have to pick someone.

What follows in this book is a series of vignettes, thoughts, ruminations and discussions of one surgeon's experience with the training and practice of surgery. The clinical part of surgical and medical training is apprentice-like. There is remarkable randomness in that we learn from whichever patients happenstance sends our way. We also learn from the relatively small number of supervising physicians in our training. Each doctor has had a widely varied mix of teachers and a wildly varied mix of patients. Yes, we all have seen numerous common problems. However, rare problems, because they are rare, only appear rarely. The randomness of the appearance of unusual cases markedly changes the experiences of each individual doctor, both in training and in practice. Each doctor has a distinct personality and intellect she or he brings to the training and practice of medicine or surgery. Each trainee's specific personality critically intersects with the experiences and flow of information in surgical and medical training in determining the training obtained, the information imparted and the lessons learned. No two doctors are alike.

The vignettes, the stories, the experiences I relate will demonstrate the breadth and the idiosyncratic nature of medical and surgical training and practice as seen through my eyes. I have no way of knowing whether my experiences in medical school, general surgical training, orthopedic surgical training, hand surgical training and thirty-seven and one-half years of orthopedic and hand surgical practice are average, duller than average or extraordinary. Looking back, I find them astounding.

I still remember with awe the first time I walked through a door labelled, "No Admittance. Authorized Personnel Only," realizing that I was now "Authorized Personnel." I never lost my childlike awe and wonder at the who I was able to become and the what I was allowed to do. I hope my vignettes, my remembrances, my thoughts and my discussions are able to transmit to you a sense of what I have lived through. In relating this information to you, I hope to impart a sense of what the training and life of one surgeon entailed. I hope to impart some of the ethical dilemmas which are inherent in the training and practice of medicine and surgery. I also hope to impart to you a sense of "The Good, The Bad and The Ugly" which occur in the practice of medicine and surgery.

For the purposes of patient confidentiality, ages have been changed, parts of the body have been changed, institutions have been changed, sexes have been changed. I have kept the core and meaning of my experiences as genuine as possible. If you, a patient, think you recognize yourself in reading this, I doubt you are right. But if you do, I also doubt anyone else will recognize you.

As I look back over my time spent writing this book, I feel as if my conscious awareness existed within a pinball machine of memories. I found myself bouncing from the lighted bumper of one memory onto the lighted bumper of another memory. I found no way to predict the direction in which my memories would next ricochet. As I opened my mind to access my past experiences, I found a continuing stream of random remembrances popping into my consciousness without control. I have attempted to provide some chronological organization to this memoir. However, many of the vignettes I describe and discuss do not easily fit into a chronological framework. For these vignettes, I could not find a way to organize these memories in any meaningful way. I have allowed the randomness of the pinball machine to determine the order in which I discuss many of my varied vignettes.

I start this book with a series of striking and intriguing experiences. I then follow with a chronological discussion of details of my training. I move on to the presentation of multiple vignettes which were difficult to corral and sort. Lastly, I present discussion of the diagnosis and treatment of some common and some rare problems.

This opuscule is a hodgepodge of reminiscences, thoughts, ideas and experiences within the awe and wonder of my many years of training and practice in the art and science of medicine and surgery. As stated above, I have wrestled and struggled to try to bring some order and organization to my memories with limited success. You will find I jump back and forth, here and there as my ideas, thoughts and whimsy pushed and pulled me hither and yon. Enjoy the ride. It was beyond my control.

PART ONE

Introduction to The Qi of the Scalpel

Qi: The force that makes up and binds together all things in the universe; the vital life force that flows through the body.

CHAPTER ONE

Saving Lives or Not; Life on the Front Line

- My First POGARF
- "You Can't Shoot Me"
- First Day of Internal Medicine Clinical Training
- The Unconscious Protocol

My First POGARF

Five minutes 'til two. Just reached the hospital cafeteria. Just in time for lunch. Closes at two. Three rules for surviving general surgical internship: One, eat whenever you can eat; two, sleep whenever you can sleep; three, repeat. I am working 120 hours a week. Between eating and occasional sleeping, I care for patients and learn. I fill my tray. I sit down. Plastic chair. Formica tabletop. Chipped brown lunch tray. Friday afternoon. A brief chance to catch my breath. Our service is momentarily quiet.

Buzz goes my beeper. There were no cellphones back then. You can never get away. In my orthopedic residency, we had two beepers when on call. Our personal beeper and the "on call" beeper. Kept you from not answering a call and claiming your battery was dead. Back to my general surgery internship. Call the number on my beeper. My senior resident says, "The POGARF we were expecting just arrived on D2."

Off I go. Running down the hall. Leaving lunch behind. Uneaten. Again. Up the stairs. Why stairs? Stairs are faster than elevators, if you're only going up a few flights. Why am I running? What is a POGARF? POGARF was our acronym for "Post-Operative Grief; Acute Renal Failure." Shouldn't objectify patients, I know. Yet, we work as a team. We have to transmit complex information quickly and accurately to each other. What did I learn from my senior resident's few words? The location of the patient. The nature of the patient's problem. The severity of the problem.

A patient may become seriously ill and require surgery or become seriously ill due to complications arising from surgery. Often, this will involve temporarily lowered blood pressure and/or bloodstream infection called septicemia. Both conditions may cause the kidneys to stop functioning, called renal failure. When it happens quickly, it is "acute" as opposed to a long-standing chronic disease. Patients with renal failure suffer a buildup of toxins in their blood and dangerous alterations in their electrolytes.

These severely ill patients are often referred to our teaching center (the Peter Bent Brigham Hospital, now merged into The Brigham and Women's Hospital; it was affectionately referred to by those of us who worked there back then, as "The Bent Peter") for further evaluation and treatment. The most common time for receiving these referrals was Friday afternoon, when continued intensive care at a community hospital over the weekend was difficult. Or was it because the original surgeon wanted a trouble-free weekend? A definite maybe.

Up the stairs. Around the corner. See the head nurse. There lies our (MY) new patient on a gurney, not yet transferred to a bed.

Why do I say "MY" new patient? I am working every other night on call. On call, all day and all night, Monday, Wednesday, Saturday, Sunday, Tuesday, Thursday, Friday. Each week I am on call two nights in a row. If I am lucky, I get two to three hours of sleep each night on call. If I am really lucky, four to five hours. Some nights—no sleep. I work steadily right through the day and night, missing occasional meals. I keep vanilla-flavored Carnation Instant Breakfast in my operating room locker and mix it in the small paper coffee cups with milk which is there for the coffee. That fills in for the missed meals. This on-call cycle repeats every two weeks. I do this for two years of general surgical training.

Back to the POGARF. This is "MY" patient because I am there, in the hospital, taking care of him or her, almost all the time. This is Friday afternoon. I had a few hours of sleep the night before. As I reach the bedside, two other physicians arrive at the same time—the head of respiratory care and his fellow. A fellow is a doctor in advanced subspecialty training.

Our patient is awake and talking. Stringy unwashed hair. Sallow complexion. Quiet. Worried. A quick check of her abdomen shows an open wound. Put on sterile gloves, gently put my hand into the open wound and palpate several open bowel lumens. Things have really come apart inside. I can tell that her previous surgery was weeks ago due to the amount of scarring. I draw blood and send it to the lab STAT. "STAT" means really, really, fast, like right now— as soon as possible. We need information quickly. POGARFs are seriously ill.

We three physicians have been at the bedside for no more than five minutes talking to the patient and examining her when she suddenly gasps, shakes a bit and arrests. Lying there. Motionless. Unconscious. Not breathing. Heart stopped.

Five seconds to recognize the arrest and call for the crash cart. I leap up onto the gurney, straddle the patient and start cardiac compression. The respiratory physicians intubate her quickly. Intubate means place a breathing tube into the trachea for control of the airway. Seemingly out of nowhere, like "apparating" in a Harry Potter novel, nurses arrive to assist. Paddles on. Step back. Shock. Check EKG. No response. More chest compression. Again. Paddles on. Step back. Shock. No response. Again. And again. And again. Continue cardiac compression. Continue administration of oxygen through the endotracheal tube. Continue breathing for the patient with an Ambu (breathing) bag. Adrenaline injected directly into the heart. Insert a long needle just under the breastbone, 45 degrees inward and up, 45 degrees to my right to hit the heart. For 25 minutes we do everything we know how to do and administer all the medicines we know how to administer. No success. No working heart rhythm.

Twenty-five minutes have passed. Pupils have remained normal size, indicating her brain continues to get enough oxygen. When the brain is starved of oxygen and dies, the pupils become fixed and dilated. Normal size pupils means we are maintaining blood and oxygen supply to the brain, temporarily at least, with the oxygen and the cardiac compression. We take turns performing the cardiac compression. Cardiac compression is rapidly tiring.

Then the labs come back. Fortunately for us and for the patient, STAT meant STAT down in the lab. They worked quickly. Potassium level 6.4. High! Way too high! High potassium levels prevent cell membranes from working properly, which prevents the heart from beating properly, or in this case from beating at all.

We inject insulin by vein. When insulin is taken up by cells, it causes the cells to take up potassium as well, thereby causing the potassium levels in the blood to drop. With a little luck, this will help the cell membranes work better. Paddles on. One more time. Step back. One more time. Shock. One more time. Successful cardioversion. Heart starts to beat normally. Patient wakes up. A "save!" There aren't many like that. This was the longest arrest I ever participated in with a good result.

What went right? Immediate attention when the patient arrived in our hospital. The luck that three trained physicians were at the bedside at the exact moment the arrest occurred. Knowing that time was of the essence. Drawing and sending off the blood for testing immediately before the arrest. A crash cart with all of the equipment and medicines we needed nearby. Well-trained and experienced nurses immediately available to assist. And, as always, luck. What could have gone wrong? Delay in any of these things. Delay in transferring the patient to a tertiary care center. In this case, minutes literally mattered. A patient able to tolerate the stress of this illness, the stress from the complications of surgery, the stress of the arrest, and the stress of the resuscitation were all also necessary for success.

Many of you have seen an accurate portrayal of a cardiac arrest resuscitation, such as I have described above. Most movie portrayals of medical topics are needlessly artificial. I have read that in the filming of the movie "E.T.," Steven Spielberg recruited emergency room physicians from the Los Angeles County Hospital for the resuscitation scene. The article I read stated that Spielberg dressed these doctors up in the white containment suits and did not give them a script. He simply told them to do a normal resuscitation. When I watched the movie, I was astounded to hear realistic dosages of actual medicines uttered by the "actors." The "acting" of the "actors" was realistic. When they stepped back just before the cardioversion shock was administered, their "acting" was surprisingly "normal."

"You Can't Shoot Me"

Another vignette. Another night. "Patient-to-be," let's call him, is in a bar half a block from the hospital. Why do I mention the half block? That will become clear as I tell the story. Mr. "Patient-to-be" gets into an argument with someone. That someone pulls a gun and points the gun at "Patient-to-be." "Patient-to-be" yells, "You can't shoot me!" The man on the other side of the argument proves him wrong. He pulls the trigger. The bullet enters the wide-open mouth of "Patient-to-be," missing his teeth and exiting the side of the throat. Excellent marksmanship!

Massive bleeding from the outside of his neck and from the inside of his throat ensues. Here is where that half block becomes important. Four friends pick him up and run with him directly to the emergency room without waiting for an ambulance. Our team is on call. We all simultaneously hear the overhead page calling us STAT to the ER. We all arrive minutes later.

Patient is lying on a gurney. Young man. Early twenties. Dark hair. Eyes darting around scared and confused. Blood-soaked clothes partially cut off. Spewing blood from his mouth. Conscious. Because he is conscious, he has been able to keep himself from drowning in the massive bleeding occurring inside of his throat. No obtainable blood pressure. Our chief resident decides to rush him to the operating room (OR) without any further evaluation. Mad dash down the halls pushing the gurney full speed. Into the OR. Senior anesthesia resident, fortunately a good one, gets an endotracheal tube into the trachea on the first attempt. This is no small feat, given the massive bleeding inside the throat. Slosh surgical prep on neck. No time for a timed formal prep. Throw on a few drapes. Incision along the neck. Find the carotid artery and jugular vein. Dime-sized holes in both. Clamp the carotid artery and jugular vein on both sides of the holes to stop the bleeding.

Pause. Stop operating. Why? Bleeding is controlled. Now we wait for blood from the blood bank. Type and cross multiple units. Multiple transfusions. Wait for the blood pressure to come up, wait for the patient to stabilize, and hope the brain has enough blood supply from the other side of the brain to keep the side we are operating on alive. Repair holes in the carotid artery and jugular vein and sew up the skin.

Patient awakens in the recovery room, now called the post-anesthesia care unit, or PACU. Why do we keep having to rename things? Anyway, patient awakens in the post-anesthesia care unit yelling, "Who shot me? Who shot me?" Then he turns to me and whispers, "I know who shot me and I'm gonna get him!" Then back to shouting, "Who shot me? Who shot me?" Leaves the hospital in two days with full recovery, except for a sutured incision on the side of his neck.

These are the heroic cases which make you feel good. Yet luck, both good and bad, are ever present. If the patient had been in a bar a block away, or a mile away, he would have died. One more thought about this case. As I was sitting in the recovery room writing the post-operative notes and orders for this patient, I checked to see if he needed a tetanus shot. Part of the trauma protocol. I note that while in the emergency room, a nurse gave him a tetanus shot and wrote it down to record it.

Imagine the scene, please. Let's let Steven Spielberg direct it. Carried by four inebriated men with bloody footprints, this patient is rushed into the waiting room of the emergency room. Blood is spurting from his mouth and the side of his neck. He is rushed to the trauma room. Imagine the controlled chaos in the trauma room with the emergency room residents making the initial assessment, starting IVs, calling for the surgical team STAT. The surgical team arrives in moments, takes one look, grabs the patient without any concern for proper "transfer paperwork," and then makes the mad dash to the operating room. Amid this tense and chaotic scene, one nurse, a really good nurse, I should add, quietly gives him a tetanus shot as part of the trauma protocol and even records it. I think I was as surprised—or more surprised—by that than by anything else that happened with this patient. What worked here? Luck, of course. But also protocols, training, excellent nurses, good equipment and again, luck.

First Day Internal Medicine Clinical Training

So, what was your first day of internal medicine clinical training like? Early in my third year of medical school, for my first clinical rotation, I was assigned to the emergency room. A young teenager was sitting cross-legged on a stretcher which had bars and a cage around her; she was shaking the cage and yelling, "It's a bummer. It's a bummer. It's a bummer." Hour…after hour…after hour. Bad LSD trip. She was in the cage for her protection. Sometimes, the best treatment is to do nothing and wait. She did not need sedation. She did need to be "caged" for her own protection. Eventually, she slept it off and was discharged home. Epiphany. You do not have to "treat" everything. Sometimes your only treatment is to protect patients from themselves.

This first day of my internal medicine clinical training at the beginning of my third year of medical school was July 1. Why is this date important? I will explain later. A man walked into the emergency room waiting area. He walked up to the reception desk. He said, "I think I am going to have a seizure." Then he promptly fell down on to the floor and began having the typical jerking motions of grand mal seizures.

We are called by the front desk. Who are we? Senior medical resident, which meant about three to four years of clinical training beyond medical school; a junior medical resident, which meant two to three years of clinical training beyond medical school; a medical intern, which meant first day out of medical school; and me, my first day of third year of medical school and my first day of clinical training. We rushed the man into the STAT room with all the equipment for emergencies.

Fortyish year-old man. Good nutrition. Well dressed. Constantly jerking arms and legs with tonic clonic movements. First—cut off his clothes with big scissors. This is important to look for injuries and to urgently gain access to his veins for injecting intravenous anti-seizure medications. We pump in the anti-seizure meds. He continued to seize. This is life on the frontlines. We are saving lives!

Oh, one other thing we do. Part of protocol. Again, I mention protocol. Just like airplane pilots have checklists to review before takeoff, we have the equivalent approach to clinical situations, like I mentioned above. We obtained his name from his wallet and sent for his old chart. You can never have too much information about a patient. Our patient continued to seize. We continued to pump in anti-seizure meds. This was clearly an unusual, difficult and thrilling case. Still on the frontlines, still saving lives! His chart finally comes up from medical records. Stamped across the front of the chart in big red letters is the word "Munchausen."

Munchausen syndrome is a psychiatric syndrome in which patients obtain positive feelings by faking illness and being treated for the faked illness. Why July 1? Our patient was "experienced." He knew that the resident staff changed completely on July 1. He knew that every resident doctor would be new. No one would know him. An experienced and, shall we say, professional Munchausen patient, and on my first day of clinical in hospital training.

So we stopped treatment. The senior resident told him we were stopping treatment and that he, the patient, should get up and go home. He opened his eyes and then expressed anger that we had destroyed his clothes when we cut them off. Lessons learned. Lessons learned quickly. Not everyone needs treatment. Not everyone can be treated. Diagnosis can be difficult. Patients do not always tell the truth. Medicine is complicated.

Another thought. I did not think of this until editing this book and marveling at my many memories. The letters of the Munchausen stamp were even and clearly came from a single stamp. That suggests that there was sufficient need for this stamp that the record room had ordered one and kept it for use.

I later learned that this patient was a legend. One story told of his attempt to get admitted to the Massachusetts General Hospital. He was recognized by the resident covering the triage desk. He was told by the triage resident that there was nothing he, the patient, could do to get himself admitted to that hospital. Wrong! Wrong! Wrong! The legend continued. This patient went out in front of the hospital and threw himself in front of a moving car. He was admitted to the hospital with a broken leg. "Showed that resident! Hah!" Some patients cannot be helped. A rare diagnosis. Rather, only rare patients suffer from this diagnosis. Even when recognized, they do not respond well to attempted behavioral treatment.

Some years later, I treated another Munchausen patient, who ground feces into his foot causing a severe infection. I operated to drain the resulting abscess. A central line—an intravenous line in front of his chest going directly into one of the large veins, which drains directly into his heart—was placed for the administration of broad-spectrum antibiotics. After a few days, when he was feeling better, the patient hobbled out of the hospital in his hospital gown with the central line in place—needless to say, against medical advice. As he was getting into a taxi, one of our great nurses tried to reach him and remove the central line. She failed. Off our Munchausen patient went with a central line in place. I never heard of or from him again. I get shivers thinking of a Munchausen patient, outside of the hospital, with a central line in place.

Back to my first twenty-four hours of internal medicine clinical training in the emergency room. A man came to the ER complaining of severe chest pain. Clearly a heart attack. Rushed him into the STAT room. Fifty-plus-year-old man lying quietly on the stretcher scarcely moving. Shallow rapid breathing. Blood pressure was low indicating a significant amount of damage to the heart muscle. The heart was not strong enough to push out a sufficient amount of blood with each beat to maintain the blood pressure.

We administered cardiogenic medicines, that is, medicines that help the heart beat stronger. When I say "we," I mean the residents administered the medicines while I watched. The patient's blood pressure returned to normal. Once again, I feel I am on the frontlines, saving lives. Our patient had a large family. They were allowed to see him briefly, but only briefly. His blood pressure trended downward. We increased the dose of cardiogenic medicines and his blood pressure came back up. This happened several times. Clearly, we have the medicines. Clearly, we were saving this patient. Again, his blood pressure sank. Again, we increased the medicines. This treatment course continued over three hours. Suddenly, the patient tensed his muscles and arrested. Our attempt at resuscitation fails.

Here is what was happening, which I did not understand. The first drop in blood pressure following the heart attack is called cardiogenic shock. This means the heart is not strong enough to keep the patient alive. The short-term survival for cardiogenic shock at that time was under twenty percent. I did not know this. After an hour or so, we had reached maximum dosages of medications and his blood pressure was still falling. A clear sign of impending death. I did not understand this. Thus, my learning curve—my really steep learning curve. The short-term survival probability in this situation approached zero. I did not know this.

I was shocked when he died. Really shocked. Stunned. By **my** loss or rather our loss. It was **my** first loss. I did not realize what was happening. The intern took me aside and explained how the practice of medicine has clear limits. We do not win them all. Important lesson. One of many, I was rapidly learning.

Another lesson I learned. Think of the family, not just the patient. When it was clear we were failing in our treatment, and it was clear that his death was imminent, we, the treating physicians, failed to allow his family back in to spend time with him, while he was still conscious. We failed in forgetting the family. We failed in not allowing the family a chance to say their final goodbyes.

When the patient arrested, why did our attempt at resuscitation fail? We were already at maximum treatment. If a patient under maximum active treatment arrests, you aren't going to succeed with your resuscitation. I was introduced to the shorthand phrase that succinctly teaches this, "If you can't keep them alive when they're alive, you can't keep them alive when they're dead." As I mentioned before, I don't like these objectifying sayings. But they do teach a point and offer some emotional distancing, which is necessary, when you fail in these stressful situations.

The Unconscious Protocol

Later in my training, I worked in emergency rooms, moonlighting to earn extra money. This was a time before there was the specialty of emergency room physician. One night a man was rushed in by ambulance, unconscious, with his arms held rigidly straight and internally rotated. This is called decerebrate posturing and "always" means there has been severe damage to the brain, often due to a massive stroke. With no history of injury, this patient clearly was suffering a severe stroke (loss of blood supply to a portion of the brain and/or severe bleeding into the brain). With the severity of the stroke, there was really nothing to do. Yet! Somehow! Fortunately! I remembered "protocol." You will find I mention protocol frequently.

I said to myself, "The patient is unconscious." So, I initiated the "unconscious patient" protocol. This includes drawing blood for blood sugar level and injecting D50W intravenously. D50W is a concentrated sugar solution. Patients with severe hypoglycemia (low blood sugar) can present to emergency rooms unconscious. This "unconscious patient" protocol prevents a physician from failing to diagnose a patient with severe hypoglycemia. Failure to recognize severe hypoglycemia can result in a patient dying, rather than being saved. By following this protocol, I was simply following rote instructions, not expecting anything to change. Twenty seconds after injecting the D50W, my patient woke up and was immediately "normal." His blood sugar level came back from the lab at 46. Severely low! Normal fasting levels are 90 to 100.

I staggered over to a corner and sat down, gasping with relief that I had not missed this diagnosis. It would have been so easy to miss. I have told the story of this unusual presentation of hypoglycemia to numerous internists and emergency room physicians. None has seen it. I do not know if further workup disclosed intracranial pathology.

I have chosen these few vignettes for this introductory chapter to demonstrate the remarkable randomness and occasional intensity of medical training and practice. I wish to emphasize the apprentice-like nature of medical and surgical training. We truly learn from whichever patients come our way.

PART TWO

Chronology: My Medical, General Surgical, Orthopedic and Hand Surgical Training

CHAPTER TWO

Some Early Medical School Experiences

- First Day Medical School Clinic
- First Physical Diagnosis Patient
- Reactive Hypoglycemia
- Introduction to the Clinic: Dr. Godwin
- Dog Lab: Introduction to Surgery and Sterile Technique

First Day Medical School Clinic

So, what was the first day of medical school like? First day of medical school we, green, unknowing medical students attended a demonstration clinic. The stated purpose of this clinic was to demonstrate the breadth of the practice of medicine and surgery by presenting unusual and intriguing patients. Three patients were presented. In the first presentation, a man was swimming in his swimming pool alone. He woke up lying on the bottom of the swimming pool. He managed to swim up to the surface and climb out of the pool on his own.

Medical workup disclosed a problem called intermittent heart block. The heart normally receives timed electrical signals through an anatomic electrical pathway. These electrical signals originate in a specific area of the atrium, which is near the top of the heart. In heart block, the signals fail to get through, and no signal reaches the rest of the heart to stimulate it to contract and beat. The brain needs a large volume of blood flow and oxygen to function. When the heart stops beating, loss of consciousness occurs quickly. Sometimes the heart stops long enough for death to occur. Sometimes the stoppage is transient. In this patient, he was probably unconscious for less than a minute, just enough time to sink to the bottom of the pool. When the heart started beating again, there was enough oxygen in his blood and lungs to pump oxygen to his brain. This allowed him to regain consciousness quickly. He then was able to swim to the surface and get out of the pool.

Our bodies do not have sensors to warn us if our blood has a low oxygen level. Evolution developed the urge to breathe by having sensors in our body measure carbon dioxide levels. If you hold your breath, the urge to breathe comes from increasing levels of carbon dioxide in your blood. It is dangerous to hyperventilate and then try to swim long distances underwater. The reason: the hyperventilation blows off a lot of carbon dioxide. You can run out of oxygen before the buildup of carbon dioxide warns you to surface to breathe. With a lack of oxygen, you can black out without warning. This is also the reason you are instructed to put an oxygen mask on yourself before your child in an airplane that has lost cabin pressure. This prevents you from blacking out and being unable to help a child traveling with you.

There are many other types of abnormal heart rhythms. When the electrical signaling system has a circular aberrant pathway, an irregular rhythm occurs called atrial fibrillation. A common problem. Treatment may include shocks to try to correct the abnormal rhythm, medicine to control the frequency of the abnormal beats and blood thinners to decrease the risk of stroke from blood clots travelling from the heart to the brain.

The terminology of abnormal heart rhythms has always fascinated me. Normally we have a regular rhythm. Beat, pause, beat, pause, beat, pause, beat. There are regular, irregular rhythms. Here is an example: beat, pause, beat, long pause, beat, pause, beat, long pause, beat, pause, beat, long pause, etc. The rhythm of atrial fibrillation is called irregular, irregular. The rhythm never repeats. Here is an example: beat, short pause, beat, long pause, beat, short pause, beat short pause, beat, very long pause, etc. There is no pattern to this rhythm.

Back to the first clinical presentation at medical school. The second patient was swimming when a motorboat ran over him causing multiple deep lacerations to his leg. He was helicoptered from the shore to the hospital. There was discussion regarding the emergency medical technician care, the system for transporting seriously ill patients to a hospital quickly, the concept of triage and the protocols for the care of seriously injured patients.

The last patient had undergone extensive surgery and chemotherapy for cancer. The nature of cancer and the multitude of therapies for cancer were discussed. The surgery required removal of her entire nose. She normally wore a surgical mask to cover the surgical defect. We were encouraged to look into the interior of her sinuses.

These three patients were all extremely grateful for the medical and surgical care they had received. They willingly came to our introductory clinic for their presentations, told their stories and answered our questions. Why have a clinic like this? Clearly our teachers picked patients with stories of high drama and unusual interest. Not a bad way to introduce us to the fact that we were entering a world entirely different from anything we had ever known before.

First Physical Diagnosis Patient

Let's move on to my first experience of a physical examination of a patient. We, a carload of medical students, report to a room at the Massachusetts General Hospital. Our instructor gives each of us a piece of paper with a different patient's name and room number. Our assignment: We are instructed to go to that patient's bed, take a history, examine the patient and report back. We then go as a group to each patient. Each medical student then presents his patient to the group and the instructor. Each medical student then examines the abnormal physical findings of the presented patient. The instructor instructs. This is, hands-on, apprenticeship-type of training. It is not sequential education, like reading a textbook from front to back. It is random and sporadic. We learn from whichever patients happen to come our way. None of us has formally taken a history from a patient or performed a complete physical examination before. Yes, we are clueless.

I go to the ward to find my patient. I use the word ward, not room, on purpose. When I was in training, many patients were placed in wards of about 30 patients. These were large rooms with beds around the sides of the room and nothing but thin hanging curtains that could be pulled around the beds for pretend privacy.

I asked the nurse where my patient was. She pointed to the far-right corner of the ward. The curtains were pulled around that bed. I walked over, opened the curtains and walked in. The patient was on his back, unconscious. Well, I thought, this saves me the trouble of trying to talk to the patient to take a history. I opened our little book of instructions on how to perform a physical diagnosis. I still have that book, "Outline for Patient Study; Department of Medicine; Harvard Medical School; 1967." A little red paperback book, 4 ½ inches by 6 ¾ inches; 43 pages, including 4 pages of accepted definitions.

Back to my first patient in my first clinical physical diagnosis course. I knew where the heart was. I had listened to my heart and my fellow students' hearts. This should be easy, I thought. The heart is, to confirm the obvious, on the left side of the chest. I placed my stethoscope over the left front of this patient's chest and listened; no heartbeat!! I listened; I listened; I listened again; Still no heartbeat!! I moved the stethoscope around a bit. Still no heartbeat!! Oh, those bastards, I thought. They have given me a dead patient as a practical joke. I moved up to my patient's face; he was breathing; so, clearly alive. So, no practical joke. But, no heartbeat, either.

What to do? The question "What to do?" is a question, you will find, I repeat often in this book. I gave up trying to examine his heart. A bit discouraging, you must admit. My first patient and I can't hear the heart! Oh well! I figured, I'll do better when I listen to the heart on my next patient. So, I moved on. The next chapter in the physical diagnosis handbook was the examination of the lungs. I figured, if my heart exam was a failure, I might as well try my hand at the lung exam. The patient was clearly breathing. So, I put my stethoscope over the right side of the patient's chest to listen to the lungs. Surprise! I heard his heartbeat.

Okaaay…I thought. There are rare cases of mirror image reversal of the organs. I figured this was not the case. Never seen a case in my whole career. Really, really rare. I looked up at his neck and noticed that the trachea (the breathing tube that runs from the throat down the front of the neck) was not running straight down the front of the throat. Rather, it veered sharply to the right, as it approached the clavicles (collar bones). I realized that the mediastinum (the contents of the chest) had shifted to the right, because the right lung was collapsed. This patient, unfortunately, had end-stage lung cancer and was in the hospital for terminal care to minimize his suffering. Actually, a perfect, first-patient examination, with dramatic physical findings, while also an early lesson that we don't win them all.

On to my second patient. Several days later. A 654-pound man in the hospital with a bleeding ulcer lying on two hospital beds placed next to each other. First patient in my career I took a history from. He told me that if he did not eat every two hours, he felt like a team of wild horses was stomping in his stomach yelling, "Feed me! Feed me! Feed me!" His words; not mine. My abilities in examining the abdomen did not improve that day. From the side of the bed, I could barely reach the midline of his abdomen. My first introduction into the remarkable breadth of differences in people's lives.

Reactive Hypoglycemia

During one of our drives from our Avenue Louis Pasteur dormitory to the Mass General, one of my classmates became increasingly irritable and verbally combative over a ten-minute period. Then he said, "Oh!", and took out and ate a candy bar. Within a few minutes his behavior became normal. He had early diabetes. This was my first "clinical" experience with the symptoms of reactive hypoglycemia (symptomatic reactive low blood sugar which occurs hours after eating).

Introduction to the Clinic: Dr. Godwin

Toward the end of my second year of medical school, the dean's office at Harvard Medical School announced a significant reordering of the curriculum, called the Core Curriculum. We all joked that the core is the part of the apple you throw away. The dean's office planned to advance the time when medical students entered hospitals to begin their hands-on, clinical training. We were the first class they were planning to move up. This would mean, for our class, that we would be overlapping with the class ahead of us in our first months in the hospitals.

A group of us medical students were concerned this change would dilute the teaching and that we would suffer from an increased student-to-faculty ratio. I was one of a group of students who brought our concerns to the dean. To his credit, he listened. Remember, this was the sixties, with student protests at their height. Normally the medical students were on vacation the summer between second and third year of medical school. For those students who wished, we were allowed to begin our clinical training at the beginning of the summer between second and third year of medical school. I chose to do this. Only a relatively few other students from my class also chose this option. We were assigned to Boston City Hospital for the Introduction to the Clinic course. There were four faculty members assigned to training seven of us.

One faculty member took the first two in alphabetical order, second the next two, third the next two and so on. As the last in the alphabet of the seven, I ended up one on one with an amazing physician, Dr. Herman Godwin. Each day, I was assigned a patient. I performed a detailed history and physical examination and wrote a multiple-page report. I attempted to make a diagnosis and then met, one on one, with my teacher, mentor and proctor, Dr. Godwin.

Let's say my patient was a severe diabetic who had come into the emergency room of the hospital in ketoacidosis. (Ketoacidosis means the blood sugar level is dangerously high.) Insulin was being given in small doses frequently to gradually to safely bring the blood sugar level down to normal. Dr. Godwin suggested I act as if I was leaving for the night and needed to sign off the patient to the resident on call that night and therefore, I should present the 30-second, brief summary containing all the pertinent information that the resident on call would need.

Thus, I might say "Mrs. X is 38 years old with diabetic ketoacidosis. She came into the hospital 18 hours ago with a blood sugar of 432. She is on hourly checks of her blood glucose level and has a sliding scale for insulin written for her. Her blood sugar 10 minutes ago was 243." This is sufficient. If the patient got into trouble in the night, the resident could consult the chart for more details.

I was then instructed to give the two- to three-minute presentation that I might give to a chief resident the morning after an overnight admission. This presentation expanded to include how many years she had been a diabetic, how much difficulty she was having in controlling her diabetes and why. I also added a discussion of her other chronic medical problems.

Then I was instructed to give an expanded presentation that I might give if the patient was being presented at a teaching conference. This included family history, mention of different methods of treatment used in the past and details of all of her other medical problems. In a teaching conference I would present a detailed account to give the attending physician running the conference a lot of material to work with.

For me this was hard. Really hard. I struggled. I had never been asked before to use the same body of information and then organize it and present it in different ways for different reasons. I had no previous experience or training in oral presentation. Over the six weeks of this course, I worked as hard as I have ever worked, not in memorizing facts, but in trying to learn how to function as a resident physician. Those six weeks were some of the most helpful, useful and wonderful training I ever had. I started out extraordinarily frustrated and ended up thrilled at how much I had learned. Yes, I learned medicine. More importantly I learned how to communicate effectively both orally and in writing. I was further fortunate that this experience occurred in a one-on-one format. I received far more individual attention than was routine.

Think about it. Most of us spend much of our lives, both at work and in our personal lives, transmitting information to others and having others transmit information to us. If you take your car in for repair, the better "history" you give, the easier it is for the mechanic to solve the problem. If the problem is difficult, one mechanic needs to be able to explain as clearly as possible what the problem is to another mechanic. The mechanic then later needs to be able to explain clearly to the customer what was found and what was done.

This communication can be oral or written. By this time in my career, I was 24 years old. No one in my entire education had ever emphasized the need to take a body of information and then organize it and present it in different ways, in different periods of time and for different audiences. It seems to me that this type of training should begin early in schooling and continue throughout. There are few jobs that do not require these communication skills. Personal relationships especially require this give and take of information. Even the job of "mime" requires communication skills, just not oral ones.

Communication is integral to our lives. We communicate with family, co-workers, friends and strangers. The better we communicate, the better our lives. Here is one failure to communicate vignette. A patient on one of the orthopedic services died during the night. The resident on call did not want to bother the attending orthopedic surgeon by waking him up to inform him. The resident figured it was OK to wait until the attending came into the hospital in the morning. By chance, the attending entered the hospital through the main lobby the next morning. He saw the family and walked up to them and told them how well their family member was doing. The family told him of the death. Embarrassing? Oh, yes! The problem? Failure of the resident to communicate in a timely manner.

Dog Lab: Introduction to Surgery and Sterile Technique

Yet another vignette. Why must teachers and instructors so often abuse the power of their position? Dog lab; second year of medical school. Before we were allowed into an operating room, we received training by operating on dogs. We needed to learn the basics of sterile technique and the "simple" details of how an operating room operates. Why is this important? One legend we medical students passed around was that a neurosurgeon at Boston City Hospital would not allow any medical students into his operating room. The legend held that once during surgery for excision of a brain tumor, the neurosurgeon moved to the side so that an unscrubbed medical student could see the tumor. The legend held that the student reached forward and touched the tumor with his non-sterile finger.

Back to dog lab. We medical students were divided into groups of four, brought into the instruction room and assigned an operating table. One of my fellow students, who shall remain unnamed here (you know who you are), picked up a large thermometer and inserted it into his mouth. He then cavorted around the room as a joke. The dogs were brought in and step by step, we were told how to prepare our dog for surgery. After anesthesia was induced, we were told to place the thermometer into the dog's rectum to allow measurement of the dog's temperature. My fellow classmate's face turned the most unusual shades of green, purple and gray. The entire room burst out laughing.

There were four dog labs. We were assigned one of four roles: surgeon, assistant surgeon, scrub nurse or anesthesiologist. A different role for each lab. Each table of four students was also assigned a general surgeon as instructor. For the first lab, I was assigned the role of assistant surgeon. Our gruff, general surgeon instructor was right out of central casting.

What is the role of a first assistant in surgery? In real surgery, the first assistant helps the surgeon by allowing the surgeon to see what needs to be seen. The assistant does this by moving retractors to push tissue out of the way and by manipulating tissue to place it where the surgeon can easily reach it. A good first assistant will also be aware of what is going on in the operating room and anticipating what will need to be done in the future. The first assistant will also make suggestions to the surgeon. Often, when I was in practice, I had one of my partners assist in a complicated surgery. While I was concentrating on the difficult dissection, my partner would be strategizing the bigger picture. In this way we complemented each other.

Back to the dog lab. In this artificial situation, our general surgeon instructor told me that as first assistant, I should hold the tissue to display it to the surgeon and freeze. I was not supposed to move at all. I was mesmerized. I had never held living tissue in my hands before. I was moving and feeling the tissue with my fingers. I suppose our general surgery instructor must have told me several times to stop moving my fingers. I suppose I must not have heard him. Suddenly, he started shouting at me to leave the table and leave the room. I and the other three medical students on my team with me looked up in surprise. None of us realized I had done anything that deserved this reaction.

I am reminded of third grade. I am in a reading group of six to eight students arranged in a semicircle in front of our teacher. I am sure I was jabbering away and not paying attention. I am sure Mrs. Maxie had told me to shut up several times. I am sure I did not hear her. I can focus really well and ignore the outside world. Suddenly Mrs. Maxie rears up and hits me on the top of my head with the reading book. One of those thick reading books. I am sure I shut up for a few minutes. I told my parents about it … ten years later. Seemed like no big deal to me at that time. In present times, I suppose, it would be considered child abuse and felonious assault and battery. I think I probably deserved it. Stockholm Syndrome, I suppose. Times and expectations of behavior certainly change over time.

Back to the dog lab. This being the late sixties, laden with protests, I stepped back from the table, but refused to leave the room. Since I wanted the instruction, and could not obtain it any other way, I told the surgeon instructor that I was paying a lot of money for this education and I would not leave the room. After a few minutes he reconsidered and I was allowed to resume my role as first assistant.

The ethics of using the dogs to teach medical students basic surgical and sterile technique skills are complex. In the course of this book, I will visit and revisit issues involving the ethics of medical training. When and in what circumstances should a medical student, intern or resident physician do something for the first time? Sterile technique is a "habit" learned from repetitive doing. You do not learn it from a didactic lecture and memorization. If you are a patient undergoing surgery, do you want a medical student in your operating room who has never practiced sterile technique in a realistic situation before? Is a dog lab the "best" way to teach this? I am not sure. Perhaps using models suffices but models are a giant step away from more realistic training.

CHAPTER THREE
Application to Medical School

The first two chapters of this book give a brief sense of what my life in the trenches of medical and surgical training was like. Let's switch topics and go back in time. What was the application process for medical school like? I did not decide to attend medical school until the summer before my senior year in college. Prior to that decision I planned to attend graduate school in biophysics. The summer before senior year of college I worked at the RISO National Laboratory in Roskilde, Denmark. I began to doubt my career path toward academic laboratory research. I found that I did not enjoy it as much as I expected. I decided to apply to medical school thinking I could still decide to do research later if I changed my mind. I applied to a number of medical schools. I don't recall how many. All of the schools I applied to required "in person" interviews. Most of the questions I was asked in these interviews seemed trite, lame, worthless. It isn't clear to me that the interviews were of much value to the medical schools in determining who to accept. Interviewing is difficult, I think, both for the interviewer and the interviewee.

I recall my interview at Johns Hopkins. The two interviewers noted I had mentioned in my application that I liked helping people. They asked for examples. I found the question insulting and trite. Without taking time to think, I overreacted. I replied stupidly that, "No, I couldn't think of any examples." I could have given them a great example. In Boy Scouts, as patrol leader, I had a deaf scout in my patrol. I worked extra hard teaching him scouting. Discussing my Boy Scouts experiences, especially while I was a patrol leader, would have been a perfect answer. I could also have referenced my experiences as a sailing counselor at a summer camp.

Unfortunately, I overreacted to the question. Back when I was applying to medical school, we did not go through the process of practice interviews. There was no such thing as video, at that time, which would have allowed us to observe ourselves in an interview situation. With experience, I now realize you should wait a beat after each question to formulate your response. I realize that I was too reactive, perhaps my reaction to the stress of the interview. I have more recently spent two hours with public relations advisors. I went through a pretend interview with journalists about the orthopedic group I was work-ing for. I then watched the video together with the PR people critiquing my performance. I was awful. An interesting and educational experience. A skill that can be learned or at least improved upon.

Part of our "education" in high school and college, perhaps even in grade school, should be practice and experience with the interview process. Part of our "education" in school should include preparation for life's known and expected experiences. Applications. Interviews. Writing reports. Public speaking, etc. I had none of that. I remember writing a paper on "destiny" in the play "The Emperor Jones" in high school. Somehow, that seems less valuable, in retrospect, than practice with public speaking and interviews would have been.

Back to medical school applications. I was originally scheduled to have two interviews at Harvard at 2 and 4 p.m. I planned on driving up from New Haven starting at 9 a.m. on the day of the interviews. I figured I would have a leisurely lunch in Boston and then go to the interviews. I received a phone call the afternoon the day before, changing my appointments to 10 a.m. and 2 p.m. Without careful thought, I decided to leave at 7 a.m., not allowing much leeway or extra time. We didn't have Google Maps to estimate driving time then. I drove through Hartford and merged onto the Massachusetts Turnpike. I am making good time, when I see a sign ahead of me, "Albany and Points West." The picture of that highway sign remains crystal clear, deeply engraved in my memory, these many years later. I realize I am going the wrong way. I have been going the wrong way for a while. Panic time. I get to the next exit, which takes ten minutes, and turn around. Now, I think, I am running late and begin to drive east at 80 miles an hour. Within ten minutes, I see the flashing lights and am pulled over by a state trooper. Not a good morning, Frank!

The trooper asks me what the rush is. I tell him I am running late for an interview at Harvard Medical School. He tells me I am not going to make it; to follow him to the station, which I do. At the station, he tells me that they are supposed to book every speeder, which takes two hours, but he is going to let me go, because he doesn't want to hurt my career. I thank him; I drive 55 miles per hour all the way to Harvard. I arrive at the medical school five minutes before 10 a.m. I can't find a place to park. I pull into a parking lot labelled "Faculty Only." I tell the attendant that I am going for an interview and can I please leave my car there. I am prepared to abandon my car and have it towed. The attendant agrees. I walk into the admissions office, one minute before 10 a.m., heart hammering away, and am immediately ushered into Dr. Hermann Blumgart's office. Dr. Blumgart was an internationally renowned cardiologist who had just retired from his cardiology practice and cardiology research and was working as a primary care physician for medical students and doing interviews for the admissions office. His Wikipedia entry describes him as the "father of nuclear medicine" for his work with medical imaging using small amounts of radioactive material.

The interview seemed to go well. I do recall discussing my three grades in the low 70s. We had number grades at Yale then. A grade in the low 70s was the equivalent to a C-minus. These grades were in second year German, a higher-level math course and a higher-level course on comparative economic systems. I recall discussing that I had lost interest in German. I also discussed my realization that taking a higher-level math course after two years without taking any math course was not a good idea. Lastly, I took a comparative economics course taught by Professor Lindblom. I often took courses based on the reputation of the professor as a great teacher. I did not take any introductory economics courses. I called Dr. Lindblom in the spring to ask his permission to take his course. He said, "Yes." This course had two names. One was a political science department name. The other an economics department name. At the first class of the course, Dr. Lindblom emphasized that the economics majors should be signed up with the economics name and the political science majors should sign up with the political science name. The reason: he was planning on giving a different exam to the students, depending on their major.

After the first class, I spoke with Dr. Lindblom and asked him which course name I should use, given that I was biophysics major. He looked at me over the top of his glasses and examined me the way an entomologist might examine an interesting bug. He asked, "How did you get into this course?" I stated that I had called him in the spring and that he had given me permission. He replied with surprise, "I did?" I stayed in the course. A great course. Learned a lot. Received the not unexpected low grade due to my lack of prior economics and political science experience. Professor Lindblom decided to give only one exam for all of the students.

I think that Harvard Medical School accepted 12 students from Yale my year. I was tied with one other student for the lowest grade average of the 12.

Why was I accepted with a lower grade average than other applicants? The most likely explanation: they made a mistake. As noted above, I sometimes took advanced courses without necessarily taking the introductory courses. First semester junior year, I took 6 2/3 courses. At most colleges you take four. At Yale five was normal. The 2/3s was an eight-hour per week science lab. In sophomore year, I took a physics course renowned as the lowest graded course at Yale. We started the first semester with 45 students and ended the semester with 28 students. There was one A, one B, grade 88, (mine), 14 Cs and the rest Ds at the end of the first semester. I also tied for the second highest grade one semester, in organic chemistry. One question on an hourly test asked for the identification of an unknown sugar determined by a list of specific test results. I was the only student who found that there were two possible answers to that question. I was given a grade of 110 on that test. Let me put this grade in perspective. For another hourly test I overslept and reached the test room one half hour late. There were three problems on the test. I could not answer one. In my haste I misread another. I received a grade of 33 on that test.

In his recommendation my premedical advisor at Yale discussed the difficulty with comparing my grade average to that of other students. My pre-med advisor recommended adding six points to my grade average for comparison. The recommendation may have made the difference. Frequently, when the people in institutions have accepted me, I have asked myself the question, "What were they thinking?"

Two years later, I came down with infectious mononucleosis (called mono, for short) and saw Dr. Blumgart again. I asked if he remembered my interview. He said he did. Some people have amazing eidetic memories. I then told him about my morning in the hour or two before the interview. I asked if he had noticed anything. He said no, I seemed calm and collected. Great man. One of the last of the "gentleman" physicians.

Back then Harvard Medical School sent out acceptance notices once a month by hand-delivered telegram. Rumor would spread around the Yale campus that a Western Union telegram messenger was on campus delivering telegrams. I was in my room with three friends when the guard of my residential college called to tell me there was a telegram for me. Telegrams at that time cost a minimum charge for the first ten words, then another charge for each additional word thereafter. The telegram was exactly ten words. "Delighted to report your admission Harvard Medical School. Letter follows."

CHAPTER FOUR

Medical School Didactic Instruction and Clinical Rotations

- Medical School Didactic Instruction
- Internal Medicine Clinical Rotation
- General Surgery Peter Bent Brigham Hospital
- Neurology Clinical Rotation
- Obstetrics and Gynecology Rotation
- Psychiatry Clinical Rotation
- More Clinical Rotation Vignettes
- National Board Exams
- Orthopedic Surgery Clinical Rotation

Medical School Didactic Instruction

The first two years of medical school involved primarily didactic education. Six to eight hours of lecture a day. Book studying the rest of the time. Memorize. Memorize. Memorize. Like learning a new language. My first internal medicine clinical rotation occurred at the beginning of my third year of medical school. I was assigned to the Beth Israel Hospital in Boston. Some of the vignettes I described in the first chapter of this book came from that rotation.

The last two years of medical school education comprised clinical rotations in various specialties of medicine. I did take an elective one-month course in advanced anatomy.

Half of my Harvard Medical School class was composed of the number one pre-med student from their college; the other half were "others." I was in the "others" group. To be the number one pre-med in your college, you had to have that remarkable kind of memory which can easily and quickly imprint any and all useless (useless by my definition, at least) trivia. With such an exceptional eidetic memory, you can answer more obscure questions than anyone else on tests. That is how you get to be the number one pre-med student in your university.

It is the night before our first test, first year of medical school, on hematology. I wander into a dorm room down the hall. Three of the number one pre-med students from prestigious universities were studying together asking each other trivia questions. Tables in the textbook that I had briefly glanced at and decided were unimportant, these guys had memorized. I walked out of the room shaking my head in disbelief.

Throughout our years at medical school, we were tested and graded. Interestingly, the tests did not ask trivia and the grades were not reported to us. If we were doing satisfactorily, we did not hear from the administration. By the end of the first semester, the trivia sessions had ended, because the number one pre-med students realized they were unnecessary. The sense of hypercompetitiveness vanished, because no one knew their grades or relative class standing.

I was fascinated to watch how the testing and grading system at Harvard Medical School dramatically and positively influenced the study behavior of the students. If students were not asked trivia or "gotcha" questions, they stopped studying trivia. If students knew they would be tested on the more important stuff, they spent more time studying the more important stuff. If grades were not reported to the students, the students could not compare class rankings. If the students could not compare class rankings, the hypercompetitiveness died out.

Speaking of class ranking, common knowledge (which is, of course, not always true) was that in reporting class rank to the hospitals, two thirds of our class was reported as being in the top one third and one third as being in the middle third. None was in the bottom third. As I said above, this was "common knowledge" or rumor. I don't know if it was true.

When I was in the first two years of medical school, we had six to eight hours of lecture a day. Listening to lectures is a remarkably inefficient method of learning facts. Lectures are good for explaining difficult concepts, but not for transmitting "facts." A popular term, used constantly by our teachers, was the word "key." As in, here is a "key" concept. Our class reacted to this. Whenever a lecturer used the word "key," the entire class spontaneously began to chant, "it's key; it's key; it's key." It helped to relieve the stress and the boredom of our prolonged sitting.

This being the sixties with the intensity of protest, our class decided spontaneously that we did not like the use of brand names of medications. Whenever a lecturer used a brand name, the lecture hall echoed with boos. I remember one guest lecturer used a brand name medicine in the midst of his lecture. As the amphitheater echoed with boos, this poor man shrunk back against the blackboard. He looked up in fear and plaintively asked, "What did I do?"

The sixties were also a time of emphasis on participatory democracy. I recall a class meeting we held to plan a class party. We spent two hours of full class discussion planning a three-hour party. I became a firm believer in representative democracy.

Internal Medicine Clinical Rotation

Moving on to more medical school vignettes. Common sense is important in the practice of medicine. Of course, it is also important in the practice of life, the universe and everything. Tip of the hat to author, Douglas Adams. In the first week of my first clinical rotation, my internal medicine rotation at Beth Israel Hospital, we were treating a patient with congestive heart failure who needed blood drawn for laboratory tests. Neither the medical students nor the residents were able to find any peripheral veins in his arms. The senior resident drew blood from one of the bulging veins on the side of his neck, the external jugular vein. In congestive heart failure, the heart is beating weakly and blood backs up in the veins. Thus, the veins in the neck distend, especially if the patient is lying down. I repeat, this occurred in my first week as a medical student on my internal medicine rotation. What did I know?

For half an hour, I stood with three other medical students, an intern, a junior medical resident and the senior medical resident as the senior resident put pressure on the side of the neck to stop the bleeding from the needle stick puncture wound. After minutes of pressure, each time the pressure was released, the puncture wound resumed bleeding. Thinking about this from a mechanical point of view, I timidly suggested sitting the patient up to decrease the venous pressure at the puncture site. The senior resident followed my suggestion. The bleeding stopped without further pressure.

When I entered medical school, I planned on specializing in internal medicine and in rheumatology, which is the area covering the medical treatment of arthritis, immune disorders and inflammatory conditions. The experience mentioned above was my first hint that maybe, just maybe, I wasn't cut out to be an internist. I remember in many of our internal medicine teaching rounds the attending and other medical students sitting around discussing the interesting aspects of some patient's problem. I found that in internal medicine, "interesting" patients often had terrible diagnoses. I often found myself sitting in a corner worrying about the poor patient and the bad diagnosis and not concentrating on the "interesting" aspects of the case. As you know, of course, I eventually found orthopedics and hand surgery more to my liking.

But before I changed my mind to orthopedics, I knew, I was certain, I was convinced, I was positive, I was without doubt that I was not going to specialize in surgery or any branch of surgery. No doubts. None at all. None whatsoever. I think I have made my certitude clear. The reason? General surgery and any surgical subspecialty required two years of general surgery training which involved two years of working on call every other night. And I was never, and

I mean never, going to let anyone subject me to that. Not the only time I have changed my "certain" mind.

General Surgery Peter Bent Brigham Hospital

My medical school rotation in general surgery at the Peter Bent Brigham Hospital was, let me state, "interesting." I was assigned to a two-month rotation in general surgery, early in my third year of medical school. The general surgery department was run by Francis D. Moore, sometimes referred to by the residents and interns among themselves as Franny Moore. Dr. Moore had an "outsized" reputation. Dr. Sabiston, chief of surgery at Duke, had recently published his "Textbook of Surgery". The first chapter covered the history of surgery. As I recall, Francis D. Moore was the only living and actively working surgeon mentioned in that chapter.

I was thrilled to get this assignment to the Peter Bent. Part of the usual general surgical rotation at the Peter Bent was two weeks on either C Main or D Main. Before the Medicare rules limiting the number of patients in a room came into effect, there were open wards of approximately 30 beds with only thin curtains pretending at privacy. In today's world this would constitute continual, massive, outrageous government privacy violations. C Main was the male ward and D main was the female ward. My mind is fuzzy but I think that "Ricky" was chief nurse on C Main and "Faith" was chief nurse on D Main. Both were amazing nurses and excellent teachers as well.

Medical students assigned to these wards were allowed to, but not required to, come in at 4:30 in the morning, make rounds by themselves, write all of the necessary orders and act, in essence, like an intern. It was the only rotation, in the entire medical school, that allowed and encouraged this. The intern then came in around 6 a.m. and rounded with the medical student, checked his work and taught. The other residents appeared around six thirty and reviewed the medical student's work and taught, instructed and chastised as appropriate. This allowed the medical student to act as an intern. Extremely educational. Superbly confidence building. I was thrilled. I eagerly anticipated this two-week rotation.

As I mentioned earlier, Harvard Medical School, at that time, was changing the curriculum to start clinical training sooner. As a result, there were more students than usual assigned to the hospital for this general surgery rotation. There were not enough slots in C Main and D Main for all of the students. I arrived the first morning and discovered, to my despair, that I was not assigned to a rotation on either C or D main. The following morning, I went to Dr. Moore's office around 6:30 a.m. and waited for him to come into his office. I expressed my disappointment and asked politely if there was any way to arrange for me to get a rotation on C or D main. Krakatoa erupts. Vesuvius blows. Mount St. Helens explodes. The asteroid of 60+ million years ago strikes. Let me put it mildly. Dr. Moore was upset.

Let me, also, these many years later, try to put this in perspective. Let me attempt to understand Dr. Moore's point of view. This is 1969. The protests of the 60s are in full war cry. For years, Harvard has been buying houses and land near the Peter Bent Brigham Hospital with plans to build a new hospital. The old hospital is pre-World War One vintage. There were originally separate buildings to minimize transmission of communicable diseases. Later the separate buildings were connected by covered hallways. The hospital is old, old, old.

Recent protests, often student led, have, in the previous months, prevented the building of a new hospital. This means Dr. Moore will never get to move into a new hospital in his career. He is not at this moment pleasantly disposed toward protesting or complaining students. Unknowingly, I plunge into his cauldron of emotion. First, Dr. Moore suggests that there is something wrong with me. I must be lazy or a bad medical student. Surprised; overwhelmed; stunned; confused: I comment that, surely, I am not lazy since I am asking for a more demanding rotation. He says he will see about it. "We" will discuss it later!

That morning my team is doing an operation called an esophagogastrectomy. A long incision is made from chest to stomach. Then a portion of esophagus and stomach are removed to treat a cancer of the distal esophagus. The procedure takes three to four hours. During the course of this procedure, the intern, the junior assistant resident and the senior resident, who are supervising me, are each, sequentially and peremptorily, called out of the operating room, down to Dr. Moore's office and quizzed about me. The intern comes back and asks me, "What is going on?" He tells me that he walks into Moore's office. Dr. Moore says to him, "Tell me about this Seinsheimer fellow." Then, before the intern can utter a word, Dr. Moore launches into a tirade about me. Later that afternoon, I am called down to his office. I walk in and say to Dr. Moore, "I don't understand what is going on." This is happening on a Tuesday. Dr. Moore replies that we will meet late Friday afternoon to discuss me.

On Wednesday afternoons at 5 p.m., we have Chief's rounds. Residents, interns and occasionally medical students present patients to Dr. Moore. He uses each presentation and each patient to teach the assembled medical students, residents and staff. Usually 20 to 30 participants attend. Wednesday morning, the chief surgical resident takes me aside and tells me that because I am having "trouble" with Dr. Moore, I will have a chance to redeem myself by presenting the patient we operated on the day before, at Chief's rounds, later that afternoon. So, I begin studying my patient and his chart carefully to prepare. Around 2 p.m. that afternoon, our patient takes a turn for the worse and becomes suddenly, seriously ill. The next three hours are ones of frantic activity trying to stabilize him. At five minutes of five, new lab data comes over the teletype printer. Five minutes later, Dr. Moore arrives.

At this point in my career, if you can call it a career, I have had less than one week of general surgical training. Shall we agree I am underprepared? I make my presentation. Dr. Moore notes that there are a lot of tubes attached to our patient. He then asks me to point to each tube, name it, state where it goes into the patient's body, what machine it is attached to, the indications for its use, the potential complications from its use, etc. If I remember correctly, there were: 1. an endotracheal tube, which goes down the trachea (breathing tube) and is attached to a respirator, which breathes for the patient; 2. a nasogastric tube, which goes up the nose and down the esophagus to drain stomach acid and any bleeding from the surgery; 3. a thoracostomy tube, which goes through the skin into the chest cavity and is attached to low intermittent suction to remove any bleeding and other fluid from the chest cavity; 4. a similar tube for drainage from the abdominal cavity; 5. a Foley catheter to drain urine from the bladder; 6. a central venous line to administer fluid and measure central venous pressure; and 7. an ordinary intravenous line for administering fluid and antibiotics. There probably were others. I forget.

Many of these "tubes" I had seen for the first time in this patient. So, one by one, I stared at each line, wondering what the heck it was. I then tried to say something meaningful. For my stage of training, I think I did OK. That is, I think I demonstrated, quite clearly, the lack of clinical knowledge of a beginning third-year medical student. After each tube I discussed, Dr. Moore turned to a PhD/MD engineer working in his lab to complete and cover everything I had omitted. To this day, I have no idea about the quality of my presentation. I learned later that I had "stumbled" into one of Dr. Moore's "legendary" tube rounds." He did not do this often, but the education was important. Dr. Moore was emphasizing the importance of each of us having intimate knowledge of the technology we were using. Educational? Absolutely! But, oh, so stressful to be the deer in the headlights.

That Friday afternoon, my whole team was called down to Dr. Moore's office to discuss me. There were cookies on a platter in the conference room we were waiting in. Each of us took a cookie and started to eat it. As Dr. Moore walked in, everybody slipped their partially eaten cookie into their pocket. Everybody, that is, except me. What the heck! I figured, I am in enough trouble already, although I didn't know why. How much more trouble can I get into, by continuing to eat my cookie? One by one Dr. Moore asked the members of my team about me. Knowing he was looking for criticism, each found something to criticize.

I was on the private service at that time. Evenings were usually quiet. I had been told to go home evenings. They would call me in if anything was going on. I had done that. I had come in when called. The senior resident complained that I was not staying in the hospital at night. I replied that he had told me to go home and that I had come in when called. You get the picture. I did not get a rotation on C or D Main. I finished my surgical rotation without further interaction with Dr. Moore.

Neurology Clinical Rotation

More ricocheting in the pinball machine of my memories. I rotated on to the neurology service in my third year of medical school at the Peter Bent Brigham Hospital. As in many of our clinical rotations the instructor assigns you a patient, you go see the patient, take a history, perform a physical exam, write up a report and then present the patient to the attending and the other medical students on your rotation. The first patient I examined on the neurology rotation suffered from increasing generalized weakness over a year or more. On exam, I noted that multiple muscles were weak. I noted fasciculations of muscles in multiple parts of her body including her tongue. Fasciculations are the flickering of multiple involuntary small muscle contractions.

I presented the patient to the attending, Dr. H. Richard Tyler, and the three other medical students on the rotation with me. Dr. Tyler's first response to my presentation was, "You know, you have just pronounced her death sentence." Wait! What? Help! I think that summarizes my immediate response to his comment. He proceeded to teach us about amyotrophic lateral sclerosis, also known as Lou Gehrig's disease. I was told that the Peter Bent as well as five other hospitals were doing a study of a medicine to see if it would help. I do not recall the name of the medicine, but it was being touted by the drug maker as a cure. It was not. Patients were being admitted to the hospital as part of the study. The study found that the medicine was worthless.

At another meeting with Dr. Tyler, he was teaching us about EEGs (electro-encephalography). When performed currently, multiple electrodes are placed all around the skull to measure the electrical activity of the different parts of the brain. In patients with seizures, abnormal spikes of electrical activity are often seen in specific parts of the brain. Dr. Tyler then told us that the first EEG ever performed was with only one electrical lead. Dr. Tyler had worked with the neurologist who had performed the first EEG. Imagine the creativity of the first person to wonder if there was electrical activity in the brain that could be measured and then set up equipment to try to measure it.

Dr. Tyler reached into the left-hand pocket of his jacket and pulled out a small reel of paper tape. He unrolled it a small amount and we could see up and down squiggles on the paper. This, Dr. Tyler informed us, was the printout of the first EEG ever done. He was in personal possession of it. When the doctor, who was studying this, discovered the electrical activity of the brain, he called in all of the employees in his office to study them. One of his employees, I think his secretary, had a different EEG pattern, with spikes of electrical activity. Dr. Tyler pulled a small reel of paper out of his right-hand jacket pocket and showed us this EEG. There were abnormal spikes of electrical activity. The secretary was known to have petit mal seizures. These are "small" seizures and usually do not involve major jerking motions. The doctor studying this immediately recognized that this different pattern of spikes was connected to the secretary's petit mal seizures.

One part of medical care involves determining who has real problems and who is faking. The Munchausen patient I discussed earlier is a classic example. While rounding on the neurology service with Dr. Dawson, we examined a patient with difficulty walking. As part of the examination, Dr. Dawson asked her to walk down the hall and back so that we could evaluate her gait. Dr. Dawson already felt that she was faking. As she walked down the hall, she began to stagger, with increasingly greater shifting side to side without falling. She turned and began to stagger back to us. Dr. Dawson whispered to us, "Here come the vapors." The patient walked to within three feet of Dr. Dawson and then collapsed, expecting him to catch her. He did not.

As we discussed this case, Dr. Dawson explained how difficult it is to determine who is faking and who is not. He once had a patient who staggered from wall to wall while walking down the hall. He did not, at first, think it was real. She turned out to have a tumor in her cerebellum, a part of the brain concerned with balance. This was in the days before CT scans and MRI scans. It is now easy to scan for these tumors.

While on the neurology rotation we treated a patient with bilateral foot drop. This means that the peroneal nerve, which runs down the front of the leg and innervates the muscles which lift the foot and toes, was not working. The "only" cause for bilateral peroneal palsy is heavy metal poisoning, except, as I sometimes say, when it isn't. This patient's tests for heavy metal poisoning were negative. In the course of this book I discuss frequently the need for asking patients the right questions. I also note the need for aware observation. This patient was a driver for the MTA. His job involved sitting all day long. Whenever we saw him, he was positioned so that his legs were crossed in a manner in which both lower legs were parallel to each other, with the outside of each knee pressing against the other. This position was causing one knee to put direct pressure on the peroneal nerve of the other knee. The problem was chronic pressure on both peroneal nerves due to this patient's method of sitting all day long. I recall sitting with him, uncrossing his legs and telling him not to cross his legs. He replied, "OK." Then within 30 seconds, he was sitting again in the old position. We could not break him of that habit.

Obstetrics and Gynecology Rotation

Obstetrics is different than all of the other medical rotations in one specific way. You are often participating in events which are normal, healthy and natural. You are not always treating abnormal pathology. I remember helping with my first delivery. As the baby's head was crowning, my mentoring obstetrician wheeled this enormous table in front of me. This deep and wide table was now between me and the oncoming infant. I had no idea what its purpose was. Out slid the baby into my hands. Never in my life have I felt, handled, held something so slippery. With deep profound understanding I understood the need for the deep and wide table. If you have ever squeezed a seed between your fingers and felt it spurt away, you will understand my fear. This baby was so profoundly slippery, I was concerned it could spurt out of my hands, into the air and onto the floor. Rapidly the nurses wiped, cleaned and wrapped the baby and the slippery risk was eliminated. These many years later I still marvel at that slippery feeling. The sense of a new fragile life in my hands was also overwhelming.

Psychiatry Clinical Rotation

I previously discussed my "exciting" rotation on general surgery. When applying for internships in my senior year of medical school I was informed that my grade for that rotation was a "C." Tantamount to flunking. More on that later. I received my highest grade in a clinical course from the psychiatry department. Imagine that! A surgeon excelling in his psychiatry rotation. I can think of two vignettes from my psychiatry rotation that may have contributed to my grade. Each medical student on the psychiatry rotation was assigned a psychiatric inpatient. We met with our patients, one on one, for an hour each day, for the one-month rotation. We, medical students, then met in groups of three or four, twice a week, with one of the attending psychiatrists to discuss our patients.

My group of three met with our attending psychiatrist in a large room on the second floor of an old Victorian house. One afternoon, our attending psychiatrist was late for our meeting. We three medical students joked that in college, you waited 10 minutes for an assistant professor, 20 minutes for an associate professor and 30 minutes for a full professor. After waiting a while, we decided that when our attending came in, we medical students would carry on our discussion normally, but we would not look at our attending. Our attending came in about a half hour late. He sat down and we began our discussion of our patients. As the discussion continued, we students talked normally but deliberately avoided eye contact with our teacher.

Our teacher became increasingly concerned. He leaned forward more. He talked louder. He clearly recognized that something was wrong but could not figure out what. Tension in the room mounted as each time one of us talked, we looked at one another but never at the teacher. After half an hour, we broke out laughing from the tension. We then explained what we were doing and why. Our attending loved it! We discussed our feelings and the importance of body language in communication.

There is a known reaction in psychoanalysis called transference. Classically, this is the situation in which a female patient develops romantic feelings for a male psychiatrist. There is a corresponding reaction called countertransference in which the psychiatrist develops romantic feelings for the patient. The patient I saw for an hour each day was a woman in her early twenties. During my third week while meeting with her, I became aware of romantic fantasies regarding her. I understood immediately what was happening. At my next meeting with my psychiatry mentor, I discussed this with him, explaining my understanding of what was happening. He was thrilled. I don't think many students were as open about their feelings with him. I suspect my A grade came from these episodes.

During the psychiatry rotation, we also spent time at a psychiatric emergency room. We initially watched and later participated in the evaluation of possible suicidal patients. We studied the difficulty in trying to decide who was a serious suicide risk, who needed immediate hospitalization and who could safely be followed as an outpatient. The critical question seemed to be whether the patient was thinking of a specific method to use.

More Clinical Rotation Vignettes

Another vignette. Another time. Our surgical team was called to the emergency room to see a patient referred from a rural hospital. A patient with a farm injury. An open fracture of a leg that became infected and was not responding to treatment. We walked into the exam room to see a teenager with extensive swelling and mottling of his right leg, oozing fluid.

This fluid was swabbed. As "the medical student," the junior member of the team, I was given the swab to do a gram stain. The gram stain technique dyes bacteria either deep purple or light pink. Bacteria are usually shaped as either dots, called cocci, or rods, called rods. A few medical terms make sense.

I did the gram stain and saw gram positive rods. Most bacteria are either gram positive (purple) cocci, such as streptococcus and staphylococcus (common causes of soft tissue infection), or gram negative (pink) rods such as *E. Coli* (a common cause of urinary tract infections.) There are few gram-positive rods. This gram-positive rod was *clostridium perfringens* or gas gangrene. Life and limb threatening. One glance down the microscope, I knew the leg needed immediate amputation. Nothing else had a chance of saving this patient. This was done within the hour. The patient survived. Some decision-making and treatment has to be done quickly. This was the only case of gas gangrene I ever saw, fortunately.

When I was a medical student, Boston City Hospital was not air conditioned, except for a few rooms. One legend described residents trying to treat a seriously ill patient during an unusually hot summer day. High temperature and humidity are stressful for anyone, but are particularly dangerous for seriously ill patients. The legend held that a group of residents barged into the office of the CEO of the hospital, took the window air conditioner out of his office and put it in the window of the room with the seriously ill patient.

When a medical student friend of mine was on a rotation there, Boston City Hospital ran out of mechanical respirators. My friend was assigned to breathe for this patient all night using an Ambu bag. He was instructed to squeeze the Ambu bag every four seconds to push air into a patient's lungs. Sometime in the middle of the night, when he was relieved for a bathroom break, he left the hospital and went home. He felt he was being abused as a medical student. Tough ethics in a situation of limited resources. I do not know if he received reprimand or other discipline as a result of his action.

More legends. The fanciest private ward at Massachusetts General was the Philips Pavilion. Food was served on bone china, drinks in real glasses. You get the idea. Many patients there had private duty nurses. Many of these private duty nurses were, let me gently state, past their due date. One legend held that a patient, in his first night of post-op, had to get out of his bed and walk down to the nurses' station to report that his private duty nurse had died sitting in her chair. Another legend held that a private duty nurse on the Philips Pavilion carefully and dutifully recorded over a period of many hours the gradual decrease in measured blood pressure until the patient died, but never called for a doctor.

I was continually learning about people and their behavior in medical school and in my surgical training. I recall talking to a woman alcoholic who had stopped drinking two years earlier and had been sober since. I commented that her husband must have been thrilled. She replied, "Oh, no. He lost a drinking partner." More education about the different milieus patients live in.

I recall treating a police officer who had been shot in the head in a part of town he was not assigned to. His wife came in to see him. I discussed the case with her. A few hours later, his wife came in to see him. A different woman. He had two wives. Neither knew of the other's existence. More education about the social lives of my patients.

Early on in my rotation on the medical service at Beth Israel Hospital, we admitted a patient with severe pain from a kidney stone. This pain often comes in waves and can be some of the most severe pain a patient ever experiences. I drew blood to send down to the lab and went to get my supervising resident. When I came back to the patient's room with the resident, the patient's pain was gone. The pain never returned. The patient said that my "shot" cured his pain. Probably this was a coincidence. Perhaps my drawing of his blood caused him to pass the kidney stone. Perhaps the drawing of his blood caused a constriction of the ureter (urine tube), which passed the stone. I doubt it was pure placebo effect, since there was a blocked stone on the X-ray.

On my medical rotation at the Beth Israel Hospital, there were phlebotomy technicians, who routinely drew blood for ordered blood tests from patients in the morning. Some patients are difficult to draw blood from. They may have tiny or delicate veins or they may be drug addicts who have destroyed their veins from multiple injections of drugs. If the phlebotomists were unable to successfully draw blood for the tests, they left the laboratory orders in a small brown wooden box at the nurses' station. We, beginning medical students who had never drawn blood before, were assigned to draw blood from these difficult patients. A great learning experience for us. After all, if you can figure out how to draw blood from a difficult patient then an easy patient is a snap. Of course, from the difficult patient's point of view, the extra needle sticks of the beginning medical student's learning curve may not have been so enjoyable. This was the way a good teaching hospital worked back then. This was the embedded ethics of a good teaching hospital. At some point in time, trainee doctors have to begin doing things themselves. We learned fast.

National Board Exams

Senior year of medical school we senior medical students took the national medical board examinations. Three days of testing. Three hours each morning. Three hours each afternoon. I am generally a fairly fast test taker. For the first three three-hour sessions, all of the questions were multiple choice and there was plenty of time to finish the test and then go back and check my answers. For the fourth session the test pamphlet started off with similar multiple-choice questions. I relaxed my pace of answering since it seemed clear that time pressure was not going to be an issue. Halfway through the test booklet, the question type changed to several paragraphs of text followed by three questions. A much slower paced portion of the test. I gasped, realizing that I was behind timewise. I began to push through the test as quickly as possible. Over the next half hour as I raced through the second half of the test, I heard gasp after gasp throughout the room as the other test takers reached the same point and realized they were far behind. I finished the last question just as time was called. Most students did not finish this portion of the test. Epiphany. Any time you are handed a test booklet, take a moment to flip through it so that you are not taken by surprise by a change in question type.

Orthopedic Surgery Clinical Rotation

I reached the middle of my fourth year of medical school without a clue regarding which field I wished to obtain further training in. As I mentioned before I expected to train in internal medicine and rheumatology. As also previously mentioned, my reaction to patients with terrible diagnoses was emotional. I found that I had difficulty obtaining sufficient distance to "enjoy" what I was doing. I also did not find staying up all night to keep a confused, senile patient alive a few more weeks to be emotionally rewarding. As I have said before, I was "certain" that I would never go into surgery because I would never accept two years of every other night on call. Pathology and radiology, which are specialties with little patient contact ,were not interesting to me. I spent a year and a half through third year and the first half of fourth year of medical school confused, worried and uncertain about my future plans.

I entered my clinical rotation in orthopedic surgery in the middle of my fourth year of medical school. I found orthopedic surgery to be "fun." Much of what we did made sense. The patients were healthier and grateful. The surgery was interesting. The residents I trained with were pleasant to be with and excellent teachers. To my surprise, I found that I had finally found my calling.

CHAPTER FIVE

Application to General Surgery Programs

Let's move forward a bit. What was the application process for general surgical internship like? In Boston in 1971, the application process included interviews, which were usually "stress" interviews. I doubt there were or are any worthwhile studies regarding how to find the best candidates for general surgical internships, especially any studies on the efficacy of stress interviews for evaluating applicants for general surgical internships. You would have to follow graduates throughout their medical careers. Even then, how do you measure success? The stress interviews were more like fraternity hazing. We've always done it, so let's continue to do it.

I was not particularly interested in Massachusetts General Hospital. My 2 p.m. medical school application interview four years earlier was with a general surgeon at Mass General. That interview was interrupted by a phone call from a general surgery resident upset that his rotations had been changed to his detriment. In addition, he was not going to get any vacation that year. The reason was that another resident was staying longer at the National Institutes of Health and would not be in the resident rotation. The surgeon, who was interviewing me, told the resident, on the phone, brusquely, "Accept it or quit."

At the start of fourth year of medical school, each medical student met individually with one of the deans to go over our past performance. I love the phrase,

"Past performance is no guarantee of future performance." I am not certain how well that phrase applies here. As students at Harvard Medical School, we were never told our grades. As long as we were performing satisfactorily, we heard nothing. So, we really did not have a sense of how we were doing compared to the rest of our class. The dean told me that I got a C in general surgery. I described, in extensive detail, my, shall we call it, interaction with Dr. Moore. Knowing Dr. Moore's reputation, the dean threw out the grade. I was advised that any and all hospitals were reasonable for me to apply to. I knew I had no chance of being accepted at the Peter Bent. Nevertheless, I applied to both Mass General and Peter Bent for the interviewing experience. I also applied to Beth Israel Hospital and the University of Colorado among others.

More on my meeting with the dean. When I met with the dean to discuss my grades, he also noted that I received a C in my pediatric rotation. We examined the written discussion of my performance together. The first paragraph stated that I was one of the best medical students they had seen that year. Excellent fund of knowledge. Hard working, etc. The second paragraph stated that I was one of the worst medical students they had seen that year. Poor fund of knowledge. Slacker, etc. The third paragraph stated that I seemed to lose interest at the end of the month. I reminded the dean that I left this rotation one week early to get married, with his permission. The dean remarked that this was a bizarrely inconsistent report. He threw out this grade also.

Back to my applications for surgical internship. As I mentioned earlier, I applied to Peter Bent for interview practice. As part of the application process, Dr. Moore interviewed each applicant individually. On vacation the previous summer, I went sailing with friends in the Virgin Islands on a bareboat charter. My friends and I snorkeled extensively. I took an underwater camera and experimented with underwater photography. As I entered Dr. Moore's office for my interview, I noticed a wall of underwater pictures and commented on them. We then had a pleasant 20-minute chat about the Caribbean and techniques of underwater photography. Dr. Moore turned on that warmth and charm that only really successful people are able to do. I, of course, recognized exactly what he was doing. I admired his ability to do it. I wasn't exactly sure, of course, why he was bothering.

Dr. Moore then asked me how I was doing in medical school. Interesting question, considering he had my entire file in front of him, and, of course, remembering my general surgical rotation. Hmm. How to answer? I answered something to the effect, "As you know, I got a C in surgery here." He replied that my grade was the only one given that year that he thought was wrong. I am thinking, "Okayyyy, if that is the case, why not call the dean's office and change the grade?" Of course, I stayed mum on that topic. We continued chatting and to my total surprise, he told me that they wanted me as a surgical intern the upcoming year. I thanked him, expressed my gratitude and left.

Now, you must admit, given the story I described above and my grade of C, an offer of internship was a wee tad unexpected. Let me, now, put his offer in perspective. Peter Bent Brigham Hospital took eight general surgical interns each year. Comparing notes with my classmates, I found at least eight of us who had been told the same thing. So, I doubted that I was high on any Peter Bent list.

Then, in the first week in January, came the interviews at the Boston hospitals. I think the one at Massachusetts General Hospital was first. The first interview at Mass General was three on one. Three surgeons on one side of the table. Me, little me, on the other. Remember, these are stress interviews. First question: "Do you know what ambergris is?" My answer, "I think it is the stuff from whales they use to make perfume." Clearly nothing to do with surgery. Second question, rapid fire: "Quite right. It is a highly olefinic compound. What do you think it does in the whale?" At the time, I thought that meant a smelly, hormone-like compound. Looking it up now I see it means a compound of carbon and hydrogen with double bonds. I wasn't far off. This would make it smelly and possibly hormone-like. If I had been a better interviewee, I would have slowed the pace and thought a bit. As it was, I blurted out, "I haven't the faintest idea." I was not an experienced interviewee.

Immediately, one of the interviewing surgeons followed up with: "I note you took six years of Latin in high school. Quote me the first ten lines of the Aeneid." I did indeed take six years of Latin. My teacher in 11th and 12th grades was Ms. Rosemary Hope. She is the reason, and the only reason, I continued Latin. Twelfth grade, there were ten of us in the class. It was like a college seminar. Senior year, our Latin class was the last class of the day. The class before us were seventh graders. We were a six-year public, special college preparatory high school, Walnut Hills High School. I fondly remember walking into class. As we entered the room, there was Ms. Hope standing with white hair looking hunched and tired, running her hand through her hair. She would look up, see us seniors walking into the classroom and immediately straighten up, smile and perk up.

First grading period senior year was important for college admission. All junior year, I received steady Bs from Ms. Hope, but first grading period, senior year, I had As on every test. Out came the report card: B. I went up to her to ask why I had received a B, when I had received As on every test. She replied, the tests are 50 per cent of the grade and class translation is 50 per cent of the grade. My class translation grade was B level, which I don't dispute. She said I was exactly halfway between a B and an A. She told me she had to decide whether I was an A Latin student or a B Latin student. The B grade was her answer. I don't dispute the fact that the best I could ever hope for in Latin was to be a B student. She was right. I still loved her. We read the Aeneid, in Latin, senior year. She told us she did not like to assign memorization; however, her one exception was to ask us to memorize the first twenty lines of the Aeneid. I recall her words, "In some bizarre set of circumstances you might find this useful."

Returning to my three on one stress interview: laughing internally, and remembering Ms. Hope with pleasure, I recited the first ten lines of the Aeneid. In retrospect, I am not sure I recited all ten lines. Today, I only remember the first four lines. So, I know I recited at least four lines. To this day, I wonder how many of them knew the lines. I know they did not challenge my recitation. After I recited the lines, they didn't blink or respond; just followed up immediately with another question, "What meter is it in." I was not sure. What to do? Decide quickly. I recalled two types of meter from English class, dactylic hexameter and iambic pentameter. Hadn't a clue which was which. Didn't seem like, "I don't know" was a good answer. I rapidly figured that a wrong answer was no worse than an "I don't know" answer. It seemed to me that I had heard of dactylic hexameter more than iambic pentameter. So, I guessed, "dactylic hexameter." Luck. I guessed correctly. On the questioning went. Those are the only questions I recall.

I passed this "preliminary" interview and was passed on to the final interview. One of my friends—smart, personable, etc.—did not pass his first interview. Although I was not witness to his interview, I have no understanding for this decision. When I saw him later that evening, he was shocked and bewildered. The decision made no sense to me. So many decisions are based on interviews. There are so many different interviewing techniques. Besides the weeding out of a small percentage of obviously unfit candidates, I wonder how effective the whole process is.

Later that afternoon, I was ushered into a room with a long table for my second interview. I sat at one end of the table. Around the table were ten to twelve surgeons: the chief of surgery and the chiefs of all the surgical subspecialties. Ashtrays on the table were overflowing. Most people smoked back then. The chief of thoracic surgery opened the questioning, "Can lung cancer present with pain as the initial symptom?" This is not an easy question. Most often lung cancer presents with complaints of coughing and/or bloody sputum. I answered that a peripheral cancer that grew to irritate the lining of the chest cavity could present with pain as the initial symptom. With additional questioning, I finally lurched and staggered into a second answer, that a lung cancer that grows high up in the upper part of the lung can grow into the nerves that go into the arm, thus causing shoulder and arm pain. This is called the Pancoast Syndrome. Rare.

The chief of neurosurgery then took over the questioning. In a hoarse and quavering voice, he asked, "You've been talking a lot about pain. Tell me, how is pain perceived?" I remembered one lecture from perhaps three years earlier on what was called, I think, the gate theory of pain perception. For 20 minutes,

I demonstrated my ignorance regarding the theory of perception of pain in multiple ways. I could not get off of a topic about which I knew next to nothing. I was then dismissed. How this "experience" demonstrated my prospective ability or lack of ability to succeed as a surgical intern continues to elude me.

It's odd that I remember little of my interview at Peter Bent. I guess it was "ordinary" and thus not memorable. I also interviewed at Beth Israel Hospital. All of the applicants from around the country came to Beth Israel early one morning, the first week in January. We were brought to an amphitheater, given a blue book (in those days blue books were used for students to write in for tests) and we were asked to "Write about ourselves." "Good God!" I thought. Do they want a detailed self-psychoanalysis or a complete autobiography? How is my answering this question going to determine my suitability as a surgical intern? I decided to bail out. My version of "Hell no; I won't go!" So, I wrote about my hobbies and non-medical interests. I avoided anything deep. One of the topics I mentioned was the Japanese board game Go.

Throughout the day, the applicants were called for interviews. My luck was to be the last interview of the day. I was tired and upset at having to sit around all day waiting to be called. It was five thirty, late, late afternoon, when I was called. I entered a room with a long table and ten or twelve surgeons sitting around the table. They had been interviewing all day. The last thing they desired was another interview. Ashtrays were again overflowing. Ties were loosened. Everybody was slouched in his chair with a dazed, fatigue-glazed expression on his face.

I was surprised to see John Nemiah, chief of psychiatry, on the panel. He asked the group, if he might ask the first question. With vague, "whatever" waves of their hands, the assembled surgeons indicated assent. Uh oh! Where was this stress interview headed? Dr. Nemiah noted that I had discussed the game of Go in my blue book answer. He had just purchased the game for his kids that Christmas and couldn't figure out how to play it. So, he asked me to discuss the game of Go. I launched into a 20-minute discussion of the game. Profoundly simple rules. Exceedingly complex strategy arising from these simple rules. Far more positional possibilities than chess. For 20 minutes, I seemed to have their undivided attention; not a single interrupting question. Then I was dismissed. Probably the least stressful stress interview in history. Did this interview transmit any information regarding my suitability as a surgical intern? I suspect they were fatigued beyond caring.

I also traveled to Duke for an interview. Common knowledge among my friends was the fact that the Johns Hopkins surgery training program was highly competitive and pyramidal. The pyramidal system meant that only a few trainees stayed and finished the program. Only those few who reached the top of the pyramid got to do most of the surgery. Common knowledge among my friends was that Dr. Sabiston, chief of surgery at Duke, was from the Hopkins program and ran his program in a similarly competitive way. I did not desire a highly competitive program but distrusted the "common knowledge."

Let me digress for a moment to discuss "common knowledge." When I was in high school, "common knowledge" among my friends was the fact that Yale was "no good," that is, not a college to go to. Don't ask! In retrospect, I cannot explain it to you. Perhaps it was because it was all male. I don't know. Perhaps it was just our parochial, midwestern herd mentality. Fortunately, my Sunday School teacher was a Yalie and talked Yale up to me. I applied to Yale, early decision. I was the only student from my high school who did. Being the only student to apply early from a nationally known public college preparatory high school dramatically improves your acceptance chances. I was accepted. The beginning of my understanding of the importance of bucking and ignoring herd mentality. The beginning of my understanding that the social process of herd mentality exists.

Back to the Duke interview. With good experience running against herd mentality, I was primed to run against herd mentality, again. So, I visited the Duke general surgery program. The day I visited the Duke program to evaluate it and interview, there were two other medical students visiting. Dr. Sabiston brought the three of us into his office together, sat us side by side on a couch opposite his desk, and began firing fact questions at us, rapid fire. He called on whoever raised his hand first, jumping up the highest in eagerness to answer his question. I immediately recognized that the common knowledge about the hypercompetitiveness at the Duke general surgery program was, in fact, correct. I felt that I was also interviewing the Duke general surgery program. I sat back on the couch, smiling, prepared to answer any questions Dr. Sabiston might direct at me personally. For half an hour this continued. Then, we were dismissed. I did not answer a single question. Clearly, Dr. Sabiston recognized that I did not wish to participate in his hypercompetitive "game" and therefore was not interested in me. I did not list Duke on my matching list. The culture of internecine hypercompetitive destructive education was anathema to me.

Internships are decided by a matching system in which each hospital ranks its applicants in numerical order. Similarly, each applicant ranks each hospital in numerical order. Then a computer crunches the data. I ranked Massachusetts General Hospital first, despite my concerns mentioned above. It is hard to row against the current of reputation. I put Peter Bent Brigham Hospital second. Again, based on reputation, with little chance of acceptance. Beth Israel third. The University of Colorado fourth. I figured I had a fair chance at being matched at the Beth Israel with greater probability for the University of Colorado.

The results of the matching process were kept secret. Late in the afternoon on one specific day in the spring, all across the country, senior medical students meet with their deans and are given sealed envelopes with their match. At Harvard, we were scheduled to meet at the dean's office at 4 p.m. No one ever knew their match ahead of time. No one, that is, except me. On "matching" day, I was sitting in the cafeteria at Peter Bent with a group of friends having lunch, when Dr. Alan Birtch came up behind me.

As first-year medical students, we were assigned in groups of four to a member of the medical school faculty. We met for one hour, one evening, each week. There was no specific course material. The purpose was a general introduction into what the practice of medicine was all about. I was in the group of four assigned to Dr. Alan Birtch. He was a general surgeon at the Peter Bent.

I remember one evening he walked us through the emergency room. I had never been in an emergency room before. He discussed what an emergency room is and how it works. There was an elderly woman awaiting treatment for a wrist fracture with an obvious swollen deformed wrist. Dr. Birtch asked the patient when she had broken her other wrist. Dr. Birtch had noted a mild deformity in the other wrist. None of us early first-year medical students had noticed this deformity.

Physical examination consists of observation, palpation, percussion and auscultation. Thus, my physical examination of a patient begins when I enter the exam room. How old does the patient look? How well or sick does the patient look? Is there deformity? Does the patient seem alert? This seemingly minor episode of Dr. Birtch noticing the mild deformity of the other wrist stands out in my first year as an epiphany. I needed to up my game. I needed to work on observation and awareness of the world around me. The next time you drive up to a red light and slow down and stop, look at the people crossing in the crosswalk in front of you. Most are looking straight ahead or at the ground. It is rare to see one of the pedestrians look at you to see if you are actually slowing down and stopping. Most people do not expand their awareness to the world around them.

In my social psychology course in college, we discussed a study about this. Researchers showed movies of people walking down the street to incarcerated muggers and asked the muggers which pedestrians the muggers would choose to attack. People walking with their eyes on the ground with no awareness of their surroundings were chosen as possible prey. People with their heads up, turning their heads and aware of their surroundings were not chosen as possible prey. Increasing your awareness of the world around you is important for your safety and allows you to see, learn and appreciate more of life.

The epiphany of Dr. Birtch noticing the minor deformity of the non-injured wrist, in retrospect a minor observation, was hugely instructive to me. You will find I frequently mention experiences which rocked me back on my heels, which led me to reevaluate myself, which led me to the knowledge that

I needed to "up my game." As minor a teaching experience as this was, this is one of those moments I recall with clarity.

I remember Dr. Birtch was constantly smoking and drinking coffee. So many were at that time. One member of my group of first-year medical students asked him one evening whether the nicotine and caffeine from the cigarettes and coffee interfered with his ability to perform surgery. Dr. Birtch's reply was priceless. He said he didn't know. He hadn't tried performing surgery without them. So Dr. Birtch and I knew each other and had a friendly mentor/student relationship.

As part of our general surgery rotation as medical students at Peter Bent, we spent two weeks on the anesthesia service. Dr. Leroy Vandam was then chief of anesthesia. He had previously been a surgeon, so I was told, but due to vision problems switched to anesthesia. My first day on the anesthesia rotation, he and I helped wheel a patient into the operating room for an upper abdominal operation. Smoothly, he assisted me in intubating the patient, which is inserting a rubber breathing tube into the trachea. Under his supervision, I adjusted the anesthesia gases to their proper concentrations. Suddenly, I noticed that Dr. Vandam was no longer in the operating room. I was "alone" with the patient. Unknown to me, Dr. Vandam was watching everything through a strategically placed window.

My first instinct: Panic! Call for help! But…everything seemed to be under control. I controlled my sense of panic. I continued to monitor the anesthetized patient. At one point during the operation, the patient became a little light and I slightly increased the anesthesia gas concentration. The operation took about an hour and a half. Just as the operating surgeon was finishing the operation, there was Dr. Vandam in the room overseeing the arousal from anesthesia and the removal of the endotracheal tube. It all seemed natural and routine to me. What I did not know, but found out later, was that Dr. Vandam did this with other medical students as well. As a general surgical intern and junior resident a few years later, I watched the scenario play out a few times. All of the medical students I watched called for Dr. Vandam to return within minutes. I was the only one I ever knew of who "lasted." Dr. Vandam became a big supporter of me.

Returning to the intern matching process. I am sitting at a round table in the cafeteria at Peter Bent with seven friends just hours before the "ritual" opening of the sealed letters with the hospital matching results. Dr. Birtch bends over and whispers in my ear. "Congratulations! I hear you are going to be with us next year." Surprise does not begin to describe my response. I stammered "Thanks," I think. Perhaps I was speechless. Many members of my class knew the story of my "run in" with Dr. Moore. It was near legend in our class.

So, why was I matched with Peter Bent. Obviously, I am not certain. My father-in-law, a chief of radiology, told me once that when you have a run in with a chief of a department, he knows you. Well, yes, but doesn't he know you in a negative way? Did Dr. Moore change his mind about me? Possible, I guess. Dr. Birtch, Dr. Vandam or others may have influenced the decision. Possible, I guess. My best guess is that Peter Bent ranked all of the applying Harvard medical students highly, including me. Though I was probably last or near last of the Harvard medical students. Then, perhaps most of the other Harvard students and a lot of others ranked other hospitals higher and got matched elsewhere. As I think about this many years later, I wonder if the story of my run in with Dr. Moore discouraged members of my class from applying to Peter Bent. Whatever the reason, I was lucky beyond any reasonable expectation of luck. Many of the vignettes I am writing about come from my two years of general surgery training at Peter Bent. You can tell by reading them how much and how quickly I was learning. I cannot imagine a better two-year experience.

Let me revisit the issue of herd mentality. Due to Dr. Moore's reputation, I think that the herd mentality of our class was avoidance of the general surgery internship at Peter Bent. I think that, once again, I benefited from my ability to buck my fellow students' herd mentality.

CHAPTER SIX

General Surgery Internship and Junior Residency

S o, what was your first day as a general surgery intern at Peter Bent Brigham Hospital like? We, the eight new general surgery interns, were asked to start a week earlier than originally scheduled. One week before July first. We then worked for one year without vacation and were given one week of unpaid "vacation" the last week of June of the following year. Where is a good union when you need it?

We came to the hospital early the first morning, met with Dr. Moore and were given our assignments. I was assigned to the service covering the Surgical Intensive Care Unit (SICU) and Dr. Moore's and certain other attending surgeons' patients. This, the chief's service, was the most difficult service and had, by far, the sickest patients. I was told that I was given it first only because I knew my way around the hospital, so my learning curve would be minimally faster. Fascinating to see me travel from harshly criticized, "Grade C" general surgical medical student to being assigned the hardest general surgery intern rotation first.

Normally, surgery started at 7:30 in the morning but on this day, surgery started at 9:00 in the morning. At 9:15 that morning, I was standing on one side of an anesthetized patient with an abdomen prepped for an open tubal ligation. This was the last year tubal ligations were performed with open surgery.

Thereafter, the laparoscope was used. To my surprise, and I do mean surprise, the surgeon handed me the knife. Wow, I thought, they sure don't mess around in teaching you surgery.

In the John Hopkins pyramidal system, the first-year intern was allowed to do little surgery. The chief resident did most of the surgery. At Peter Bent Brigham Hospital, the intern did more surgery, in number of operations, than any of the other general surgery residents. As you advanced in seniority and experience, you did the more complicated surgeries. On the transplant service, the senior general surgical resident did all but the first kidney transplant operation.

For my first operation, John McArthur was the attending surgeon. Leroy Vandam, the chief of anesthesia, was standing close by watching to see what I was going to do. I had only used a scalpel once in dog lab and then to remove small lumps on two human patients, as a medical student. These many years later, I have difficulty finding words to describe my sense of surreal, disbelieving excitement. Yes, I was now enrolled in a general surgery training program, but I seemed to know so little about what I was doing or going to do. I did not know the "simple" things like "how hard do you push the scalpel when you make an incision?" The patient was obese, so there was little chance of making an incision too deep. I made an incision about half an inch deep to start. This was actually about right. An artery spurted and blood hit Dr. Vandam in his mask. He was leaning over close to observe me carefully. Both he and Dr. Macarthur began razzing me in a good-natured way. I did the entire operation under constant and careful supervision. Wow! What a way to start your first day of surgical training! What a way to start your first hours of surgical training!

There are two aspects to surgical training, which occur in parallel. One is learning the motor skills, the anatomical knowledge and the craftsmanship of the actual performance of surgery. The other is the medical side: the diagnosis and non-surgical management of the patient. Within the first week of my internship, I was assisting on a thyroidectomy (removal of the thyroid gland from the front of the neck). In the front of the neck, there are innumerable small vessels, which bleed a lot during this surgery. Think of how easily and how much bleeding you get after a small nick when shaving. Multiply this amount of bleeding times 50. In typical surgery a cautery instrument is used to stop the bleeding from each of the small vessels which have been cut. In this teaching program, at the beginning we were not allowed to use cautery. The purpose was to give us extensive practice in knot tying.

Back to the thyroidectomy. Each of these tiny blood vessels was clamped with a small mosquito clamp. As the second assistant and beginning surgical intern, I was handed a roll of 5-0 plain catgut suture to use to tie off each vessel. In naming the size of the suture, in this nomenclature, the bigger the number the smaller the suture. A 5-0 plain catgut suture is thin and breaks easily. It is easy to pull the suture too hard and break it. In addition, the soft tissue of the inside of the neck is fragile and tears easily. Even gentle pulling on the suture, while tying a knot, will pull the knot off of the soft tissue.

I had never used 5-0 plain catgut suture before. I knew how to tie knots for surgery but had never tied a knot in an actual operation with suture this fine. I had always practiced on bigger, stronger sutures. This was far more delicate than anything I had attempted before. It took me about half an hour of attempting to tie the knots without either breaking the suture or pulling on the knot and tearing it off of the soft tissue before I finally "got it." The surgeon and other resident stood quietly without criticism or complaint while I mastered this technique. They knew that the time spent learning this early would pay off the rest of the year. Given my past experience with a general surgeon in the dog lab and with Dr. Moore, I was surprised and pleased with the patience they demonstrated. Really strange. Not a word of criticism or impatience. I guess it was like watching your baby take her first steps.

Friday afternoon of my first week of internship, I overheard one of the general surgeons screaming at the senior resident of his service, that the intern on his service couldn't tie knots. Because the intern couldn't tie knots, the surgeon couldn't give him surgery to do. The surgeon told the senior resident that if the intern was not tying knots by Monday morning, he, the senior resident, was not getting any surgery. Guess who spent that weekend teaching his intern to tie knots? The desperate desire to teach and to give the interns surgery, as early and as often as they could, was impressive. Despite my previous interaction with Dr. Moore, I was already impressed and thrilled with his teaching program.

We interns were given all the appendectomies, half the cholecystectomies (removal of the gallbladder) and half the hernias among other surgeries. During my time there, the interns and residents did all of the cholecystectomies except one. What was special about that one? A little over one year previously, a man was admitted for this surgery. While waiting in the preoperative area, he developed crushing chest pain and suffered a myocardial infarction (heart attack). The surgery was cancelled and he was allowed to recover from his heart attack. A little over six months later, this same man returned for his cholecystectomy, having recovered from his heart attack. While waiting in the preoperative area, he again developed crushing chest pain and had another heart attack. This was treated with emergency coronary artery bypass surgery. He was given another six months to recover. Now, he was coming in for his third attempt for the surgery. This was what it took for a staff surgeon to do the operation himself. Curiously, this patient—unfortunately—suffered a complication called a bile leak, which resolved. This was the only patient that year who suffered that complication. Boy, did we, interns and residents, razz the attending surgeon about that.

There was tremendous enthusiasm and hard work amongst the surgical interns. This came from the fact that we were learning so much so quickly. There never was a sense we were being used or taken advantage of. The closest we came to being "used" occurred when patients with severe respiratory failure were placed on a machine called a membrane oxygenator. This only occurred rarely. A membrane oxygenator is a machine which puts oxygen into the bloodstream and removes carbon dioxide from the bloodstream without using a mechanical respirator to aerate the lungs. This was a research project trying to save patients with respiratory failure so severe that the lungs were unable to keep the patient alive despite 100% oxygen and a respirator. When patients were on the membrane oxygenator, we, general surgery interns, were required to stay awake all night at the bedside. No patient with respiratory failure that severe recovered despite the use of the membrane oxygenator while I was there. The membrane oxygenator was only used on a limited number of patients.

Sometime in the first week of internship a patient arrested on the medical service and a STAT for a surgeon was called over the PA system. I raced down the hall to respond. Another surgical intern arrived at the same time I did. This patient had difficult veins and the medical doctors were unable to establish an IV to administer drugs. In a situation like this a surgeon may make a small incision over a large vein at the ankle and access the vein for an IV. With the patient continuing under CPR I started a cut down on one ankle while the other surgical intern did the same on the other ankle. We both got our IVs in quickly. I don't remember who won the race. This was my first cut down. I had only seen one done before.

I am left-handed. From the first, it seemed obvious to me that I should practice becoming as ambidextrous as possible. There are situations where it is easier to use your left hand if you want an instrument pointing to the right and easier to use your right hand if you want an instrument pointing to the left. Otherwise you end up back handing the instrument in an awkward manner. The gallbladder is on the right side of the upper abdomen. For an open operation (before endoscopy) it is natural to use the right hand to reach the right upper abdomen from the right side of the patient. To use your left hand, you have to stand on the left side of the operating table and reach across the abdomen to reach the gallbladder.

Sometime in my first month or two of surgical training, I was operating to remove the gallbladder using my right hand. My supervising surgeon seemed to feel that I was too "awkward" using my right hand and instructed me to move to the other side and use my left hand. After a half hour of struggle from the far side, I begged to be allowed to return to the patient's right and use my right hand. My request was granted. The operation went smoothly after that.

Back to the first day of internship. The afternoon of my first day as an intern, a patient on the neurosurgery service arrested. A stat was called and we, the new interns, ran pell-mell up to the patient's room and began CPR. We performed chest compression, intubated the patient, hooked up an EKG and were administering correct drugs without success. About 20 minutes into this, I looked up and saw all of the senior residents leaning against the walls, watching us, but not participating in the code. I said, "Hey guys" to the other interns, who then looked up as well. We looked at the senior residents. They shrugged.

This patient had end-stage brain cancer. She had been expected to die soon. The senior residents were letting us get practice in a situation where it did not matter since the patient was terminal and would not respond to the code. I have often wondered about the ethics of this. I can see both sides. On the one hand, we were doing unnecessary "treatment" to a dead patient without permission from the family. On the other hand, if an arrest happens at night or if other residents are tied up with emergencies, we, the new interns, may be the only doctors available at an attempted resuscitation. If you were that patient, would you want to be my first or would you want me to have more experience? If you want me to have gained more realistic experience, how do I obtain it? How does the surgical training program provide it?

What is the best way to train surgeons, or more generally doctors? There always has to be a first time you, the trainee doctor, do something with a supervising mentor present. There also always has to be a first time you do something alone without a supervising mentor present. What preparation and training should you have? There always has to be a first time you do something. I repeat, there always has to be a first time you do something alone. There has to be a first time you make an incision in a patient. There has to be a first time you perform CPR by yourself. There has to be a first time you perform surgery by yourself.

I remember when I was an orthopedic resident at Massachusetts General Hospital, three of us, residents, and the attending surgeon stopped by to see a patient the evening before surgery. The patient told the attending surgeon that he only wanted the surgeon to operate. He would not allow a resident to operate on him. The attending orthopedic surgeon replied that this was a teaching hospital and that residents did most of the surgery. He, the attending orthopedic surgeon, would be there the entire time. The attending repeated that this was a teaching hospital. If he, the patient, wanted surgery at this hospital, with his, the attending surgeon's involvement, the patient would have to agree to that. We, residents, silently cheered. The patient agreed.

I also recall scrubbing on a case as a surgical intern on a physician from out of town, who was a Nobel laureate. This was clearly a case in which I would be holding retractors. I was quite surprised when the attending surgeon handed me the knife to perform the operation. This was clearly a teaching hospital and quite clearly a dedicated surgical teaching program. By the end of my internship year, I had even performed several bowel cases, which required delicate suturing of the bowel. Much of this surgery is now done with stapling machines. We were allowed to do more and more difficult cases as we improved and advanced in our training.

How do you evaluate complex systems? I recall as a young boy watching over the shoulder of a TV repairman. In those days, TVs were big and heavy. Repairmen came to the home. Solid state electronics had not been developed yet. The back of the TV was crammed full of vacuum tubes. To me, at that time, unknowably complex. I watched as the repairman found a "blown" tube. He removed the tube but did not replace it. The TV, which before did not work at all, now worked perfectly. "How can this be?" I asked, "How can you remove a vacuum tube, not replace it, and then the TV works?" He replied that this specific vacuum tube provided a refinement of the image which was finer than the eye could detect. With this specific tube broken the entire complex system of the TV was broken. With this tube absent the TV worked fine. This was my first introduction to the evaluation of complex systems. Not unlike the situation in which a hand can work well in the absence of a finger but a "bad" finger may significantly disrupt the overall functioning of the hand. A seriously ill patient is like a complex system with multiple parts of that system broken. I was taught to separate out the individual subsystems: heart, lungs, blood red cell levels, electrolytes, infections, etc., and then analyze each subsystem individually.

More ricocheting in the pinball machine of my memory. I did warn you. On your first day of general surgical internship, who were your first patients? Recall, I'm the C student who was assigned the most difficult rotation, the chief's service, first. The chief's service covered the Surgical Intensive Care Unit (SICU), as well as other patients. The severity of illness and disease of the patients in the SICU was so great that their mortality rate averaged about 70%. My first patients included a man who had undergone emergency surgery for an acute ruptured abdominal aortic aneurysm many weeks earlier. In an acute ruptured abdominal aortic aneurysm, the largest artery in the body blows out causing immediate massive internal bleeding. A high mortality diagnosis. Following emergency surgery, this patient had the following problems: 1. kidney failure—he was on dialysis; 2. a type of heart failure—his heart could not beat on its own; he required a pacemaker to stimulate his heart to beat; 3. respiratory failure—he could not breathe on his own and needed a respirator. 4. He was also continually unconscious with unknown brain injury from lack of oxygen when the aneurysm blew and his blood pressure dropped. Four system failures. This situation had remained ongoing for more than six weeks on the day I started my general surgery internship.

Eventually the pacemaker stopped working. The cardiologists felt that there was no point in replacing the failed pacemaker. The patient would not survive without a new pacemaker. The surgeon in charge disagreed. The cardiologist still refused to insert a new pacemaker. The patient died that day, rather than sometime later. Another ethical dilemma. When is it appropriate to discontinue care in a terminally ill patient? In this case, I do not recall any family who visited him or who were available for consultation. There was intense disagreement between treating physicians.

We had a patient in his 30s with a 35% burn. A rough calculation of mortality in burn patients at that time consisted of adding the age and the percent of body burned. Thus, the mortality estimate for this patient was 65%. I spent an hour every day in the shower debriding dead, burned skin to expose underlying healing granulation tissue to prepare him for skin grafting. It took about three months to fully cover all of his burns with skin grafts.

During that time, he did not wear clothes due to the frequent debridement and grafting treatments. In the last weeks of his hospitalization, he was allowed to leave his room and go to the ICU kitchen for food and snacks. His body had tremendous need for calories. One evening, he wandered down to the kitchen for a snack but forgot to put on a robe. He was so used to being naked. A nurse looking down the hall called security because there was a naked man walking in the hospital.

Another patient was trapped in a burning car. He suffered massive burns including fourth-degree burns. First-degree burns are just redness. Second-degree burns include blistering. Third-degree burns are death of the full thickness of the skin. Fourth-degree burns are death of tissue down to bone. We kept him alive for about a month. He eventually died from overwhelming infection including infected heart valves.

There was a man with severe bowel disease whose bowel had become inflamed and leaked in multiple places. He had undergone multiple previous unsuccessful operations. He was possibly the longest survivor, at that time, on intravenous hyperalimentation. He was receiving all of his nutrition by IV. There was little of his bowel remaining. The day before I started my internship, he had just undergone another attempt at reconstruction of the remaining bowel. Over the course of my first week of internship, his bowel developed six leaks which were handled with six low-pressure intermittent suction drains. The intravenous was a central line. This line was his lifeline. Every three days the dressing covering the entry point of this line was carefully washed with antibacterial solution. Maintaining this line was a priority for each intern on the chief's service.

Sometime later, he was taken back to the operating room. He had undergone many operations and was terrified of more operations. Dr. Moore consented to administering light general anesthesia in his room and taking him down to the operating room while under light general anesthesia. An anesthesia resident administered the anesthesia. Then he and I rolled the patient with the anesthesia machine down to the elevator accompanied by a swarm of other personnel. The anesthesia resident and I got on the elevator with the anesthetized patient and the anesthesia machine. The elevator went down half a floor and got stuck. Recall, this building was a pre-World War I structure. The elevators had the accordion type metal doors. The anesthesia resident and I were the only ones in the elevator with the patient. The patient was stable. We could awaken him, if we needed to. We heard the shouting and confusion of everyone else outside of the elevator. It took about 20 minutes to get the elevator working. The anesthesia resident and I were the only calm ones for those 20 minutes.

I recall at some point this patient developed a total body skin rash. The dermatologists were stumped. Finally, someone figured out that this patient was zinc deficient. There was no zinc in the hyperalimentation solution. When zinc was added the rash went away.

My first night as an intern, I was on call. We admitted a 75-year-old woman with burns covering 75% of her body. She had fallen asleep, drunk, while smoking. For a rough estimate of her mortality probability at that time we added the patient's age to the percentage of the body burned. Based on that calculation her mortality probability was 150%. Not a good prognosis. We worked hard to save her. She died after three weeks despite our best efforts.

These were some of the early patients I teethed on in my first weeks as a general surgical intern. Faced with a complicated patient with serious problems with multiple systems, it is easy to become overwhelmed. I was taught; I learned to separate out each system individually and evaluate it on its own. Thus, I learned a general approach to complicated problems. Divide and simplify.

Another vignette. On the transplant service. First transplant surgery of the senior resident's rotation on to the transplant service was done by the attending. All others were done by the senior resident. Many of the transplants worked amazingly well. Some failed and were surgically removed. There were occasional infections. We had one patient whose failed transplant had been removed and who had an open wound in his left groin, which we were allowing to heal in naturally, called healing by second intention. One Saturday morning, around 6 a.m., I was startled awake by my beeper beeping, overhead page shouting my name and pounding on the door of my on-call room. The triple sign that something serious and urgent is happening. I ran full speed to the ward. Significant bleeding spurting from the groin wound. Blood pumping a foot or so high. Put on sterile gloves. Put hand into the wound. Wipe away blood. See the femoral artery with a pinhole in its side. Put my finger on the hole and push. Bleeding stops. I feel like the little Dutch boy with his finger in the dike. Tell the nurses to call in the team, certain the patient will need to go to the operating room. Wait for the team to come into the hospital. Half an hour goes by. The whole team assembles at the bedside. I have been applying continuous pressure for over half an hour. As the team watches, I remove my finger. No bleeding. Did not need to go the OR. Never bled again. Healed in. I suppose there was sufficient clotting of the hole in the artery that the patient was able to continue healing the wound without further bleeding.

I marvel at the wondrous ways people injure themselves. Gentleman is locked out of his girlfriend's apartment. Gentleman wants in. Gentleman climbs out on to ledge of apartment building six stories up. Gentleman reaches window of girlfriend's apartment. Gentleman falls six stories. Never clear whether he was helped by girlfriend. Lands on a child's toy, hitting it with his hip and pelvis. Defenestration (out the window) cases result in serious injury. The severity of the injuries rapidly escalates as the distance of the fall increases. A 12-foot fall usually results in at least one serious fracture. By three stories, the mortality rate soars. This was six stories.

Large open wound in the inguinal area. At emergency surgery, six areas of torn bowel were found just from the "sloshing" impact on the bowel. After reconstructive surgery the open wound is packed open. Days pass. Patient is surviving, but there is intermittent bleeding from the packed wound. There is a low-grade infection in the wound. To be safe we, the residents in charge of his treatment, keep a minimum of four units of blood typed and crossed in the blood bank. We physically go to the blood bank each day to ensure the blood is there, in case we need it quickly.

One morning, my team is in the operating room operating on a big case. I am not in the operating room this day. We always have one member of the team out of the operating room to cover emergencies. The service is temporarily quiet.

I am in the record room dictating charts. I have mentioned that Peter Bent is pre-World War I architecture and is spread out longitudinally. The record room is as far away from the surgical ICU (SICU) as you can get and still be in the hospital. I am caught up on my charts but am dictating another resident's delinquent charts. In order to motivate residents to dictate their charts on time, the hospital has begun deducting from the salary of interns and residents five dollars for any chart more than one month overdue. If the chart is dictated in the next month, the five dollars is refunded. If a second month goes by, the five-dollar fine is permanent. Then, any resident can dictate the chart and earn the five dollars.

You would think this policy would work and stimulate all of the interns and residents to dictate their charts on time. Wrong! The law of unintended consequences overwhelms. One of our residents is trust baby wealthy. Once he realized that it would only cost five dollars a chart to skip a dictation, he stopped doing all of his dictation. I, on the other hand, needed the money. I was more than happy to dictate his charts for five dollars each. I could dictate a chart every five minutes, earning up to $60 an hour. Unfortunately, there weren't that many charts which required my dictation. This is what I was doing. I was earning $11,000 a year as a surgical intern. Working perhaps 120 hours a week for 52 weeks. Thus, I was earning slightly less than two dollars an hour most of the time.

Back to the guy who fell six stories. So, there I am dictating charts. My beeper goes off. Simultaneously, I hear my name in a stat overhead voice page for the SICU. Never good news. I call the SICU. The head nurse tells me that there is massive bleeding coming from this patient's open wound. I have worked with this nurse for a while. She is experienced. She does not get excited easily. She is describing a massive hemorrhage that if untreated will cause death quickly. I race out of the record room and run down the hall. The blood bank, fortunately, is on my way. I run into the blood bank, past the counter over to the refrigerator. I grab all four units of blood. I do not wait to sign them out. I do not sign any of the formal paperwork. I run down the hall towards the SICU, holding the four units of blood. Picture the drama of this scene. I am chased all the way through the hospital by a blood bank employee, screaming and yelling, because of my breach of protocol.

I reach the ICU. The bleeding is as described. Insert four large bore IVs into each arm and leg and begin pumping in all four units of blood into this patient. There is a nurse at each IV with a three-way stopcock and a 50-cc. syringe. Rotate the stopcock valve. Pull blood into the syringe from the blood bag as fast as you can. Rotate stopcock valve. Push blood into the IV as fast as you can. Repeat. Four nurses. Four IVs. Call the OR. We need the next operating room that opens up for this emergency. The bleeding is from a location too deep for direct pressure to help stop the hemorrhage. My team gets out of the OR 20 minutes later. Patient still bleeding, but temporarily stabilized by the blood transfusions. Down to the OR. Explore the wound. A large amount of poor-quality tissue. Cannot find the actual bleeder. Put in some large sutures with blunt liver needles and pack deeply. The bleeding stops.

The chief resident then consults all of the "grey hairs", i.e., the oldest and the most experienced surgeons in the hospital. He seeks advice. Namely, how long to leave the packing in. All advise, "As long as possible. Until you can't stand the smell." Packing left in for weeks. Then removed. Never bled again. Patient healed and left the hospital. Remarkable save for a six-story fall. Regarding my breach of protocol at the blood bank. No reprimand. My superiors approved of my actions. An "appropriate" breach of protocol.

While a general surgery intern on the orthopedic rotation, I treated a man with a wrist fracture. Treatment included the injection of numbing medicine into the fracture, manipulation of the fracture back into proper position and the application of an arm cast. The whole process took about 45 minutes. During this entire time, I was subjected to a continuing harangue about how terrible doctors and hospitals were. This patient told me that he was on the Massachusetts board that regulates and controls hospitals and doctors. Think of this. Most patients want their doctor to like them, hoping the doctor will treat them well. This patient had such an intense hatred of doctors that he had gotten himself appointed to the board that regulates doctors and hospitals. His hatred was so intense that even in the midst of his treatment, he was continually spewing his vitriol. Wow!

More vignettes. Random synaptic firings in my brain. No clear order or organization. Many of you have seen the movie "Serpico." At the end of the movie, Serpico, a police detective, is shot in the face, right in the nose. When I was on the neurosurgical service, I was called to the emergency room to see a patient who was unconscious. This patient had been shot in the nose. There was a bullet entry at the front of the nose and no exit wound. The patient was unconscious.

The most basic functions of the body and brain are controlled by the area of the brain called the brain stem. This structure is at the bottom or base of the brain. In evolution, this part of the brain evolved first and controls the most basic functions of the body. This patient's pupils did not react to light. This is a primal, basic function. The nerves to the eyes were not working. There is a test called the Doll's Eye maneuver. If you turn a patient's head quickly to one side, the eyes will tend to stay looking in the direction they were originally facing. If there is no brain stem function, the eyes will turn with the head. That was the case in this patient. Both the reaction to light and the Doll's Eye maneuver are basic brain stem reflexes. They were absent in this patient.

Another brain stem reflex test is called calorics. If you put warm or cold water or warm or cold air in the external ear canal, the fluid in the semi-circular inner ear canals will circulate in response to the temperature change. In an awake patient this will cause a sense of dizziness and the patient's eyes will move to the side in a staggered manner called nystagmus. Our patient had negative calorics, indicating further lack of brain stem function.

The neurosurgical resident performed all of these tests as part of the examination of the patient. He was also demonstrating these brain stem reflexes to me, the surgical intern, for my education. The neurosurgical resident was demonstrating to me the total lack of brain stem function. In essence, he was demonstrating to me that this patient, by exam, was brain dead. We called for a portable X-ray, expecting it to show that the bullet had entered the brain and spun around the inside of the skull.

While we were waiting for the X-ray, the patient suddenly blinked his eyes and woke up. He quickly became as awake and alert as we were. Given that it was the middle of the night and we were sleep deprived, perhaps it didn't take much to be as alert as we were. X-rays later showed the bullet had travelled along the side of the face and ended up in the mastoid, the bony bump behind the ear. It was a low velocity .22 caliber bullet. The passage of the bullet just outside of the skull must have caused a shock wave, which temporarily knocked out the brain stem function (like temporarily being knocked unconscious) without permanent damage to the brain stem. The only permanent damage was loss of hearing in one ear. Only with a low velocity .22 bullet could you ever see something like this. Most unusual.

Fatigue was my constant companion of every other night call, year in and year out, for two years. Stumbling home, for love and sustenance. Thank God, Lynne was there. Choices made without conscious thought. If I sat at the dining table first when I got home, I would eat then sleep. If not, I would sleep and miss a meal. My routine was to stumble home, sleep Saturday afternoon and then have some rested time Saturday night and Sunday to spend with my new love. About one day and a quarter of rested time every two weeks. Simple pleasures. One Saturday, friends visited from out of town. I had been on call both Thursday and Friday night with little sleep. Because friends were visiting, I missed my Saturday afternoon nap. We were with our friends Saturday afternoon and went out for dinner together Saturday night. I am told I lasted through the main course. I am told I fell asleep with my face literally in my dessert. I have no recollection. I slept through it. They left me there until they were ready to leave the restaurant. Great company, I was.

More early training vignettes. At the time of my surgical internship, the hospital did not have IV nurses. That is, there were no dedicated nurses or technicians who started IVs. Any IV that was needed was started by the intern. Me. I had to do it. However long it took. I was it. No calling for a senior resident for help starting an IV. Ever. Period. End of discussion.

There are some patients with few superficial veins. Then there are the intravenous drug addicts who have destroyed almost all of their superficial veins. When a patient needed an IV for antibiotics for a serious infection, you kept at it. Two a.m. and a difficult IV could take an hour and a number of sticks to work. I learned to ask the IV drug addicts where their best vein was. Sometimes it was a small vein on the back of the base of one of the fingers. Desperate to make each IV last as long as possible, I treated the IVs like pediatric IVs. First, get a rigid arm board and a roll of gauze. Put the roll of gauze under the palm and tape the back of the hand and forearm to the arm board. Then use the smallest butterfly needle. Get into the vein. Gently tape it down. Take a cardboard sputum cup. Cut out two C shapes on the open side. Invert and place over the hand and forearm and tape in place. A lot of effort, but I got more sleep that way. I prided myself that my IVs lasted longer than anyone else's.

One 4 a.m. IV I started in the midst of dense fatigue ran well. When I came by at 6 a.m. on rounds, I noted that I had neglected to take off the rubber band used to restrict blood flow to start the IV. The IV was running fine. I removed the rubber band. In the midst of severe fatigue, it is easy to make mistakes. Today trainee physicians do not work the same long hours we worked back then. Perhaps fewer fatigue errors. But less total training experience. I am not sure where the optimum trade-off lies.

Similarly, in the midst of dense fatigue, I once ordered fresh frozen plasma to be given to the wrong patient. We had an anephric (no kidneys) dialysis patient who had been operated on for perforated diverticulitis. In perforated diverticulitis, bowel contents spill into the abdominal cavity. Due to inflammation of the bowel and abdominal lining, there was need for frequent infusions of plasma to cover losses of plasma into the abdominal cavity. With an

80

anephric patient, fluid intake needs to be carefully monitored, since there is no kidney function to excrete excess fluid. The fresh frozen plasma was kept in a refrigerator in the SICU.

I was deeply asleep when called about a postoperative patient with decreasing urine output. In the midst of dense fatigue and roused from deep, deep sleep, I confused the two patients and ordered the plasma on the patient with decreasing urine output. Normally this would have been treated by increasing IV fluid. I fell back asleep. When I was awakened for another reason an hour later, I realized my mistake and checked on the patient. Fortunately, no harm was done. This was a mistake resulting from deep, dense fatigue. These two mistakes are the only two I ever made that I was aware of. Both the result of deep and dense fatigue. Fortunately, no harm done. I was told that the anephric patient with perforated diverticulitis was the first patient with that combination to survive.

In my general surgery internship year, we were required to take a national medical board exam. I was on call the night before the exam. All of the senior residents volunteered to cover for their interns the night before the exam so that we interns would be rested for the exam. All of the senior residents, that is, except mine. I had to trade night call in order to be off the night before the test. Given our every other night on call schedule, as the result of the trade, I ended up being on call three nights in a row. I was on the thoracic surgery service. By the third night in a row of being on call, I was in serious fatigue trouble with no one to turn to for help. By serious fatigue trouble, I mean serious fatigue trouble. I was staggering. I was beyond functioning.

We had three patients that night with abnormal rapid heart rate rhythms called atrial fibrillation. These three patients needed EKGs run by me, every two hours to measure their heart rates, in order to decide how much heart rate-lowering medicine, digoxin, to give them intravenously. I was instructed to take the EKG myself and to administer the IV digoxin myself. Sometime in the wee hours that night, probably around 2 a.m., I staggered into the surgical ICU, fell into an empty bed and collapsed into deep sleep. I woke around 7 a.m. the next morning, vaguely remembering having been shaken awake, shown EKGs, mumbling orders and falling back asleep intermittently throughout the night.

The nurses in the surgical ICU, bless them, knew I was on my third night in a row on call. They knew I was spent; knew I was incapable of functioning. On their own initiative, they called the other floors, arranged for the EKGs to be run by the nurses, arranged to have the EKGs brought to the ICU. When they had all three, they then awakened me, had me mumble orders, transmitted the orders, had the nurses administer the digoxin IV. When I rounded on the patients and checked the charts that morning, all of my orders were correct. Thank God!

Putting me in this situation was a serious failure of management at multiple levels. Had I made a serious mistake, however, I would have been personally blamed and the nurses would have been blamed. The nurses were heroes. I was so staggeringly exhausted, it took me days to even realize what the nurses had done. I repeat, this situation was a failure of management at multiple levels. There was no one I could turn to for help. Seeing the situation, the nurses clearly did not feel that they had a way to express their concerns to management either. This was quite simply considered business as usual.

Yet another sleep deprivation vignette. When I was on the neurosurgery service, a patient was electively admitted to the hospital around 2 a.m. She was from South America and had been traveling for two days to get to Boston. I reached her room around 2:30 a.m., sat down in a chair and began to take her history. She had had little sleep while traveling for the past two days. Likewise, I was seriously sleep deprived. I woke up about two hours later still sitting in my chair. She was asleep. I think we both fell asleep at the same time. I woke her up and finished taking her history.

Some of the problems we treat as surgeons involve congenital abnormalities. As part of my anesthesia rotation as a surgical intern, I was assigned to administer anesthesia to a patient scheduled for a reduction mammoplasty (partial removal of each breast to decrease breast size). From the simple name of the operation, this seemed to be a good surgical intern anesthesia case. Thus, I was assigned to provide general anesthesia for this case. Some women, for genetic reasons, have breasts that are exceptionally large. This is enlargement far, far beyond sexual attractiveness. These patients have chronic neck and shoulder pain. The weight on their shoulders from their unusually large breasts causes drooping of the shoulder area. As a practicing orthopedic surgeon, I, occasionally, was referred these patients for orthopedic examination so that I could write a letter to the insurance company certifying that the reduction mammoplasty surgery was medically indicated and not a cosmetic procedure. With this certification, the insurance company paid for the procedure.

The patient I was to give anesthesia to came to the operating room. Her problem with excessive breast enlargement exceeded any I have ever seen. Her breasts were so large that when she was sitting, her breasts rested on her thighs. They extended beyond her knees. They were so big and heavy that she could not breathe if she lay down on her back. Normally when general anesthesia is administered, the patient lies on her back. This allows easy access to the airway. In this patient, we had to administer anesthesia and intubate her in an upright sitting position. Each breast when removed weighed 35 pounds. Post-op, she was a happy woman. It is sad that she did not get her surgery earlier.

A contrasting story to this patient was a patient I saw on my plastic surgery rotation. She was 45 years old, admitted to the hospital for an augmentation mammoplasty. The typical "boob" job. As I took her history, I asked why she was having the procedure. She explained that her husband was playing around and she hoped this would help her hold on to him. Sad. I do not think this was a good reason for the surgery. Better to dump the bum. I, of course, did not tell her this.

A friend who became a plastic surgeon told me of a case which involved the question of who should have surgery. There is a rare congenital anomaly in which a female is born without one breast and without the pectoral (chest) muscles which normally lie underneath the breast. As a young teenager this patient underwent an augmentation mammoplasty to attempt to give her a breast on the affected side. Without muscle to anchor the prosthesis, the breast prosthesis slipped upward. She had suffered dislocation of the breast implant twice before and was coming in for her fourth operation. On my friend's physical examination, the prosthesis was far out of position, resting just below the collarbone. The front of her chest on that side was crisscrossed with scars. Her other breast was normal. Without any surgeries, she would have been beautiful, though unusual, with only one breast. With the multiple scars, she was now disfigured. The attempts at surgery made her significantly worse. Let me introduce a common surgical saying, "The enemy of good is better." Sometimes it is better to accept the who and what you have. Not every problem is correctable. It is easy to make patients worse.

After surgery, patients are often unable to void (urinate). This almost always occurs in men with enlarged prostates. It occurs rarely in women. Nurses were generally responsible for the insertion of catheters to drain urine from the bladder when necessary. We, interns, were only called when the nurses were unable to do this. For men, there is equipment called filiform and followers. You pass a thin solid rubber tube up the urethra. You maneuver this tube up the urethra and pass the area of constriction. You then screw on a slightly larger rubber tube. You keep screwing on slightly larger tubes and passing them past the constriction and up into the bladder until you reach a size that is hollow. This then allows the urine to drain. There are no more grateful patients.

I was called one evening to the female ward because the nurses were unable to catheterize a woman who could not void. I inspected the usual anatomic location for the opening of the urethra. I noted that there was no opening. This explained why the nurses were unsuccessful with their attempts at catheterization. I could not find the urethral opening. Again, that question. What to do? Middle of the night. I am the surgical intern. Do I try to figure it out for myself or call for help? Not good, not good at all, to call a senior resident in from home in the middle of the night, unless really, really necessary.

I pushed on this woman's distended bladder and noted urine trickling out of her vagina. Clearly the urine was coming out somewhere. Normally in a vaginal exam, a gynecologist inserts a speculum, which gently distends the vaginal opening up and down to allow visibility of the cervix. I ended up utilizing a speculum in a sideways fashion to visualize the anterior (front) wall of the vagina. Using a bright light for visibility, I pushed on the bladder. I could see urine trickling from an opening part way up the anterior (front) wall of the vagina. I obtained long clamps from the operating room. Using two of them, I was able to insert a catheter into the urethral opening and feed it up into the bladder to relieve the distention. I have actually seen this anatomic abnormality and had to catheterize it twice. To be an effective intern or resident, you have to be willing to take initiative and responsibility for decision-making. If I have seen this congenital abnormality twice, I assume it is not that rare. All my medical school teaching of congenital abnormalities and they did not teach me this one. Somehow, I think I should have been taught about this possibility without having to figure it out for myself.

More on naive, little me. While on my gynecology rotation, I saw a young woman with an infected abscess on one breast. There seemed to be crusted puncture wounds above the abscess. I asked her what had happened. She told me she had been bitten by an animal. Naively, I asked what kind of animal. She smiled coyly and said, "A nice animal."

In the early 1970s the women's liberation movement was in full war cry. I think that is a fair description. Among the strident calls for feminine empowerment was the complaint that men should no longer hold the door for women. I recall holding a door for a woman at Saks Fifth Avenue in Boston and being subjected to a particularly virulent lecture on the error of my ways. At the time I was a general surgical intern at Peter Bent, there were no gynecology residents. So, we, general surgery interns and residents, rotated on to the gynecology service, attended the gynecology clinic and scrubbed on all the gynecology cases. At that time, almost all of the gynecology doctors were male. The women's liberation activists, as I recall, were quite vocal about trying to eliminate the "mystique" of the male gynecologist versus the female patient. The women's lib activists recommended that patients throw the sheet off of the bed and stare at the gynecologist while he was performing the pelvic exam. I actually had a patient do that. Not sure what the maneuver gained. The patient certainly was able to see everything I did. Talk about awkward.

Even more on naive little me. Many patients came to the gynecology clinic with complaints of bleeding from the vagina. The most common causes were fibroids and incomplete, spontaneous abortions. One patient on exam had abrasions up and down the walls of her vagina. This was an unusual cause of vaginal bleeding. Something I had never seen before. In taking a history from a patient, it is important to figure out what questions to ask. Sometimes a broad question is best. I simply asked, "What's been going on?" She stated she had had sex with multiple partners the night before. The only time in my career I lost my professional demeanor. Mind you, this was early in my first year. I guess it was a reflex. I asked if she'd had fun. She replied, "Oh, yeah!" Never lost it again. Not good professional manner. Nobody is perfect. She did not seem to mind. My treatment? Advised her to "Let it rest awhile to heal itself."

When I was on the gynecology service, we had a patient with severe rheumatic heart disease, a disease in which the heart struggles to push out blood during pumping due to damage to the heart valves. The heart valves are narrowed (stenosis) by scarring. The narrowing of the heart valves limits the amount of blood the heart can pump out. The patient had been previously advised not to get pregnant. Pregnancy puts a great deal of stress on the heart, particularly around the eighth month of pregnancy when the heart is beating for two people. This patient became pregnant. As she reached the eighth month of pregnancy, she began failing. The heart was having trouble pumping out enough blood to keep her and her baby alive. To save her life and the life of her baby, it was necessary to perform a Caesarean section (incision in the lower abdomen, vertical incision in the uterus, pop out the baby, sew everything up). This patient was so ill that she could not tolerate general anesthesia or spinal anesthesia.

She was brought to the operating room. At the head of the table was the anesthesiologist, although she was not there to give anesthesia; she was there to administer medicine as necessary to try to support the patient. Next to the anesthesiologist was her cardiologist, also to help with her medical support. Only time I ever saw a cardiologist in a regular operating room. Local anesthetic (like Novocain) was injected into the skin and fatty tissue of the lower abdomen. Incision in the skin and fatty tissue of the lower abdomen. Incision in the uterus. Physiology lesson. The skin has nerves which cause the sensation of pain when these skin nerves are cut. This obviously is necessary from an evolutionary point of view so that we know to protect ourselves from injury. In contrast, deep tissue can be sharply cut without causing the perception of pain. Thus, a surgeon can cut deep tissue without anesthesia. A normal, healthy baby was delivered and the mother survived, at least, for the short term. We did not have successful treatment for severe rheumatic heart disease at that time. Today, heart valve replacements are an option for treatment.

I have talked about doctors' dependence on our assisting personnel. One Saturday morning, as an intern, I had a severely ill patient who was temporarily housed in the recovery room because the ICU was full. Lab reports at that time normally came over a teletype machine. The labs did not come. I called the lab and was told by a young man working the weekend that he had already sent the labs over the teletype. I told him that I had not received the labs and asked him to read the results over the phone. He refused. I ran down to the lab to ask him for the lab results. He refused and closed the window through which we were talking by slamming it down. I finally realized that he had probably sent the labs to another ICU. I ran up there and found the labs. On Monday, I complained to the head of the lab about the assistant's behavior. Her response? "He's such a nice boy. You know, he wants to go to medical school." I hope he didn't get in, but he probably did. I wonder what kind of a doctor he became with that attitude.

As a junior resident in general surgery I rotated on to the plastic surgery service. The ability to move tissue, manipulate tissue and reshape tissue was fascinating. One day I was operating with Dr. Joseph Murray. He had won the Nobel Prize for early work in kidney transplantation. We were doing routine cases, which, given the nature of our training program, I should have been doing, but he just went ahead and did them. I was frustrated and angry and trying to figure out how to respond in a way that might work positively. Simply complaining would not work. So I said to Dr. Murray that I was really concerned. I felt that he didn't think I was any good. That he was afraid to give me cases because I wasn't any good. He said something to the effect of, "No, no, no, that's not true. In fact, I have a parotid tumor excision coming up next week. I'd like you to do it. I have a movie on how to do it. Watch the movie."

Parotid tumors are rare. At least, back then they required a special technique of teasing them away from the facial nerve with small blunt hooks to keep from injuring the facial nerve. Now, the chief resident in plastic surgery had never done one. The senior surgical resident had never done one. All that week, they went crazy over the fact that Dr. Murray had decided to give me that case and not them. The operation went well. Good training for me.

Yet another vignette. This one an awkward vignette. Really awkward vignette. Awkward for me, that is. Most awkward of my training. Most awkward of my career. I was on the plastic surgery service. The plastic surgeon and I were finishing an operation at one hospital. We had a second operation scheduled at another hospital. The second operation was a reconstruction, which involved the rotation of skin and soft tissue flaps. The second operation was scheduled as a combined orthopedic and plastic surgery operation. We were running late with the first operation. The plastic surgeon instructed me to go over to the second hospital and move that case along. I drove over there, met the attending orthopedic surgeon and examined the patient. The operating room was open, so the attending orthopedic surgeon immediately took the patient back to the operating room. I went along.

I was expecting the plastic surgeon to turn up momentarily. The patient was anesthetized. I stood at the operating table waiting for instructions from the orthopedic surgeon. The orthopedic surgeon told me that this was a plastic surgery case. That! I was the representative of the plastic surgery department. That! I should begin to operate. Now! I explained that I had not discussed this case with the plastic surgeon. I did not know which type of skin flap he was planning to use. No sign of the plastic surgeon. No cellphones. No email. No way to reach the plastic surgeon. The orthopedic surgeon ordered me to begin operating, using the strongest possible language. What to do? What to do? What to do?

Talk about an uncomfortable situation. Talk about awkward. There is a situation which occasionally arises in chess called zugzwang. Zugzwang refers to a position in which the obligation to move is a profound disadvantage. You are forced to move. In being forced to move, you lose. You cannot pass. I felt like I was in a zugzwang position. Except. In real life. In an operating room. My two choices were: 1. refuse to start operating, or 2. start operating. The imperative I felt from the attending orthopedic surgeon was overwhelming. I felt impelled to start operating. Expecting the plastic surgeon to arrive any minute, I slowly marked out the flaps, I felt were correct. Then, slowly, I began to operate. I had been operating for perhaps half an hour before the plastic surgeon arrived. He was held up in traffic by a bad accident. He approved of my flaps but extended them to the different flaps he was planning on using. All these many years later, I still marvel at how I was inadvertently placed in such an awkward real life "zugzwang" situation.

When I was an intern and general surgery resident, there were three known types of hepatitis: A, B and non-A–non-B. Hepatitis is a viral infection of the liver. The number of known types has now expanded. Hepatitis B can be transmitted by blood contact and was a known risk for working doctors, surgeons, nurses, interns and residents. I was always one of the most careful to minimize possible exposure to disease. For example, when I washed my hands, I then dried my hands and turned off the water with the paper towel. As part of a research project at Peter Bent, blood samples were drawn on all of the house officers. I received a call that my blood test was antigen positive and antibody negative for Hepatitis B. Antigen positive means that there is actual "living" virus in your blood. Antibody positive means your body's immune system is reacting to the virus. Antibody negative means there is no evidence that your body is reacting to the virus. I was having no symptoms.

I immediately consulted with a staff internist, who was an expert in this field. Earlier that year, a dialysis nurse in our hospital died from acute yellow atrophy. That meant the hepatitis virus completely "killed" her liver. She died in days. We drew blood tests for my liver enzymes. Mine were minimally elevated. There is a disease called chronic active hepatitis. I was convinced I had that. Life expectancy for chronic active hepatitis at that time was three to five years. They took me off night call. Over the next three weeks, my liver enzymes went up a little and then came back to normal. The antigen titer turned negative indicating no more "live" virus in the blood. The antibody titer turned positive indicating normal immune response to the virus infection. I never had any symptoms except fear regarding the diagnosis.

I went back to taking night call. The researchers had serendipitously picked up a mild, asymptomatic case of hepatitis B infection. I spent three weeks terrified that I had something more serious. My internist kept wanting to do a liver biopsy for research purposes. I kept declining.

There is a hormone gland in the lower neck region called the parathyroid. Para means nearby, so parathyroid means near the thyroid. This gland secretes parathormone, which is important in the control of calcium levels in the blood. There are four parathyroid glands. Abnormalities in the parathyroid, in which too much parathormone is being secreted, may require surgery to remove essentially three and one half of the parathyroid glands. This is an uncommon surgery and in surgical training programs only performed by the senior residents.

At the time I was a surgical intern at Peter Bent Brigham Hospital, it had, I was told, the largest dialysis population in the world. It was in the early days in the development of dialysis for the treatment of chronic renal failure. It was also the early days of kidney transplantation surgery.

Before I continue with this story, another side story. A carpool of dialysis patients was on its way to the hospital for dialysis when it was involved in a serious motor vehicle accident on the Massachusetts Turnpike, with multiple severe injuries to multiple patients. We received a panicked phone call from the Newton Wellesley Hospital ER. In those days, few physicians had experience treating patients without working kidneys. With Peter Bent having a large population of dialysis patients, we were comfortable treating patients without working kidneys. We told the physicians at Newton Wellesley Hospital to send all of the patients in by ambulance. We joked with each other, "At least, we don't have to worry about kidney failure."

My memory is that early in my internship, the dialysis physicians discovered that the phosphate concentration in the dialysate (the fluid used in dialysis) needed adjustment. The doctors treating these patients discovered that most of the patients on dialysis at that time had developed hyperparathyroidism. That is, the parathyroid gland was reacting and producing too much parathyroid hormone on its own. For treatment of this problem, three- and one-half parathyroid glands needed to be surgically removed from perhaps 100 patients. The general surgeons on the private service began to admit two patients a week for this "rare" surgery. After the chief resident had done enough, and the senior resident had done enough and the junior resident had done enough, this "rare" case became a "routine" intern case. I have discussed before the randomness and the apprentice-like nature of medical and surgical training. We learn from the patients happenstance brings our way. This is a perfect example of that. I probably performed more parathyroidectomy operations as a surgical intern than most general surgeons perform in their careers.

CHAPTER SEVEN

Application to Orthopedic Residency

If you were in good standing in one of the general surgery programs at one of the Harvard hospitals, admission into the Harvard Orthopedic Residency Program was pretty much assured. There hadn't been a denial in recent memory. I was part way through my second year of general surgery training. Still feeling like I was newly married. Life was good. Lynne was working as a physical therapist at Peter Bent Brigham Hospital with a salary of $11,000 a year. As a junior assistant resident, I was paid $11,000 a year. My wife and I had little excess money.

I interviewed with Dr. Henry Mankin, the chief of orthopedics at Mass General. In my interview, I asked Dr. Mankin if it was advisable or necessary for me to apply to other orthopedic programs. He said, "No." So I didn't. Trusting, naive, little me. As a general surgical intern and junior resident, I worked with Dr. Drennan Lowell at Peter Bent Brigham Hospital while on my orthopedic rotation. I asked Dr. Lowell to write a letter of recommendation for me. He told me that he would be glad to do so.

Then I received a letter telling me that I had been turned down for the Harvard Orthopedic Residency program. Surprise! Unexpected! Disappointment! Shock! I need to check my thesaurus for a few more descriptive words. I called Dr. Mankin to inquire about this turn of events. He told me I should call Dr. Lowell. I called Dr. Lowell. He told me he would need to talk to some people, whatever that meant. A few days later Dr. Brooks, a general surgeon at Peter Bent, stopped me in the hallway and said he had heard I was having difficulty with my application to the orthopedic program. Dr. Brooks said he had heard someone had written a blackballing letter about me. I asked whether someone had spontaneously, without prompting, written such a letter. Dr. Brooks responded, "No, No, No!" I followed up, asking whether one of my requested letters of recommendation had blackballed me. Dr. Brooks stuttered and stammered that he hadn't meant that at all.

Lynne and I went out for dinner that night to Natalie's, a cozy restaurant on Mass Ave., in Cambridge. Red and white checked tablecloths. Cheap wine bottles overflowing with candle drippings. Good food. Intimate atmosphere. Our favorite haunt. Lynne and I discussed and strategized. Lynne, working as a therapist at Peter Bent, had once heard Dr. Lowell engage in an anti-Semitic rant. Today, I don't even know if Dr. Lowell knew I was Jewish. He may have had a personality issue with me. I recalled assisting him on a case when I was on the orthopedic service with him as a general surgery intern or resident. There was a bleeder from the hip capsule he was having trouble controlling. I watched him struggle for half an hour to control the bleeder. Finally, without asking permission, I asked the scrub nurse for a long-handled clamp, reached in and clamped the bleeder. Perhaps that had ticked him off.

After thoughtful discussion and analysis Lynne and I concluded that Dr. Lowell had probably written the blackballing letter about me, despite having agreed to write a supportive letter for me. I called a number of orthopedic programs; spent money to fly out and interview. They did not have openings. I wasted money. I don't know why they bothered to have me come out.

Dr. Francis Moore was still my chief of general surgery. He heard of my predicament and called me down to his office. First thing, he assured me that there was a place for me as a senior resident in his general surgery program, if I wanted it. Second, he said he would find a place for me in a plastic surgery residency, if I wanted it. Wow! Such support and just when I needed it.

Third, he called Dr. Clement Sledge, one of the chiefs of the Harvard Orthopedic Residency program down to his office. As Dr. Moore later told me, "I kept him waiting half an hour in my waiting room." Then Dr. Moore told him "You don't treat people that way." And specifically, "You don't treat one of my boys that way." The next week, I received an acceptance letter from the program.

A year later, "working in the lab late one night," I accessed my file. There was Dr. Lowell's recommendation letter. "I recommend Dr. Seinsheimer for the orthopedic program." Nothing more. There then followed multiple comments, "If Dr. Lowell doesn't want him, I guess we shouldn't take him."

Further follow up to this story. I am a junior resident in orthopedics. My senior resident on a rotation is having dinner at my house. He is applying for an academic position. He tells me, by chance, that the chairman of the department he is applying to has asked him to have Dr. Lowell write him a letter of recommendation. My senior resident is Jewish. I predict that Dr. Lowell will write a blackball letter. My senior resident does not believe me. The next time the senior resident returns for a follow-up interview at the academic institution, the chairman of the department brings him into a room, sits him at a table, shows him Dr. Lowell's letter and asks, "Can you explain this?" It is a blackball letter.

As the senior resident told me later, he did not believe me. But! Having heard my warning, he was prepared. And with that preparation, he was able to tell my story. And with my story, he was able to discount the letter. He got the job. Who can you trust? I was fortunate and my senior resident was fortunate that Dr. Lowell was not successful in interfering with our careers. I presume we were not the only trainees in Dr. Lowell's career he took a dislike to. I presume, that there were others he successfully harmed. During my orthopedic residency I never was aware of any backlash or negative effect from the issues which arose during my application process to the orthopedic residency.

I find it fascinating that my relationship with Dr. Moore began in such a confrontational and adversarial way with nowhere to go but down. To this day I cannot figure out why I put Peter Bent at number two on my matching list. Yes, I know. Reputation and all that. But, really! What was I thinking? One of the better decisions of my life. Asking Lynne to marry me being the first, of course. I cannot imagine why Dr. Moore listed me high enough that I was matched. Really! What was he thinking? Perhaps he truly recognized that my evaluation as a medical student had in fact been unfair. Perhaps, reputation again. Perhaps he listed all of the Harvard medical student applicants high enough that I was matched. At the end, my relationship with Dr. Moore was as positive and supportive as I could possibly hope for. I was lucky beyond any reasonable expectation.

CHAPTER EIGHT

Orthopedic Residency

For the first six months of our orthopedic residency we, the beginning orthopedic residents, were assigned to the Children's Hospital in Boston. In addition to caring for patients and operating, there were a series of lectures and demonstrations instructing us in the "specifics" of orthopedic surgery. For example, I recall one demonstration solely devoted to the analysis of gait. The way in which you walk may be altered by pain, muscle weakness, stiffness of one or more joints and differences in leg lengths. The simplest gait abnormality is the antalgic or painful foot gait. If you have a nail in your foot you will shorten the amount of time you put weight on that foot. In orthopedic parlance this is manifested by a shortened stance phase of gait. My wife, Lynne, had similar training in her physical therapy program. Many a time, Lynne and I have sat sipping our cappuccinos and americanos at a sidewalk cafe while analyzing the gaits of passersby.

In the orthopedic clinic at Children's Hospital we frequently saw children whose parents were concerned that their children were in-toeing or out-toeing too much. We learned to distinguish between normal variations in rotation of the legs, moderate variations for which splinting or bracing might help and the rare severe variations for which surgery is indicated. It was difficult to reassure parents of children with milder variations that no treatment was indicated.

We were taught that many professional football running backs and quarterbacks were mild in-toers. There was a sense that mild in-toeing was an advantage in sports requiring rapid changes in direction. Infants who have mild in-toeing tend to walk earlier. Out-toers tend to start walking later.

One of our nurses in the orthopedic clinic had been placed in special shoes for over a decade as a child for mild in-toeing. The special shoes did nothing except waste her parents' money. We often brought her in to see parents as an example that first of all, not every mild abnormality needs treatment. And second, not every treatment works.

Scoliosis is a problem of abnormal increased curvature of the spine. This occurs most often in teenaged girls. When mild, no treatment is indicated. When moderate, bracing may help. When severe, surgical straightening of the spine, temporary fixation with stretching rods (Harrington rods) and bone fusion are indicated. This surgery was done frequently at Children's Hospital when we were residents there. About a week after surgery these patients were placed in a plaster body cast which extended from neck to hips. These patients were brought into the plaster room and placed on a narrow frame. Four orthopedics residents, two on each side, working together as a team applied the plaster body casts. This was before the days of fiberglass cast material. The chief plaster technician's name was Charlotte. She oversaw our application of the body casts. Her other job was teaching us how to use plaster for casting.

When applying plaster, it is important to smooth the plaster to eliminate air pockets. Air pockets weaken the strength of the plaster cast. Charlotte's frequent exhortation to us residents was "Rub it like you love it. Rub it like you love it." Over and over and over. Her voice still echoes in my brain. Thank you, Charlotte, for your excellent training. I apologize. I never thought to thank you when I was a resident.

A normal body cast is somewhat cylindrical and totally flat in the front of the chest. There was a mirror placed above the patient's head so that she could see what we were doing. As we finished each body cast, we asked each patient if she wished any plaster "breast sculpture" on the front of the cast. Most did and were quite appreciative. A body cast is the exact opposite of a feminine figure. It is more the shape of a golem. Each patient directed us regarding the size of "breast sculpture" she desired. This gave the golem-like body cast a minimal sense of a female figure.

I have in my possession a small pamphlet titled "Outline of Orthopedic Examination." This is a small 6 5/8 by 4 ¼ inch gray, 21-page booklet from Mary Hitchcock Memorial Hospital, Dartmouth Medical School and the Hitchcock Clinic. First published in 1953 and revised in 1962. I do not recall whether I was given this during my medical school rotation in orthopedic surgery, my general surgery internship rotation in orthopedic surgery or at the beginning of my orthopedic residency. Somehow, I think it was handed out at the start of our orthopedic residency. We residents used it initially as we were learning the details of a complete orthopedic examination.

I inserted a motto at the beginning of this book. The last line of the motto states "Become your own teacher." This advice is mentioned in "The Book of Five Rings" by Miyamoto Musashi. Musashi was a famous samurai and sword duelist in the mid-1600s in Japan. History records that he fought about 50 sword duels to death and won them all. In many of his later duels he used a wooden sword against a "real" metal sword. Once, he is said to have used a wooden oar and won. The advice to "Become your own teacher" resonates with me. At some point in your training in any activity, you will stall at a certain level of ability, unless you psychologically begin to think independently. You have to have the "arrogance" to believe in yourself. This doesn't mean you stop learning from others. However, you do have to become comfortable with the value of your own ideas.

I know that throughout my life, I have had a persistent inner urge to constantly "up my game." I don't know where it comes from. I remember in fourth grade fighting back against a bully, who was bigger than me, not willing to be bullied. I matriculated at Walnut Hills High School, a six-year special college preparatory public high school, which required passing an entrance examination for acceptance. I started there in seventh grade. The school accepted students from all over Cincinnati. Over 700 seventh graders started the first day I attended. I recall sometime in the first weeks of school sitting down at a long table of strangers in the lunchroom. Some fellow student grabbed my bag of potato chips and threw it to someone else. I was small for my age. This was seventh grade. I had late puberty. Everyone at that time was taller than me and bigger than me.

With the speed of thought, the virus of bullying spread around the table. Instantaneously, the "crowd" determined that I was going to be the "goat." Angered, I went from student to student, as my bag of potato chips was thrown from one student to another student. The situation then evolved so that the biggest student of the bunch stood holding the bag of potato chips behind his back with both hands. I screamed at him to give me my bag of potato chips. He said, "No!" Back and forth; multiple times. There were no adults in the lunchroom. These were the days of no adult supervision. Not caring for future consequences, with my eyes closed, I reared back, swung and punched him, I suppose, somewhere in the head. My eyes were closed, when I swung and hit him. So, I don't know where I connected.

When I opened my eyes, my tormentor was flat on his back. A bag of potato chips was already on my tray. I took my seat and ate lunch. I had expected my tormentor to get up and destroy me. He was bigger and stronger. Why didn't he? Somehow, I had cowed him. I had obviously impressed the other students at the table sufficiently that one of them had immediately taken his own potato chip bag and put it on my tray. The whole class must have seen this. It clearly served as an "anti-bully" vaccination. No one ever bullied me again.

I have been accused of arrogance in the past and should probably plead guilty. It takes a certain degree of arrogance to write this book. I find there are two types of arrogance. There is the brash, in-your-face arrogance that I think is often the result of deep-down insecurity. Then there is the quiet self-confidence type of arrogance. I think I tend to have the latter.

As I stated above, the first six months of my Harvard orthopedic residency were at the Children's Hospital in Boston. John Hall, M.D., was chairman of the department of orthopedics and in charge of our training. John Hall was a renowned, international expert in scoliosis surgery, with the expertise and ability to operate through the abdomen and chest without a general surgeon or thoracic surgeon present.

When performing this surgery, there are large, short arteries that run along the front of the spine. These arteries need to be clamped, divided and carefully ligated (tied) to prevent major bleeding during or immediately after this surgery. There are a number of ways of tying surgical knots. There is a two-hand method of tying knots. I was taught at Peter Bent Brigham in my general surgery training that the two-hand method is safer. I was taught to use the two-hand tie in "delicate" situations, that is, situations where you really, really, really want the knots to hold. There are one-hand knots which work well. I use them often. They are flashier. They are faster. You cannot hold tension on the first throw as well when throwing the second knot. Thus, the one-hand tying technique is not as safe in "delicate" situations.

I am in my first week in my orthopedic residency. I am assisting Dr. Hall in one of these transthoracic (through the chest) cases. I am using two-hand knots to tie off these large short spinal arteries. Dr. Hall begins to make fun of me. Like, I'm a "wuss" for using two-hand ties. He instructs me to use one-hand ties. Wow! My opinion of him plummets. Mind you, he is world famous. He is my mentor; my teacher; my chairman. Have I said my opinion of him plummets? Have I mentioned I have been accused of arrogance? Another one of my many "What to do?" situations. Amazing how often I have had to ask myself that question. Safety in surgery was pounded into my DNA in Dr. Moore's program. I refused Dr. Hall's direction to tie these spinal arteries with one-hand knots. I continued to use two-hand knots. Oh, what a way to begin my orthopedic residency! And in my first week, too. Really awkward situation. To me, this was a "Become your own teacher" situation. I was comfortable disagreeing with Dr. Hall, despite my junior status.

Fast forward six months. We were supposed to have a formal review of our progress in a meeting with Dr. Hall. I am in a clinic with Dr. Hall. He calls me into a supply room. "Frank," he says, "if you were as good as you thought you were, you would be really good." That one sentence was the total extent of my six-month review. As I said, I have been accused of arrogance, but this time, I was being accused by a really arrogant doctor.

I remember the day I "felt" I had become an orthopedic surgeon. I was on call in the orthopedic room in the Massachusetts General Hospital emergency room. We were sufficiently busy to have an orthopedic resident assigned to the ER full time. A nurse came in and asked me to look at a patient with an ankle fracture before he was wheeled to the X-ray department. I walked out into the hall. There was an elderly patient with his ankle angulated 60 degrees to the side. With this degree of displacement and stretching of the soft tissues, there was no significant blood supply reaching the foot. The foot was blanched and bluish.

Restoring blood supply to the foot immediately by straightening the ankle was important. I told the patient I was going to straighten his ankle, that it would hurt some. I then pulled gently on his foot to apply traction and separate the fracture fragments. I then slowly straightened his foot. As I did this, I heard multiple gasps around me. I looked up in surprise. There were three pediatricians, whose room was across the hall, who had come out to look. There were three civilians walking down the hall who had just seen me do this. What I had just done seemed the most natural thing in the world to me. My reduction of the ankle fracture had shocked the six bystanders. The nurse, who had asked me to look at this patient, knew the importance of straightening the ankle before X-ray and had seen this done many times before. Rather than being shocked, the nurse specifically came to get me because she knew I was going to do this. I looked up at the shocked bystanders and said to myself, "I guess I am an orthopedic surgeon."

While operating as a junior resident with one of the attendings at the Mass General, I was amazed at how often this attending pointed out anomalous anatomy during an operation. His knowledge of the anatomy seemed superior to others because he so often found anomalous anatomy. By the time we residents rotated on to his service as senior residents we realized that he really didn't know his anatomy and that the anatomy was all normal. Behind his back we referred to him as "Dr. Anomalous Anomaly."

The Harvard Combined Orthopedic Residency covered both Massachusetts General Hospital, Peter Bent Brigham Hospital and Robert Breck Brigham Hospital. When rotating through Massachusetts General Hospital, we residents were expected to attend breakfast with Dr. Henry Mankin from 6:30 a.m. to 7:00 a.m. These breakfast meetings were partially a teaching conference and partially a chance for Dr. Mankin to browbeat the junior residents. At least, that was my perspective, as a stomach churning, browbeaten junior resident. I remember during one of the breakfasts, Dr. Mankin was showing X-rays of children with various congenital abnormalities. He put up one X-ray and proceeded to browbeat one of my fellow junior residents. He kept pushing and pushing for him to rapidly describe what he was seeing. Then, after allowing the resident to demonstrate his lack of knowledge, Dr. Mankin pointed to a structure on the X-ray which was the bones of a tail. The X-ray was of a monkey.

I found the breakfasts difficult. Another theme in my story: my difficulties with overweening authority. Particularly authority which is simply authority that seems to glory in demonstrating "I have power and you don't. Isn't that sweet?" My issues with authority get worse when there is browbeating or intimidation. So I stopped coming to the breakfasts for a week or so. Breakfast conference was encouraged, but not required. Each time I returned to breakfast, Dr. Mankin turned his laser focus on me for that breakfast. I would then pass for a week or so. My intermittent attendance went on for my six months' rotation as a junior resident in orthopedics at Mass General. Neither of us commented on my intermittent attendance. Each of us fully understanding, I assume, the nature of our interaction.

As I approached my rotation onto his service as a senior resident, I knew that he was not looking forward to it. I was friendly with his secretary and she passed this information on to me. Dr. Mankin was active in developing methods of removing large segments of bone involved with bone cancer and replacing them with matching cadaveric bones. Each senior resident on his service was required to obtain permission from the family of a patient who had just died in the hospital to harvest bones from their deceased family member for use in other patients. This is similar to the use of hearts, kidneys, livers and corneas for transplantation. As a junior resident, I had seen the failure of the senior residents to do this become a serious issue of contention.

The day I rotated on to his service, I was determined to make my transition as smooth as possible. My first night on call, as a senior resident on his service, two patients died on other services. I was able to convince the grieving families to allow me to harvest certain bones for Dr. Mankin's work. I remain profoundly grateful to these families for their willingness to allow their loved ones to aid others. Needless to say, Dr. Mankin was impressed when he came into the hospital the next morning. No resident had ever done that for him before. A good start. We were operating together a day or two later, when he looked up, smiled and said, "I'm a little easier to get along with the second time around." I agreed. He clearly was remembering my intermittent breakfast routine of the previous year.

A patient of Dr. Mankin unfortunately developed an infection surrounding one of the implanted cadaver bones. We were operating to remove infected bone. I did not think he was removing enough bone. I realize now that Dr. Mankin knew, based on the operative findings, that the patient was going to need an amputation and therefore did not need more bone removal. I was too young and inexperienced to recognize that. After pushing him to remove more bone, he looked up at me and said, "Frank, you don't know when to shut up, do you?" So, I shut up. Fast forward three or four years. I am applying for a position as an orthopedic and hand surgeon. One of the doctors called Dr. Mankin for a reference. I was accepted.

Some years later I was recounting the story of being told I didn't know when to shut up to one of my partners. He laughed and told me that Dr. Mankin had given me his highest recommendation but did add one thing. He told my partner, "Sometimes he doesn't know when to shut up." He was obviously remembering that incident also. A number of years later, after I had left Dr. Mankin's program, I told him that I thought he had run an amazingly good teaching program and wanted to thank him. I told him that was not something I could have ever said to him when I was under his power. He smiled and said, "Frank, you were never under my power." I am sure he was remembering some of the experiences I have recounted above.

Some people in life think for themselves. Others seem to just follow rules. Most seem to follow herd mentality. Have I mentioned this before? In the mid-1970s, one of the orthopedic surgeons at Massachusetts General Hospital was Carter Rowe, M.D. He had developed a specific method of performing an operation for recurrent dislocation of the shoulder called the Bankart procedure. Today, much of this surgery is performed by arthroscopic surgery. Back then in Boston every orthopedic surgeon I trained with seemed to follow Carter Rowe's method. In the published description of his approach to this operation Carter Rowe meticulously describes finding a large vein in the upper arm, the cephalic vein, and tying it off. This was done to prevent inadvertent damage to the vein during surgery and unexpected bleeding from the torn vein. The cephalic vein can be easy to find but not always. It is often hidden in a fold of muscle. As I progressed in my training, my supervising surgeons had me spend up to half an hour searching for this vein as part of the exposure for this operation.

Later in my training, I was fortunate to rotate on to Carter Rowe's service at Mass General. In the first Bankart procedure I did under his direction, we spent no more than three minutes looking for the cephalic vein. Then he said not to bother and showed me where to split the muscle to gain access to the deeper tissues. Epiphany! Every orthopedic surgeon in Boston was making a fetish out of finding the cephalic vein as part of the opening because they thought they were doing what Carter Rowe was doing. But he had moved on to a more sensible approach or maybe he had never been compulsive over finding the cephalic vein in the first place. What Carter Rowe was demonstrating to me was common sense. What everyone else was doing was rote following of cookbook instructions. Wow! I write about the little random bits that make each surgeon's training so different. This is yet another example. The other half needed is, of course, the open mind that learns from the random bits.

Seriously, think about it. I am training at one of the foremost medical institutions in the world. The Bankart procedure, at that time, was probably the most commonly performed procedure used for recurrent dislocation of the shoulder. Carter Rowe was performing this procedure in a common-sense manner. Most of the other orthopedic surgeons at Harvard that I scrubbed with were "wasting" time searching for the cephalic vein as part of their opening because they thought Carter Rowe was doing it. It boggles my mind. It is so important to think for yourself. At the beginning of this book, I inserted a four-line motto. The last line is apropos here. At some point you should become your own teacher.

One more vignette about Carter Rowe. For his Bankart operations he used white cotton suture, an old-fashioned suture, for his capsule repairs. No one else in Boston that I trained with used white cotton sutures. I asked Dr. Rowe why he used white cotton suture. With a hint of his southern accent, he replied, "Ah always use white cotton." Not really an answer. His patients did well. Never saw a complication from his use of white cotton suture.

As a senior resident in orthopedics, I was operating on a patient who had suffered a fracture and dislocation of the right hip a year previously. Due to other injuries and other reasons, treatment had been delayed. The fracture/dislocation was a year old and had healed far out of position. The leg had shortened and rotated. There was intense scarring, making the dissection extremely slow, tedious and difficult. The goal was to perform a total hip replacement. First, identification of the important structures was necessary. This is difficult if there is thick intense scar.

There is a general principle when operating in an area with thick scar: Start your dissection away from the scar, in normal tissue; identify the important structures (i.e., the nerves and blood vessels in normal, unoperated tissue); and then follow the important structures into the scarred areas.

The first part of the procedure on this old hip fracture dislocation was to open the leg far enough down toward the knee so that all of the tissue initially seen was uninjured and without scar. At the beginning of the operation it was important to find the sciatic nerve, the main nerve to the leg, in normal tissue and then slowly follow the sciatic nerve up toward the hip and free it from scar. Failure to do this would have led to a high risk of injury to the sciatic nerve.

So the attending surgeon is allowing me to do this extremely difficult and delicate operation. I am naturally thrilled. He is holding the retractors to give me visibility, while I dissect up into the dense scar. Every five minutes, it seems, the retractors relax, the sides of the wound cave in and the attending surgeon comes around and looks in to see what I am doing. This means, of course, that I am not accomplishing much, since I cannot see much for more than a short period of time. Frustrating.

After at least a half hour of this, I say to the surgeon that I really appreciate him allowing me to do this case, but that I am having trouble because he keeps letting go of the retractors. I can't see long enough to make much progress. He replies that he understands, but it is such a great case, he keeps wanting to get a better view. He still allows me to do the whole case. Superb training.

While in my training, as the orthopedic representative of a combined orthopedic and neurosurgery case, my supervising neurosurgeon and I were operating on a multiply operated back. Slow meticulous dissection down through dense scar. The problem was that bone had previously been removed from the back of the spinal canal in multiple previous surgeries. Without bone protecting the back of the spine we surgeons might inadvertently move deep into the spinal canal and injure nerves without knowing it. The spine was also severely curved, a condition called scoliosis. There was serious risk that while dissecting down into the spinal canal, we would cut nerves in the spinal canal without knowing it. Our plan was to go down the side of the canal to find bone first then dissect out on top of the bone to find the edge of the spinal canal. This would allow us to orient ourselves. Finding the side of the spinal canal was not straightforward due to the scarring and the severe curvature of the spine. As I carefully dissected down, I finally found a ledge of bone. From this point it should be easier. You follow the bone left and right until you find, on one side, the edge of the spinal canal. Then you follow the bone the other direction until you fall off an edge; that will be the center of the spinal canal.

Having found the ledge of bone, I dissected one way and fell off an edge of bone. This should have been the center of the canal. I then dissected the other way hoping to find the side of the canal. I fell off another edge. What was going on? We finally figured out that a previous surgeon had left an island of floating bone at the back of the spinal canal, which you are not supposed to do. It took a lot more careful dissection to find our way safely into the spinal canal to perform our surgery.

As a medical school student, I watched a resident reduce a dislocated shoulder. As a first-year orthopedic resident, I coached a medical student in performing the reduction of a dislocated shoulder. I later performed my first reduction of a dislocated shoulder by myself. Our informal training motto was, "See one; do one; teach one." This is or was how good teaching institutions worked. I prided myself that I once changed that to, "See one; teach one; do one." The patients all did well. This is what training is like, or rather was like. I don't know what it is like today.

One of our rotations in orthopedics was at West Roxbury Veterans Hospital. This was an acute care VA hospital. There was one orthopedic open ward of about 30 patients which was always full. We admitted patients one or more days before surgery and kept them in the hospital for one or more days after surgery. The VA hospital was reimbursed by Washington for each day a bed was occupied by a patient. On my first rotation there, as a junior resident, the senior resident and I found that we were not seeing enough patients in clinic to stay busy or to learn. We were only seeing about 15 patients a day in clinic. We asked the administration to schedule more patients. The administration refused. Understand, we wanted to do more work. It would not cost the VA more. What to do?

The senior resident and I allowed the beds in the orthopedic ward to empty. Then, we waited quietly. It took two days for the administration to discover this. An administrator came storming down to complain. Recall, for each empty bed, the hospital received less money from Washington. The senior resident and I explained with mock sincerity that we were not seeing enough patients in the clinic to keep the beds full. The administrator then asked how many patients we wanted to see each clinic. We told him 25. He acquiesced. We then kept the beds full, only discharging a patient when we had an admission. Such machination, just to work and train harder. Such inefficient bureaucracy. Another example of watching and learning as a senior physician solves a problem.

There is a disease called Dupuytren's contracture, in which an abnormal scar-like tissue forms in the hand. Each cell of this abnormal tissue seems part muscle and part scar. It develops on the palm side of the hand most often involving the ring and little finger. A terrifying moment occurred during my training. The scar-like Dupuytren's tissue often densely surrounds the nerves in the fingers. I was performing a Dupuytren's surgery one afternoon at the VA hospital as a junior resident with a senior resident assisting me and I was unable to find the nerve on one side of a finger. The senior resident and I are convinced that I have inadvertently cut the nerve. I have a momentary vasovagal reaction. I feel nauseated and faint. Large sweat beads break out on my forehead. The senior resident leans forward and looks at me intently through his magnifying surgical loupes. He comments, "Those are awfully large beads of sweat on your forehead." Fortunately, with further dissection I found the nerve. It was a false alarm. I still feel that temporary feeling of horror these many years later.

A marvelous teaching example regarding the question of surgical reconstruction of the hand, was presented in a teaching conference I attended led by Dr. Lewis Millender, a hand surgeon at Harvard. He presented the case of a man who was confronted by an assailant who pulled a gun on him, the patient. The patient to be put up his hand in reflex. The assailant fired the gun. The bullet passed through the center of the patient's hand. He survived without other injury. The bullet shattered multiple bones, divided multiple tendons and injured multiple nerves. After the wounds were healed, that is, covered with skin, the patient came to Dr. Millender for follow-up care.

Having presented the case, Dr. Millender then asked the assembled medical students, interns and residents for their suggestions regarding reconstruction of this injured hand. This method of teaching involves asking the attendees for their opinions in ascending order from the least trained up to the most experienced. Everyone's recommendations included multiple operations, usually three or more, and up to two years for completion.

After everyone had their say Dr. Millender pointed out that one of the important issues to consider is the patient's life expectancy. This patient was a member of an underworld gang. Someone wanted him dead. Someone had not succeeded the first time. The probability was high that there would be another attempt. In fact, the patient was killed six months after consulting Dr. Millender. Extensive reconstruction was not indicated in this patient. Decision-making can be complicated. It is not always straightforward. A wonderful teaching conference, which I still remember clearly, these many years later.

Another example: When to perform complex reconstruction? When to perform salvage? A patient presented for evaluation with the following history when I was in training. He had suffered a laceration of the base of the middle finger deep enough to cut both of the flexor tendons and both of the nerves of the finger. He did not seek medical attention for treatment for this injury. The wound was never sutured and remained open and contaminated with bacteria. With both nerves cut there was no protective sensation to the finger. Approximately one week later this patient "self-treated" his finger by soaking it in hot water. He then presented to our emergency room with second-degree burns of the entire finger. The entire finger was covered with one large blister from the second-degree burn.

What to do? What to recommend for treatment? In order for any patient to do well following reconstructive surgery of the hand he needs to be reliable. He needs to come to therapy regularly. The attending felt that this patient had demonstrated a serious lack of these characteristics. Given the double injury, our attending recommended amputation of the finger. As I write this paragraph, I am reminded of a different patient I had when in private practice, who missed his first post-operative hand therapy visit and did not call to cancel. A few weeks later he came in and apologized. He had been in jail. Not all patients follow up for therapy in an ideal way.

Most, if not all, orthopedic training programs have a fracture conference as part of the didactic education. A difficult fracture is presented and treatment is discussed. I have attended fracture conferences in which the treating surgeon presents a difficult fracture. He then shows pretty X-rays of a complicated reconstruction. The presentation stops there. There is no further discussion. I find limited educational value from this type of presentation. In fact, this type of presentation tends to encourage the residents in training to use the "fancy" techniques shown without considering the expected results and the possible complications of the presented treatment.

The fracture conferences at Massachusetts General Hospital during Dr. Henry Mankin's tenure, as chief of orthopedics, were run differently. All of the cases were presented by senior orthopedic residents. A minimum of six months' follow-up was required for each case presented. The senior residents were responsible for finding and presenting these cases on a rotating basis. Obviously, it is far more interesting and educational to present cases that did not go well. In fact, I can't remember ever anyone presenting a case that went well. Knowing that this responsibility lay ahead, junior residents kept records of patients who had complications from fracture treatment. These patients' names were jealously guarded.

In a typical presentation, the senior resident showed the X-rays of an acute fracture. Then we went around the room from least trained medical student, up through junior and senior orthopedic residents and then to the multiple attending orthopedic surgeons, who also came to this conference. Opinions often differed widely and wildly. In many of these cases reasonable people had significantly different opinions. There is tremendous education in seeing the reasoning of excellent orthopedic surgeons as they analyze complex problems. There is tremendous education in seeing that there can be more than one way of treating a problem.

I am going to shift gears for a moment. Many years ago, a pediatrician and I admitted a two-and-a-half-year-old child to the hospital with a spontaneous infection in one of the bones in her leg, called osteomyelitis. This type of infection is most common in children between the ages four to six. In that age group the most common bacteria causing the infection is staphylococcus. In younger children, such as our patient, other bacteria, which require different antibiotics for treatment, are also common. The pediatrician and I chose a specific antibiotic, which would not only cover staphylococcus but also would cover the other possible bacteria types. This was not the antibiotic normally used in the four to six-year-old age group.

Saturday morning, I come into the hospital to make rounds. The child's mother says she needs to talk to me. She is a nurse. She is a national expert who advises hospitals on how to avoid legal problems with patients. Her husband is an attorney. That morning, before I arrived at the hospital, the pediatric resident covering the patient sat down with the mother and told her he was refusing to continue covering her child because of our terrible care. The pediatric resident felt that the pediatrician and I were using the wrong antibiotic. He had not called me or the pediatrician to discuss his concerns with us. I explained to the mother the reason the pediatrician and I had chosen the specific antibiotic we had chosen. I offered to arrange transfer of her child to a major medical center. She stayed with us. Her child did well. The field of doctoring can be so much fun!

Later, the pediatrician discussed the resident's actions with the head of the pediatric residency program. This was not the first time this resident had had a problem with recognizing there might be more than one way to treat a patient. The intersection of a trainee doctor's personality with the training and experience of medical and surgical training is important. This particular pediatric resident had a sufficiently "rigid" personality that he was not open to calling the treating physicians for discussion and education. Once he learned something, he was not open to alternative approaches. The experience in the fracture conferences with multiple opinions and alternative approaches was refreshingly open and educational.

Before I return to discussing the fracture conferences, one more vignette with the pediatrician. She referred me a patient, four years old, with onset of leg pain of only a few hours' duration. This child also had a spontaneous bone infection in his leg. The pediatrician and I recommended immediate hospitalization and intravenous antibiotics. This was the standard treatment for this child at that time. The child's parents raised an unusual, complicating factor. Earlier that same day they, the parents, had just come home from the hospital with a new baby in the family. They desperately did not want the psychological impact on their four-year-old child that would result from the new baby coming home and then their four-year-old child essentially being "evicted" from the home and admitted to a strange, scary hospital with painful needle sticks for IVs.

Another of those "What to do?" situations. Also, another interesting ethical question. The pediatrician and I listened to the parents and agreed with their concerns. We decided to try high dose oral antibiotics and leave the four-year-old at home. Understand, this was clearly non-standard treatment. The pediatrician and I each saw the child daily in our offices for examination and measurement of temperature. At the slightest hint that he was not improving, we were ready to immediately admit him to the hospital to start intravenous antibiotics.

What made this case even more memorable to me was the following. Close relatives of the family included a pediatrician and an infectious disease specialist, each attendings at separate major university medical centers. I received multiple, blisteringly critical telephone calls from both of these family members for several days until it became clear the child was doing well. The ethical question concerned the increased risk to the child that we might fail in treating the infection early versus the unknown psychological risk of admitting the four-year-old to the hospital, the day his baby sibling came home. Had the pediatrician and I been rigid or overly safe or uncaring, we would have admitted the child to the hospital. Fortunately, everything worked out well. Decision-making in medicine is not always straightforward.

Now back to the fracture conferences. Following the presentation of the fracture and the initial discussion, the senior resident then shows the X-rays following surgical fixation of the fracture. Discussion then goes around the room from least trained to most experienced, asking for a critique of the treatment. Discussion again ranges widely. Then X-rays are shown of some complication of treatment and/or failure to heal properly. Discussion again goes around the room. Discussion centers on, "What happened? Why? What do you recommend we do next?" There are often several treatments and failures of treatment that follow.

Profoundly educational to see the many ways in which a patient might fail to heal properly. Sobering to realize that not every patient does well. Educational to see errors in treatment discussed. Educational to understand there might be more than one correct way to treat a problem. Educational and humbling to see well-trained, intelligent surgeons make mistakes. I always feel we should learn from our mistakes. I just want "our" mistakes to be someone else's mistakes.

The fracture conferences were a weekly occurrence. During the many fracture conferences I attended, I became cognizant of the fact that a significant number of subtrochanteric fractures (fractures of the thigh bone about two to four inches below the ball of the hip joint), treated with a specific type of hardware device, the AO blade plate, were failing frequently. The X-rays after the operation looked excellent. The fracture fragments were reduced into excellent position. The positioning of the fixating hardware device was excellent. Yet, with greater frequency than desirable, the fractures were failing to heal (called a non-union) and the thick, strong metal plates were breaking.

If you take a paperclip and bend it back and forth, around the sixth or seventh time you do this, the paper clip will break completely. This is called metal fatigue. Any material, if bent back and forth, even a little bit, will eventually break. This is the reason airplane wings are replaced on a regular basis. Otherwise, the wings would fall off from metal fatigue. As I write this, the news is filled with another catastrophic failure of a jet engine due to metal fatigue of a spinning part in the engine.

The primary reason the metal plates were breaking in the patients mentioned above was failure of the fracture to heal; not a problem with weakness of the fixation plate itself. Once the fracture fails to heal, the micro-motion of the surgical plate at the position of the unhealed fracture leads to metal fatigue and breakage of the plate. It seemed to me that the blade plate was "too good." It seemed to be holding the fracture fragments apart.

For my senior resident thesis in my orthopedic training, I looked up the records and X-rays of all of the subtrochanteric hip fractures I could find that had been treated at Mass General. I found 56 and studied those that had failed to heal. I found a pattern of fracture that was unstable. I also felt this kind of fixation was not an optimal solution for treating this problem fracture. I wrote a paper for publication, "'Subtrochanteric Fractures of the Femur'; Seinsheimer, Frank; J Bone Joint Surg AM; 60(3); 300–306."

A major theme of my paper was the recommendation that this type of device no longer be used for this problem fracture. This was a popular device at the time. In fact, I think it was the most popular. I was a "nobody" writing a paper recommending against this popular treatment. The editors of the *Journal of Bone and Joint Surgery* disagreed with me and refused to publish my paper unless I removed my recommendation against the use of this plate. I removed my recommendation and the paper was published emphasizing my new fracture classification and the demonstration of one specific problem fracture.

My classification of subtrochanteric fractures is still published in textbooks. The paper would have been much better the way I originally wrote it. It is hard to fight orthodoxy. This is an example of herd mentality. The editors had it and would not allow me to publish a challenge to it. The AO blade plate is no longer used or only rarely used today. I have not seen an X-ray of a hip with an AO blade plate in many years.

While I was an orthopedic resident at Children's Hospital, a young attending took a young child with a displaced fracture of a bone on one side of the elbow to the operating room to put the fracture back in place and hold it in place with pins. He put the fracture in place seven times; pinned it seven times; X-rayed it seven times; no position of the pinned fracture on X-ray was satisfactory to the young attending. He called the chief of pediatric orthopedic surgery into the operating room to assist him. The chief scrubbed in; reduced the fracture; pinned the fracture; X-rayed the reduced and pinned fracture; said it looked good; left the operating room. The position of the reduced and pinned fracture which the chief of pediatric orthopedic surgery had accepted was not as good as five of the reductions the young attending had not accepted. This case was discussed in detail at the weekly complications conference.

The lesson! You have to know what is acceptable! Perfection is not required! Perfection is not obtainable! I have mentioned before the saying in surgery, "The enemy of good is better." By trying to make something better, you can make it worse. The problem here, the error here, if you will, was that the young attending did not know what was acceptable. There is another saying in surgery, which is equally important: "Don't meddle." That means, only do what you have to do and nothing else. Nothing else. Nothing else. Nothing else. I repeat for emphasis, nothing else. A book called "Fractures and Dislocations" by Rockwood and Green was our bible in training. This book has extensive discussion regarding what is acceptable for each and every known fracture, dislocation and fracture dislocation. I frequently refer to the vagaries and randomness of surgical training. The discussion about this elbow fracture case was another of those "epiphany" moments in my training. The concept of "knowing what is acceptable" is perhaps more important in orthopedic surgery than in most other medical specialties.

Arthroscopic surgery is minimal incision or puncture wound surgery of joints. One of the early pioneers of arthroscopy was a Japanese orthopedic surgeon, Dr. Masaki Watanabe. One of the first arthroscopes he developed had a bare glass bulb at the end. This was before the days of fiber optics. One day at the VA hospital, our fiber optic arthroscope broke. The patient was under anesthesia. The hospital still had an old Watanabe scope, which I used. You had to be super careful not to push against anything with the glass bulb or it would shatter. At Mass General in the late 1970s one of the young attendings was Dr. Dinesh Patel. He was performing multiple arthroscopies several days a week. At the time I was a resident, Dr. Patel did not have a resident assigned to him. Whenever I had free time, I went over and scrubbed with him. He taught me and allowed me to do many knee arthroscopies under his guidance. I gained a lot of experience with arthroscopy that I would not otherwise have gained. Arthroscopy, at that time, was in its early days. It was frowned upon by the old-time orthopedic surgeons. It was not felt necessary to teach it to the residents. I disagreed. It was my reason for seeking out Dr. Patel and asking for his instruction.

The orthopedic outpatient clinic at Mass General was often staffed by three or four attending orthopedic surgeons and six or eight orthopedic residents. I recall an elderly woman who came into the clinic complaining of a fall, hip pain and inability to walk. The hip was painful with motion. We residents and attendings were convinced that she had a hip fracture. X-rays were obtained and did not show a hip fracture. Tomograms were obtained. Before the days of CT scans and MRIs, tomograms were used. They are multiple X-rays, each focused on a specific plane through the body. The tomograms did not show a fracture of the hip. I recall three attendings and six or seven residents all crowded around the X-rays and multiple tomogram films looking at the hip joint trying to visualize the hip fracture they were sure was there. I was in the back of the disordered scrum. I was unable to get close enough to look for the fine detail of a subtle hip fracture. I was only able to see the big picture. So I was just generally scanning the multiple films. I then saw a fracture of the front of the pelvis that was present on most of the films. I pointed this out to the attendings and other residents, who agreed. What happened? Tunnel vision. Everyone was so convinced that there was a hip fracture that nobody bothered to do a complete scan of each image. I was saved from this mistake because I was unable to get close to the images. When looking at an X-ray or other diagnostic image, I was taught as a medical student to always look at the edges and to always look everywhere you are not interested in before focusing on the area of your interest.

The purpose of this is to avoid missing an abnormal finding such as happened to everyone else in the clinic that day.

As a general surgery intern on the orthopedic service I was allowed to perform many of the orthopedic operations. By chance we had a run of ankle fractures when I was on the orthopedic service. By the end of this rotation, even before starting my orthopedic residency, I felt comfortable with my knowledge and skills in the operative treatment of ankle fractures. I talk frequently about the randomness and vagaries of medical and surgical training. We learn from the patients happenstance brings our way. In my orthopedic residency, we junior residents sometimes traded cases with each other. Since I had previously had extensive training in operating on ankle fractures, I often traded an ankle fracture with a fellow resident to gain experience in another area of orthopedics in which I felt I needed the experience.

Approximately two years after finishing my training I flew to Chicago to take the orthopedic board examination. We used to joke that passing the boards was like wearing a pair of pants. If you walk down the street wearing pants, no big deal. If you pass the boards, no big deal. If you walk down the street without pants, big problem. If you fail the boards, big problem. Months of studying, endless hours, preparing for the board exams. A written, 200-question exam; then six 30-minute oral exams. I had never had an oral exam before, other than the general surgery stress interviews.

I was taught a strategy for taking oral exams. If you get on a topic you know, give the longest answer possible. Spend the most time talking about something you know. If you get on a topic you don't know, try to get off of that topic as quickly as you can. In the orthopedic residency program, we had a one hour per week seminar on orthopedic pathology. I remember being taught about the different ways in which tumors or infection may erode bone. I remember being taught to distinguish between "bear bites" and "rat bites" in evaluating X-rays. Extensive time was spent on the evaluation of "small cell" tumors which could include infection.

At the oral pathology exam, I was shown a slide of a "small cell" tumor along with an X-ray. While I did not know the exact diagnosis for sure, I had a "small cell" tumor lecture prepared. I was able to spend 20 minutes of the 30-minute session on this one question. There was not enough time for two of the questions. The strategy worked.

CHAPTER NINE

Hand Surgical Training in Residency and Fellowship

During my orthopedic residency, I rotated on to the hand service and trained with Dr. Richard Smith at Mass General both as a junior resident and as a senior resident. Dr. Smith did not have a hand fellow in training at that time. In his office we orthopedic residents saw each and every patient of his before he saw them, and we were then in the examination room with him when he saw his patients. He taught continually with each patient. Later, I heard that he took on a hand fellow and only taught at the end of clinic and that his teaching suffered because of this. My time with him was special. He served as my inspiration to specialize in hand surgery. I enjoyed the intellectual challenge of hand surgery. For complicated hand problems, it is difficult or impossible to obtain excellent results all of the time. I was attracted to this challenge.

A few years later, after working for two years in the US Army as an orthopedic surgeon, I received further training in hand surgery with Dr. Jim Hunter at Thomas Jefferson University Medical Center in Philadelphia. Dr, Hunter's training served to further refine my interaction with patients, the craftsmanship of my surgical skills, my approach to hand therapy and, of course, the entire field of hand surgery. There were three of us hand fellows training with three hand surgeons. We were on call every third night. Half of the nights that we were on call we were up all or most of the night operating on emergencies. Many of these emergencies were amputated fingers or hands, which were treated with microsurgical replantation.

More vignettes. More training. More education. More epiphanies. When I was an orthopedic resident at Massachusetts General Hospital one night, we had a patient come to the hospital emergency room. He had fallen off a roof. One wrist had a complicated fracture and dislocation of the small bones in the wrist called a trans-scaphoid perilunate fracture dislocation. The big names are not important. I only use them for the occasional orthopedic or hand surgeon who reads this book. The other wrist had a pure dislocation of the wrist at the junction of the forearm bones and the wrist bones. A pure wrist dislocation. This is a rare injury. The only one I ever saw.

Both wrists were quite swollen. Initially in the emergency room the neurologic exam was normal. Within half an hour the patient developed numbness and tingling, with loss of feeling in both hands, particularly involving the thumb, index and middle fingers. The wrist with the complex fracture and dislocation required surgery, with incisions on both the palm side and back of the wrist. Part of the approach to this fracture dislocation automatically releases the nerve at the wrist. This nerve is called the median nerve. It goes through a tight tunnel called the carpal (wrist) tunnel. Release of the nerve is called carpal tunnel release.

The pure wrist dislocation could be treated with "simple" closed manipulation. No open surgery was necessary for treatment of the dislocation. The question arose, "Should we do immediate open surgery at the same time as the manipulation to release the nerve (carpal tunnel release)?" We, the residents on site, wanted to do the open nerve release as well as the closed manipulation. I was a junior orthopedic surgery resident at that time. The senior resident consulted with Dr. Richard Smith by phone and was instructed to just do the closed manipulation. We did as we were told.

The patient's wrist with the complex fracture and dislocation had immediate improvement in nerve function after surgery. The hand with the wrist dislocation continued to have severe impairment of nerve function. The nerve was eventually released a few weeks later but had limited improvement. It remained permanently impaired.

I continue to write about the vagaries of medical and surgical training. I continue to emphasize that we learn from the patients whom happenstance brings our way. I learned two important principles from this experience. First, if a patient develops significant nerve impairment soon after an injury, release the nerve quickly. I joke that in trauma, if the nerve is under pressure, you release the nerve, like voting in Chicago, early and often. I also learned a second important principle. The decisions people make at a distance, when they are not physically present, are often different and inferior to on-site decision-making.

Friends of ours had a daughter away at college who developed an infection in her foot. Our friends asked me to speak with her doctor. The primary care physician was treating her with an antibiotic which did not cover many possible bacteria. The primary care physician told me she was consulting, by phone, with an infectious disease specialist who agreed with that treatment. Based on my previous experience, I asked if the infectious disease doctor had seen the patient. I was told no. I insisted that the infectious disease doctor come over and see this patient. She did. Then, she changed the antibiotics and also called in a surgeon. The infection required surgical drainage. Again, the experience of different treatment if the doctor is on site. Perhaps, on site, there is a greater sense of "I am responsible for this patient. Therefore, I need to be more prudent and careful." On site, the examining physician also obtains more information through the interaction with and examination of the patient.

There was another patient I was involved with as a junior resident during my orthopedic surgery residency training, for which there was disagreement in treatment decision-making between the treating resident physicians and the off-site attending. A patient came to the emergency room with a severely injured index finger. Both of the flexing or gripping tendons were cut. Both of the straightening or extending tendons were cut. The bone at the base of the finger was shattered into many pieces. One of the two nutrient arteries had been cut. Both nerves to the finger were cut. Essentially, this was an incomplete amputation with just a small amount of soft tissue and one artery connecting the finger to the hand.

Decision-making in these types of cases is not clear cut. Honest and reasonable differences of opinion are expected. The patient did manual labor and needed the best possible hand for any hope of returning to work. We, the residents on site, made the decision to perform what is called a ray amputation of the index finger. The second metacarpal, the hand bone that supports the index finger, is severed at a level near the base of the thumb. The index finger is then removed and the skin trimmed and closed. This creates a cosmetic hand with a thumb and three fingers. It is not only cosmetic but quite useful. This converts the serious injuries to bone, tendons, nerves and artery to a wound that only requires skin healing. The patient was back at work in three weeks. Dr. Richard Smith was out of town and not available for consultation at the time of the emergency.

In later discussion Dr. Smith disagreed with our decision. He felt we should have tried to reconstruct the finger. As part of the group of residents involved with this patient's treatment, I participated in our discussions about our disagreement with Dr. Smith. We, the residents, respected his knowledge and judgement. We listened to his comments. We still felt we had made the right call. Reasonable people can reach different conclusions in cases like this. Our reasoning: the patient was actually back at work three weeks after injury; following extensive reconstructive surgery, he still would have had a lousy finger; he never would have returned to work.

One bad finger can seriously interfere with the functioning of the other normal fingers. Open your hand completely with the fingers stretched out straight and back as far as you can. Now grasp your middle finger and pull it further backwards. While holding the middle finger far back try to make a fist with your other fingers. Can't do it. At least most of us can't do it. There are interconnections between the tendons and muscles. If one finger is moving poorly, the interconnections can interfere with the motion of the other fingers. In the case discussed above, we residents felt that the one badly functioning finger—which would have been the final result after reconstruction—would seriously interfere with the functioning of the whole hand.

As a hand fellow I once saw a patient who was an obstetrician and gynecologist. His dominant index finger had been severely injured and treated elsewhere. He was disabled from his medical practice because of an inability to perform surgery or vaginal examinations. I was not responsible for decision-making in his care. I have often wondered if a ray amputation of that injured index finger would have allowed him to resume practice.

Many years ago, I read the results of a survey of surgeons asking if they were missing fingers, how many and if they were able to operate. I don't remember the number but quite a few were actively performing surgery with one missing finger. I think there was one active surgeon missing two fingers. The principle here is that often one bad finger is much worse than missing one finger.

This principle becomes important in the decision regarding whether to replant a single completely amputated finger. When I was in training, we only replanted single-digit amputations if it involved the thumb. The thumb is so important to the use of the hand that a bad thumb is better than a hand with no thumb. Also, a thumb does not have significant interconnections with the finger tendons. A stiff thumb will not interfere with finger motion.

There are surgeons who perform single-digit finger replantations. Based on my experiences noted above, I disagree with this decision-making. A hand surgeon once told me, "If I didn't do replantations of single-digit amputations, I wouldn't make any money." Not a valid reason! Again, I repeat the question, who can you trust? What are a hand surgeon's motivations for recommending a single-digit replantation? If the number of surgeries and the length of time to reconstruct a serious injury takes years, the end result may be a "professional" patient. Patients who are out of work for a year or more often become depressed, lose their sense of self-worth and lose their work ethic. The longer the rehabilitation process, the less likely it is that a patient will return to work. The question concerning whether to attempt complex reconstruction or proceed to early amputation also arises in the treatment of severe mutilating injuries of the legs.

A good amputation with a good prosthesis may function and feel better than a severely traumatized leg.

The words "tedious" and "meticulous" are often used to describe the performance of difficult surgery. There is an operation for Dupuytren's contracture of the hand, part of which involves dissecting nerves free from dense scar-like tissue in the hand. This surgery requires slow and methodical dissection. I have taken as long as half an hour just to dissect one inch through this tough tissue. When I was working with Dr. Richard Smith, chief of hand surgery at Mass General in the 1970s, he once asked me to explain the difference between the words tedious and meticulous. I forget my answer. He replied something like, "Tedious is when you are assisting me in this surgery. Meticulous is when I am doing it." A great teacher and hand surgeon. Tragically lost to brain cancer. He used to love riddles and asked riddles of residents while doing surgery. I am the only resident I know who dared to ask him riddles in return.

I chose Dr. Jim Hunter for my advanced training for several reasons. I should add that, fortunately, he chose me. It seems trite to say he was a superb teacher and excellent hand surgeon. He was. The Hand Rehabilitation Center was a storefront in downtown Philadelphia. There was a bar a few doors down from us. Dr. Hunter often ran two to three hours behind in his office practice. He never seemed to look at his watch and took infinite pains to teach regardless of how late he was running. Patients had to show up and sign in at the reception desk before they went on the waiting list. Many of our patients had suffered work-related injuries. These patients checked in at reception. Then they went down to the bar. When it was ten minutes before the patient was ready to be seen, the receptionist called the bar and told the bartender to send the patient down to us. I don't recall any drunk patients but the bar was an unusually congenial waiting room.

The first day I arrived to start my hand fellowship with Dr. Hunter at Thomas Jefferson University Medical School in Philadelphia, I saw this large hand therapy area. I did not, at that time, see the need for such an extensive hand therapy program. My initial thought: "What a racket." I then spent four months working with Dr. Jim Hunter, four months with another attending hand surgeon and then four months back with Dr. Hunter. I did 90% of the surgeries for both hand surgeons. My results with Dr. Hunter were dramatically better than my results with the other attending. I was doing 90% of the surgery. What was the difference? The difference could not have been a difference in the surgeon.

Dr. Hunter began therapy on all of his patients within two to three days of surgery or injury, if possible. The other attending did not begin therapy on his patients for three weeks. This was the only difference in treatment I could perceive. Recall, I was doing most of the surgery. The difference could not be a difference in the quality of the surgeon. Therefore, I decided, the reason for the difference in results could only be the difference in when post-operative therapy began. I came out of that training program a devotee of early hand therapy. Not everyone has the same definition of early hand therapy. There are some hand surgeons who seem to think that starting therapy at three weeks is "early." To me early is early, namely, a few days. I continue to discuss the vagaries and randomness of medical and surgical training. Perhaps few hand surgeons have had the experience I had, which allowed such a clear comparison of the results of hand therapy started at a few days with hand therapy started at three weeks.

Dr. Hunter was constantly encouraging patients, telling them how well they were doing. Even if they weren't. Patients responded to this by working harder. I saw the benefits of the physician acting as cheerleader. We had a teenager who found a blasting cap. He wondered what would happen if he banged it on the sidewalk. He found out. Much loss of soft tissue in his palm with nothing to sew together. I watched as Dr. Hunter treated him with immediate early motion in hand therapy rather than turning to immediate flaps for skin coverage. The wounds healed on their own. The patient finished treatment with near normal motion. Yet another epiphany on the value of early hand therapy and especially the value of early motion. I was also introduced to Dr. Hunter's precept, "Don't let the wound get in the way of motion."

I recall a patient who lacerated two large nerves in his upper arm when cut by a broken plate glass window. Dr. Hunter and I operated routinely with 4.5 power magnification loupes. Dr. Hunter repaired one of the nerves. I repaired the other. Visualize this. It is now about 3:30 a.m. All I am thinking about: "Any chance of getting home to grab three hours of sleep that night?" We have a full day in the office tomorrow. Dr. Hunter does not seem to be worried about getting any sleep that night. Dr. Hunter spends additional time bringing in the operating microscope to compare our nerve repairs under 10 to 12 power magnification. We have each placed eight sutures carefully through the outer tissue which covers the nerves. Dr. Hunter's sutures are within a degree of being spaced exactly 45 degrees from each other. Remarkably even spacing! My sutures are within perhaps plus or minus 5 degrees of being evenly spaced. Functionally, both repairs are equally good. Dr. Hunter's placement of sutures clearly demonstrates superior craftsmanship. He says nothing. Another epiphany. The lesson is clear. Up your game.

We had a patient with a congenital contracture of one of his fingers that Dr. Hunter wanted to straighten operatively. We reached a point in the surgery in which everything had been released except the vessels, nerves and tendons. Dr. Hunter decided to step cut the tendons to lengthen them. I disagreed with this decision.

I reached across the hand table. I placed my hand on his wrist. I said across the hand table, "Dr. Hunter, you don't want to do this."

He replied, "I do."

I repeated my statement, "Dr. Hunter you don't want to do this."

He replied, "I do."

Ditto, for a third round. "Dr. Hunter you don't want to do this."

Again, his response. "I do."

I withdrew my hand and subsided into silence. The patient did not do well. I never said anything. Six months later, out of the blue, Dr. Hunter asked me if I remembered that patient.

I replied, "I do."

Dr. Hunter then said, "You were right."

Few attending surgeons admit their mistakes so openly.

I have mentioned before how difficult it can be to make correct diagnoses. When I was a hand fellow, Dr. Hunter and I saw a woman who had suffered a large laceration near her wrist and a small puncture wound of her upper forearm. This injury cut the flexor tendons to her ring and little fingers just above the wrist. The tendons were surgically repaired elsewhere, but she never regained more than a flicker of motion in either finger. She had two repeat operations, each by a different hand surgeon to free up her tendons from scar. This type of operation is called a tenolysis. These operations were done under general anesthesia. She never gained more than a flicker of motion. She was then referred for psychiatric care under the assumption that she was unwilling to try to move her fingers and unwilling to participate in therapy.

After thorough evaluation, Dr. Hunter and I explored her arm under local anesthesia, with the patient completely awake. Only the skin was numbed. Initially we freed the tendons from scar. We were then able to pull on the tendons from above the wrist level and the fingers pulled in fully. This indicated that there was no block distal to the wrist. The tendons were gliding normally and the joints were not stiff. We opened up the forearm from the wrist to the elbow. With the patient completely awake, we asked her to move her fingers. When she tried to move her fingers, we could see the muscle that was connected to the tendons contract, but not enough to move the fingers. She was clearly trying to move the fingers because we could see the correct muscle struggling to move. This was clearly not a psychiatric case. The small puncture wound she had initially suffered in her proximal forearm had injured the small nerve, which innervates the muscles, which control those tendons. The small nerve was not repairable. The initial tendon repairs of the cut tendons and the later tendon-freeing operations did not work because the motor, (i.e., the muscle attached to those tendons) did not work well. We helped her by performing tendon transfers.

Among the many excellent advances in surgery the ability to perform microsurgery has been a technological breakthrough. Microsurgery involves the suturing together of the ends of tiny blood vessels, one to two millimeters in diameter, in a way that allows blood to flow through the anastomosis without significant leakage of blood. In order to perform this surgery, the surgeon needs to be completely relaxed. If she is tense, she will tire quickly. When you tire, your hands begin to shake. Under a 10x power operating microscope, it takes only a little shaking to look like a major earthquake. Even when under time pressure I was taught to take my time and make sure the operating hand table was at a comfortable height, my sitting stool at a comfortable height, the eye pieces of the operating microscope the right distance apart and at a comfortable height. You then place sterile towels under your forearms so that your forearms can rest without any tension of shoulder or upper arm muscles to keep the forearms in place. Then place sterile sponges under your hands so that you do not need to use forearm muscles to keep your hands in place. All of this eliminates most of your normal tremor. Then, only the hands and fingers move the minimal amount necessary to manipulate the pick-up (tweezers), needle holder and scissors. The needle holder can be locking or non-locking depending on surgeon preference. The suture size 10-0 is so fine that the suture does not hang down with gravity but the free end drifts sideways in the room's air currents.

Dr. Henry Mankin allowed me to use the microsurgery practice lab at Mass General while I was working at Fort Devens in the US Army. At first you start practicing on rats. At least that was the way I started to learn. Under anesthesia you cut the femoral artery to the hind leg of the rat. Then you suture it up with microvascular technique. If the rat's leg survives, your repair was successful. If not, then not. The operating microscopes have foot pedals that allow you to zoom in and out, focus up and down and move the area of view up and down or left and right. You can do all of this with your feet so that you can keep your hands placed where you need them. In cases involving replanting multiple amputated fingers or a case involving an amputated hand, surgery can last 14 to 16 hours. In my fellowship training the attending hand surgeon and two hand fellows rotated two hours operating, two hours assisting and two hours resting and/or eating until the case was done.

Think about your reaction to my discussing the use of rats to learn microsurgery. Both rats and dogs are living, breathing, feeling animals. Yet the ethics of operating on dogs for training seems much more problematic than the ethics of operating on rats. It is obvious, of course. Nobody likes rats. Without the use of rats for learning microsurgery, I am not certain how one could learn to do it. There are too many failures at first. There is a long, shallow learning curve. This is another situation in which the question arises: "How much training is necessary and what is the quality of craftsmanship that is required before operating on real patients?" How exactly does a trainee surgeon obtain this experience and training? How exactly should a trainee surgeon be evaluated prior to performing certain exacting procedures on patients?

While in my hand surgery fellowship Dr. Hunter and I saw a teenager who was had been splitting wood with a hydraulic wood splitter. The teenager put the wood on the rack and a second person triggered the wood splitter. Due to a mix up in timing the teenager's hand was caught by the wood splitter, amputating three fingers. Sharp amputations result in injury only where the cut occurs. An injury such as this, which results from relatively slow pulling, causes injury at a distance from the actual amputation. Thus, vascular repairs often fail. Working in shifts, we spent 15 hours replanting the three fingers. None survived. Knowing the low risk of success due to the method of injury, we still thought the attempt at replantation worthwhile due to the young age of the patient.

We did treat a patient whose hand was amputated by an extremely sharp blade used for cutting the edges of books. Very little injury at a distance. The cut was through the proximal row of bones in the wrist. We removed the first row of wrist bones to shorten the wrist and then repaired arteries, veins, nerves and tendons in that order. Another marathon procedure with a surprisingly functional result.

As mentioned previously, there is a diagnosis called Dupuytren's contracture, in which an abnormal hard tissue forms in the hand, in which each cell seems part muscle and part scar. It develops on the palm side of the hand most often involving the ring and little finger. Approximately 90 percent of people who have this diagnosis have known Scottish, English or Irish ancestry.

In evolutionary biology, there is a principle called the founder's effect. A small group of animals may enter a new niche and expand, spread and multiply within that new niche. Ordinary statistics predict that the average characteristics of this small group will be different from the average characteristics of the much larger group they have left, even without any new mutations. New mutations over time will increase the differences. Presumably, one or more of the early Celts or other tribes that crossed the English Channel and spread through the British Isles had the genetic tendency for Dupuytren's contracture.

Some years ago, a French woman in my office with Dupuytren's told me this couldn't be true. In a most French way, she told me, "I'm pure French, pure French, pure French." I operated on her and she did well. About five years later, she returned to see me for a different problem. In the interim she had had genetic testing. Sheepishly she laughed and told me that she had been astonished to discover she was three fourths Anglo-Saxon.

In the classic appearance of a hand with advanced Dupuytren's contracture, the ring and little finger are pulled in toward the palm. This leaves the thumb, index and middle fingers able to fully extend. This is the classic posturing of the right hand of a Catholic priest when blessing the faithful. Richard Smith, chief of hand surgery at Mass General, wondered aloud to me whether an early Pope had had Dupuytren's and held his hand that way because of the contractures, and had every priest since simply copied him.

One of my patients with Dupuytren's contracture, who I operated upon, returned to my office every few years with a new, significant problem requiring surgery. Every time, and I mean every time, this patient appeared with a new complaint, I found a new problem severe enough to require surgery. Following one of these surgeries, I commented to his wife about my "wonder" at the number of orthopedic problems her husband was continually developing. His wife introduced me to an Irish saying for people with bad luck, "If we had ducks, they'd drown." I have laughed about that for years.

Another complex finger vignette. Many of you may know what a ganglion is. It is a benign fluid-filled cyst on the back of the wrist that may come and go and change size. It may be painful or may not cause any pain. Treatment may consist of benign neglect (that is simply following it), needling to break it or surgery to remove it. Surgery has a five per cent incidence of recurrence. Similar benign fluid-filled cysts occur on the volar radial aspect of the wrist, the base of the fingers and elsewhere.

Similar cysts occur on the back of the distal joint of the fingers and thumb. When they occur there, they are often called mucous cysts. The skin on the back of the distal end of the finger has marginal blood supply. Pressure from under the skin from a mucous cyst may cause the skin to separate and allow the cyst to drain through the skin. When this happens, there is an open conduit connecting outside air to the underlying joint at the end of the finger. Occasionally bacteria enter this conduit and cause infection in the joint and the neighboring bone. To prevent the risk of deep infection I always recommended surgery to remove mucous cysts of any significant size.

Many years ago, an international businessman came to my office with the following history. Ten days earlier, following the rupture of a mucous cyst, the distal end of his little finger became swollen and red. He continued traveling and did not seek medical attention. After a few days the finger drained pus and seemed to improve. So, he continued to travel and ignore it. The infection then spread out of the joint and down the soft tissue of much of the finger. This led him to come to my office. There was pus and infection involving the soft tissue of the distal three fourths of the finger. X-rays showed extensive erosion of the two distal bones of the finger. Tendons had been destroyed by the ignored infection. What to recommend? There was sufficient destruction of the finger that I recommended amputation. Recall, one bad finger is worse than no finger. The patient did well after the amputation. He was willing to stay in town for five days to ensure the amputation wound was healing without infection. Then off he went. I never saw him again.

CHAPTER TEN

An Opportune Meeting

- Hand Therapy; Hand Therapist and
  Hand Surgeon Partnership

One December evening in 1968, in my second year of medical school, I wandered into the Countway Library of Medicine to study for some big test. The center of the library was open space with enclosed study spaces overlooking the atrium. The second floor was an informal space with alcoves of seating of comfortable chairs in conversational groupings. This was my preferred area in which to study. My routine was to circle the second floor to see who was there and to see if there were any date-worthy women on the floor. This, you should understand, was completely useless, time-wasting behavior. At that time, there were only a handful of women in my medical school class. I knew them all and they were not interested in me. There were precious few women in graduate school. So, I never, ever, saw even a single "eligible" woman in the year and a half I had been doing this. So, I was just going through the motions. Like some demented dog circling his bed a few times before settling down for a nap. Some primitive reflex with no present useful purpose.

This particular night, as I made my pathetic, purposeless circle, I happened upon an unanticipated vision sitting in one of the alcoves. An attractive and attracting women was sitting in one of the chairs, with a book open studying. Unknown to me, at that time, physical therapy students from Simmons College were permitted to study at the Countway Library. Who knew college bureau-crats could be so brilliant?

I sit down on a chair opposite her and begin to study. At least, I try to study. The miniskirt she is wearing is considerably distracting. In my adolescent puer-ility, masquerading as cool sophistication, I figure I shouldn't appear too eager. I figure I will wait a half an hour before I ask if she wants to take a study break. After 25 minutes, she gets up and takes a study break on her own. Hmmm. Has she even noticed my existence? Probably not. Two and a half hours go by. She hasn't left the library. She left her books and notebook behind. I have a test tomorrow. I keep studying. Ten minutes before the library closes, she comes back. Time for my clever opening gambit, "Boy, that was a long study break." She had met friends and chatted the evening away. I managed to get a name and phone number.

At this stage of my life, I was in what I now think of as "the becoming stage of my life." The only accomplishment, the only thing I had "become," was a student at a medical school, which is at best a way station, not a final destination. All else in my future were possibilities. Things I might or might not become. I had had romantic relationships before, but none had matured into long-term permanency. I was adrift in that no man's land of uncertainty we all inhabit as we grow and mature.

Again, not wanting to seem too eager, I waited four days before calling. No cellphones then. No texting. No Facebook. Not even landline phones in your dorm room. Just one landline phone per dorm floor. Lynne wasn't there. Left a message. She was organizing a charter flight to Europe for a group of students for the following summer in order to get a free flight for herself. I was just one of many messages left for her each day. We finally made contact and I made a date. First date: horrible play, parking ticket, otherwise simpatico. Within a month, dating steadily. Within months, realizing we were into something special.

That summer Lynne traveled to South Africa to visit family. We arranged for me to meet her at Logan Airport on her return. A few days before her return, I come down with a severe case of infectious mononucleosis. I am in the Harvard infirmary; temperature 103; literally bedridden; on shots of Demerol for severe headaches. I was taught that there are three types of mono. The most common is the pharyngitis or sore throat type. There is a hepatitis type with inflammation of the liver. Finally, there is a typhoidal type with big swings in fever and temperature spikes. That is what I creatively came down with.

I manage to call her roommates to ask for one of them to meet Lynne at the airport. They say they will. I collapse back into bed. Lynne arrives at the airport. Remember, no cellphones. No email. Also, no Frank to meet her. No roommate either. Lynne figures, "That bastard. I guess, it's over." Only when she gets to her apartment do her apartment mates tell her I am in the infirmary. They could not be bothered to go to the airport.

Fast forward to 1979. We are married. We have two children, one a newborn. I am in Philadelphia for my year of hand fellowship. Lynne is trained in physical therapy. She becomes interested in hand therapy. She comes into the hand therapy department frequently over the course of the year and informally trains in hand therapy with some of the pioneers of hand therapy, Evelyn Mackin and Anne Callahan, among others.

In 1980, when we moved to Maryland, Lynne and I set up as a team, hand therapist and hand surgeon working together. We continued working as a team for 37 and a half years. I have discussed above the experience during my hand training, which led me to become a religious devotee of hand therapy. My 37 years of practice have continued to confirm and reinforce that opinion. Together, Lynne and I never had a serious case of complex regional pain syndrome (severe chronic pain) in our practice. Why? Perhaps, we were lucky. Perhaps, we were attuned to the risk and were proactive. Perhaps, we were careful about "true" early motion, careful to use casts that did not prevent motion, careful about removing casts quickly that were tight, careful about quick carpal tunnel releases in early post-traumatic carpal tunnel syndrome and careful about early desensitization in patients with early hyperpathia (excessive, severe pain).

A contrasting vignette. I evaluated a patient for a second opinion who had developed complex regional pain syndrome following a wrist fracture. I reviewed his records. He had suffered a displaced wrist fracture which was treated with standard closed manipulation and casting. He called his orthopedic surgeon that night complaining of severe pain and was put off until morning. He was seen the next morning with complaints of severe pain and numbness and tingling. He was treated with Neurontin, a medicine used for chronic pain. The cast was not split. This patient should have been seen the first night he called with severe pain. The cast should have been split immediately. The patient should have been treated with an immediate carpal tunnel release. Failure to address these problems quickly resulted in the chronic pain syndrome.

Back to my partnership with Lynne. I was also fortunate that Lynne was creative and intelligent in the way she approached hand therapy. Many therapists, unfortunately, approach hand therapy like a cookbook. They use a rote formula. Here is an example. I had a patient with minimally displaced fractures of the proximal phalanges (the bones of the fingers nearest the palm) of three fingers of one hand. Despite my pleas that this patient travel to see Lynne, this patient chose to see a hand therapist near to where she lived. Despite several phone calls to the therapist, requesting early active motion and only early active motion, the patient came to my office, one visit, with all three fingers held straight wrapped in coban (an elastic wrap.) When I called the therapist to ask why the fingers were wrapped in coban, she told me she was treating swelling. The patient had little swelling. The wrapping of the coban was preventing the patient from moving her fingers. The final result was about 50% of total motion of each finger. I believe Lynne would have achieved better. Here was a situation where, despite my orders, despite my phone calls, despite my exhortations, despite my pleas, I was unable to get this hand therapist to give the specific therapy I desired. The patient did less well than I wanted.

Occasionally patients develop pain, which can become severe and disabling. Pain can truly ruin your life. This chronic pain syndrome was previously called causalgia or reflex sympathetic dystrophy and is now called complex regional pain syndrome. As I asked earlier, why do we keep renaming things? Perhaps it gives us a feeling of control or understanding and allows us to fool ourselves.

I don't know. Chronic pain following traumatic injury was first described in injured soldiers in the American Civil War by a doctor Weir Mitchell.

Any patient of mine who developed unexpected pain or unusually severe pain after injury or surgery was seen by Lynne immediately. Many patients, especially those with pain, are terrified of going to a therapist because they are afraid that the therapist will hurt them. Unfortunately, this is often true. The most important aspect of the first visit to a therapist is for the therapist to gain the patient's trust. The therapist gains the patient's trust by not hurting the patient. There are many therapists who practice "hard" therapy, which hurts. There are few circumstances in which painful stretching can help. Many patients will not return to painful therapy.

Here is an example of a "non-standard" first hand therapy visit. Lynne was confronted with a new patient I referred. The patient presented with an acute anxiety attack. Hyperventilation; forehead profusely sweating; terribly afraid. What "hand therapy" did Lynne provide during the entire first hand therapy visit? Meditation and relaxation exercises only. His hand was not touched. Then, the patient was able to return for more routine hand therapy with confidence.

Not all patients do well after injury or after surgery. Surgery is, after all, a controlled injury. Assuming the injury is not too severe and assuming the surgery has been properly performed, there are a number of reasons why a patient may not do well. One reason is that they may not be doing their therapy at home. Lynne taught me a good way to tell if patients are doing their therapy at home. Ask them to demonstrate their exercises. If they are unable to perform and demonstrate their exercises, you know they are not doing them.

When you have had a traumatic injury or surgery, your body becomes an active scar factory. Think of the classic, introductory economics class new widget factory. It first orders the raw supplies needed to manufacture the widgets. Then after the supplies arrive, the factory begins to produce the widgets. The body works similarly. After injury, the body needs time to ramp up the production of scar-forming precursor metabolites. Then it begins to manufacture scar. I visualize cement trucks lined up at a construction site pouring in cement. Starting at about a week, the body begins laying down scar. Each day some of the scar tissue is removed and new scar tissue is laid down. The reason that early therapy works is that the motion prevents adhesions that will permanently prevent motion. Young scar has a high turnover rate. Gentle therapy and motion allow the scar to lengthen. Thus, motion is gained. "Hard therapy," with forceful stretching, injures tissue causing increased scarring.

There is also a psychological reaction to injury or surgery. I once had a patient return for a first post-op visit following carpal tunnel release surgery with her hand hidden inside her blouse. She was so upset with the way it looked, just bandaged, that she did not want anyone to see it. This is the type of patient who may end up with a terrible result, with little motion and with severe pain. Immediate referral to Lynne. Patient did well. My typical carpal tunnel release patient did not go to hand therapy.

Some of you, readers, may have noticed that if you keep a bandage covering the pad of one of your fingers for a few days that when you take the bandage off, the pad of your finger is more sensitive to light touch for a few minutes. Our brains are rapidly adaptable. First, our brains are designed to pay attention to changes not to steady state conditions. There is an overwhelming amount of information constantly assaulting our senses. Evolutionary development has led to the following solution to the information overload problem. There are nerve cell endings just under our skin which send a signal toward the brain when it detects touch. The next cell back in the sensory awareness cascade receives these "I am being touched" signals. This second cell only sends a signal up the sensory cascade if there is a change in the "I am being touched" status. Thus, the next nerve cell only signals for the following states: "I have just been touched" or "My continual touching just stopped." The first cell continues sending "I am being touched" signals. From the point of view of importance, it does not matter if the shirt you are wearing stays in place. It may matter if a mosquito starts to bite you. Similarly, our peripheral vision is oriented toward detecting small movements even in low light. It is not designed to detect detailed vision nor colors at night. This makes functional sense. Picking up motion to the sides at night is a protective ability.

This type of process also occurs in the awareness and feeling of pain. Actually, the use of the word "pain" in the United States is ambiguous. Many of my patients only use the word "pain" to describe an unpleasant feeling which is severe in intensity. Another large percentage of people comfortably use the word "pain" to describe unpleasant feelings which may range from mild to severe. Probably 95% of patients coming to an orthopedic surgeon's office complain of pain or discomfort somewhere in their body. The other 5%? Something does not move properly, such as the spontaneous rupture of a tendon or a painless bump. When I first went into practice, I asked patients if they were having pain. Many patients said, "No." This left me confused. It took me a while to learn that people use the word "pain" differently. If a patient states she is not having pain I now know to immediately ask if she is having any discomfort. This was not something I learned in medical school or in my surgical training.

Following injuries to hands, as well as to other parts of the body, many patients develop pain. There is a tendency to protect the injured, painful part. This seems instinctual but is absolutely the wrong thing to do. If protected, that part of the body becomes increasingly more sensitive to touch and more painful. Increasing stimulus to the injured part is the optimum approach.

When a patient comes to a therapist for treatment, it is imperative for the therapist to reassure and relax the patient that they will not be hurt unnecessarily in therapy. The patient needs to be assured that while they may have some pain while trying to do an exercise in therapy, they will be in control of what they are doing and how much they are doing. Patients need to know that they are in control. Patients need to know that they can stop at any time. Breathing exercises during therapy may also help.

For treatment of a chronically painful area such as an amputation stump, the chronically painful area is exposed to gradually increasing levels of unpleasant stimuli. This is called desensitization. Among other effects this treatment resets thresholds in the brain for what sensory input is considered noxious. The treatment starts with minimal stimulation. Often a facial tissue is stroked over the hypersensitive area for the beginning treatment. The patient is instructed that we, Lynne and I, want to cause a level of discomfort that is unpleasant but which the patient will tolerate and be willing to continue. We ask the patient to do this for five minutes every hour while awake. As the patient gets used to this stimulus and the stimulus no longer feels so noxious, we gradually increase the intensity of the stimulus used. We use different textures and harder rubbing. Sometimes for a last noxious stimulus, we advance to using uncooked rice in a shallow pan as the rubbing surface. Once I had a patient who had suffered an amputated finger in an industrial accident come in near the end of treatment and tell me I didn't know what I was doing. Not the only patient who has ever told me this. Maybe these patients are on to something! This patient on his own had obtained pea gravel, placed it in a shallow box and was rubbing his "previously" painful amputation stump on the pea gravel. Obviously, with his intelligence and positive proactive attitude, he did well. He returned to work at full duty.

Some hand surgery patients seem to lose the normal connection between their brain and their injured hand. It seems like they are denying their hand or distancing themselves from it. When you ask them to move their hand or make a fist, they move into an awkward posturing. In order to treat this, Lynne has them gradually use their hand in their previous normal patterns of motion.

One of the keys to preventing the development of severe pain is listening to the patient and being proactive in response to their complaints. For example, any patient in a cast complaining of severe pain needs to have that cast split open immediately. My teaching was, and I continue to follow it: split the cast on two sides and make sure that the padding or lining is split all the way down to the skin. Better to accept loss of position of the fracture than end up with long-term nerve injury or pain.

I have black belts in three martial arts: Tae Kwon Do, Aikido and Japanese Jujitsu. I teach my own amalgam of the three, "Unarmed Defense Against Weapons," with emphasis on the asymmetric situation in which you are attacked by someone with a weapon or attacked by multiple adversaries. I do not teach the competitive martial arts with rules. There are some simple exercises that I teach to beginners, which are counterintuitive. In one exercise, I hold my partner's wrist firmly at waist level and ask him to elevate his hand upward. He is unable to do it. He is pulling as hard as he can with his arm muscles. His arm muscles are not strong enough. Then, I ask him to scratch his nose. Up comes his hand. He scratches his nose. I cannot stop him. What is the difference? When he goes to scratch his nose, he is using a pattern of muscles in a familiar combination. This pattern of muscle use is essentially preprogrammed. When muscles work together in a familiar, preprogrammed combination, they are more powerful. Simply, because this motion is intuitive, the muscles work together smoothly. Actions close to your body are also more powerful than actions when your arms are extended.

Similarly, in hand therapy if you have patients perform familiar patterns of motion, they will do the movements more easily, more powerfully and with greater degrees of motion than if you ask them to perform an artificial motion, which they have never done before. Lynne incorporates familiar patterns of motion into her therapy. If the patient is a violinist, Lynne will have the patient bring the violin in to the office as soon as is reasonably possible and incorporate the violin into the exercise program.

During the 37 years I was in private practice, I tried to convince my orthopedic partners to use early motion with their patients, without success. The efforts of Dr. Jim Hunter to popularize the use of real early motion (i.e. a few days) seems to have failed, since I continue to see references in the academic literature to early motion being three weeks after injury or surgery. I find this unfortunate.

PART THREE

A Cornucopia of Vignettes

Many of my vignettes do not fit easily into obvious manageable categories. In the chapters that follow, I have attempted to group these many vignettes into broad categories. I am unable to organize them into a logical sequence. Thus, these vignettes can be read in any order. Each vignette stands on its own.

CHAPTER ELEVEN

The Art, The Science, The Thrill, The Confusion of the Practice of Medicine and Surgery

- Dupuytren's Contracture of the Hand: Surgical Approach
- Communicating with Patients
- A Severe Bunion
- A Careful Second Opinion
- Sometimes My Best Treatment is Simple Advice
- Dealing with Families; Lumbar Spinal Stenosis
- How a Practice Grows
- Car Jacking Patient
- The Wild and Wacky Ways People Injure Themselves
- My Personal Experience with the Patient Side of Medical Care
- Long Term Follow Up After Treatment
- "You Think Your Leg Hurts; Take That!"
- When Should You Get a Second Opinion?

Dupuytren's Contracture of the Hand: Surgical Approach

I have previously discussed Dupuytren's contracture of the hand. In my training, I was exposed to different ways of performing the surgery for releasing the contractures of Dupuytren's and removing much of the abnormal tissue. The operation is actually called a partial palmar fasciectomy. The tough tissue is called fascia and much but not all of it is removed. It is dangerous to try to remove all of it. When the contracture has been present for a long time—think years—the skin has also contracted. As a result, there is less skin on the palmar side of the hand. After the contractures are released and the fingers are brought out straight, it is difficult to get full closure of the skin. There are many techniques described to try to solve this problem.

I was an orthopedic surgeon in the United States Army for two years after my orthopedic residency. During that time, I performed this operation using standard zigzag incisions. Zigzag incisions heal better than straight incisions if the incisions cross the joints on the palmar side of the hand. During my time in the army one of my patients developed bleeding in the palm and two skin flaps became necrotic from pressure caused by the underlying blood collection. Necrotic is a fancy word for dead. I debrided the dead tissue and then treated the patient with standard sterile saline washes for wound care. The wound, which was about an inch in diameter, closed nicely over three weeks. The patient continued moving his fingers and exercising throughout the healing process and had a superb result with complete recovery of motion of his fingers. I echo again Dr. Hunter's commandment, "Don't let the wound get in the way of motion."

My experience with the patient I just mentioned led me to reevaluate which method of Dupuytren's surgery I wanted to use in the future. A technique initially devised by an Australian hand surgeon, Dr. McCash, called— no surprise—the McCash technique, involves leaving a horizontal incision at the distal palmar crease open and unsutured at the end of the operation. This technique leaves a gaping transverse wound at the distal end of the palm. With twice daily sterile saline soaks, the wounds all heal in three weeks. Patients keep moving their fingers and do well.

Over the years, I have treated numerous patients who had surgery on one hand by a different technique, then had surgery by me on the other hand using the McCash technique. These patients did better, with better motion, after the McCash technique than they had done with their other hand. I don't think that the McCash technique is commonly used. Psychologically it seems "wrong" to leave a portion of the wound open. Having tried other ways and having seen the McCash technique during my training, I became a devotee. I had continuous positive feedback from patients who previously had different techniques on their other hand that they liked the McCash technique better. My patients all started hand therapy within a few days of the surgery.

As a physician and surgeon, it is important to be willing to constantly evaluate your results. If some treatment or operative procedure is working and getting good results, why switch to a newer, cooler procedure? However, if some treatment is not working well for you, not getting good results, having more complications than you should, then admit that to yourself and search for other approaches.

Communicating with Patients

I fondly remember a surgical ICU (intensive care unit) nurse on whom I performed a total hip replacement. The surgery went well. She did well. I saw her the day she was to be discharged from the hospital. I gave her a list of precautions. Activities and leg positions to avoid. She said she was going to do her own thing and wouldn't follow my instructions. I said, "I don't want you to do them." She continued to say she would. After three repetitions and three refusals, I did not seem to be connecting with her.

Sometimes, you have to play-act to communicate with patients. We had metal charts back then. I slammed the chart on the table, making a loud noise, and said, "I don't want you to do that." I repeated this maneuver three times. She stood there, smiling throughout my performance, then quietly said, "I'm an

ICU nurse. That doesn't scare me." With my play-acting I did get through to her. She was careful. She did well and the hip lasted 17 years, while she continued working on her feet all day long. Not bad for a patient with rheumatoid arthritis.

A Severe Bunion

What are appropriate indications for elective surgery? Bunions, also known by the medical term *hallux valgus*, are common. Surgery is indicated for significant persistent foot pain and/or sufficiently severe deformity. The angle between the forefoot bone of the big toe, the first metatarsal, and the line of the big toe is normally less than 15 degrees. An angle greater than 15 degrees does not automatically require surgery. The greater the angle, the greater the difficulty with obtaining a comfortable fit with shoes. The greater the angle, the greater chance of severe foot pain.

A man was referred to me by a rheumatologist for surgery for a bunion. This patient carried a diagnosis of severe, chronic rheumatoid arthritis. The bunion angle was 115 degrees. This is not a misprint. The angle was 115 degrees. That means the tip of the big toe was facing backwards toward the heel. The big toe was overlapping the lesser toes and part of the forefoot. I asked the patient if he was having any pain. He said, "No." I asked if he was concerned about the way his foot looked. He said, "No." I asked if he was having trouble with fitting his shoes. He said he was happy with his specially made shoes. I then said, "I don't think you need an operation." He said, "I agree." If he was not having any pain, one result of surgery might be a painful foot. For the hand, feeling, manipulation and dexterity are important. For the foot, you want a painless platform on which to stand and walk.

I later performed between 10 and 13 operations on the severe bunion patient for other valid reasons. He and I used to joke about counting the number of operations I had performed on him. It was never clear to us whether two operations through one incision counted as one or two operations. It also wasn't clear if two operations done through two incisions at the same time counted as one or two operations, thus our joking about the indeterminate number of operations.

A Careful Second Opinion

Another vignette. Still jumping around with my memories. An internist referred a patient to me who had been operated on by another orthopedic surgeon. A man had developed a herniated disc in his lumbar spine causing severe leg pain. There was a large bulge on his MRI. In a herniated disc, the shock-absorbing material between the bones of the spine degenerates, breaks into pieces and bulges into the spinal canal. In this patient the bulge was pinching a nerve. The previous orthopedic surgeon performed a percutaneous lumbar discectomy. In this procedure a tube is inserted through the skin into the disc space. A rotary suction device then removes disc material to try to decrease the bulge. This procedure was popular some years ago.

Following the percutaneous discectomy, there was no improvement in this patient's severe leg pain. The original orthopedic surgeon ordered a new MRI of the lumbar spine. The radiologist read the MRI as normal, indicating successful surgery with no remaining bulge. The patient was referred for psychiatric evaluation and pain management. The patient's internist referred the patient to me for a second opinion.

After my first visit with the patient, I asked him to obtain both of his MRIs and bring them with him to the next office visit so that I could look at them myself. When I looked at both MRIs, I saw the large bulging disc on the first MRI. On the second MRI the large bulging disc was unchanged. I strongly disagreed with the radiologist's reading of the second MRI. My opinion was that there was a clear anatomic explanation for this patient's continuing leg pain. Open surgical removal of the bulging disc was indicated; not psychiatric treatment. I recognized that my reading of the second MRI was diametrically opposite to the reading of the radiologist. I personally reviewed this MRI with three other independent radiologists. All agreed with my reading. I operated and the patient had complete relief of pain.

Three years later, I was rounding on patients on a Sunday morning. I happened to see the internist who had referred this patient. I said, "Hi." He reminded me of this patient. He told me he was impressed at how well the patient had done. I told him I was happy too. Three years later he remembered how well this patient had done. Yet I never saw another referral from him. Go figure!

The other orthopedic surgeon had a good reputation. So, what happened? Why did he fail to recognize that the large bulge was unchanged on the second MRI? Obviously, I don't know for sure. I suspect that he accepted the original radiologists report and never looked at the second MRI himself. Most of the orthopedic surgeons I have worked with insist on reviewing all of their patients' imaging studies. I do the same. The old trite statement that a picture is worth a thousand words is true. But more than that, there is a constant stream of incorrectly read imaging studies. Another pair of eyes, another review, decreases the risk of this type of error. The other orthopedic surgeon was a good doctor with an excellent reputation. Perhaps the other orthopedic surgeon relaxed a little this one time and failed to insist on looking at the MRI. It is also possible that he looked at the MRI but failed to notice the large bulge. Second opinions are often valuable.

Sometimes My Best Treatment is Simple Advice

I had a police photographer patient with chronic neck pain. His equipment weighed 60 pounds. Sometimes he had to carry his equipment half a mile across rough terrain to a crime scene. I encouraged him to buy or make a cart with big wheels to use to transport his equipment. He kept refusing. The male ego thing, you know. Especially in a macho police department. Finally, after six months, my police photographer patient relented and followed my advice. He came in later to tell me that the cart made a world of difference. That he had been a fool to resist my advice. All my wonderful training, all my wonderful surgical skills, my best treatment is often just simple advice. Marked relief in his neck pain. Don't stand on ceremony or worry about your ego. Be a smart consumer. Find ways to make your job less stressful. Tile setters and carpet layers often get infections in little sacs in the front of their knees called a prepatellar bursae. This can be prevented or at least made less likely by using pads to kneel on.

I had an electrolysis specialist as a patient many years ago with chronic neck pain. She could not contort her neck into the positions necessary to remove hair from the parts of the body of her clients that she needed to access for her work. I asked her to come to my office in a full body leotard and told her I would work with her in trying to solve her patient positioning problems. With a chaperone present we spent a half hour. First, I recommended surgical loupes, which would allow her magnification and the ability to work with her head further away from the area of her work. Then she told me which parts of the body were a problem. Using common sense, I then demonstrated possible ways of positioning her patients to treat a specific body part that allowed her to work with her neck straight.

Years later, she returned with another problem. She told me I had saved her career. She also told me that my recommendation for using magnifying loupes had spread through the local electrolysis community. We both had a good laugh remembering the "non-standard" office visit. This is an example of out-of-the-cage thinking in the practice of medicine. This is also another example that sometimes my best treatment involves "simply" giving advice.

Dealing with Families; Lumbar Spinal Stenosis

Many of you know that in degenerative arthritis, joints often develop bone spurs which bulge out of the bone. This same bone-spurring reaction to degenerative arthritis also occurs in the small joints of the spine. In the lower or lumbar spine, the bone spurs may protrude into the spinal canal. With sufficient protrusion into the spinal canal, the canal narrows, called stenosis. When severe enough, the narrowing interferes with the blood supply to the nerves inside the spinal canal. Patients with lumbar spinal stenosis are often asymptomatic when sitting at rest. However, they are most symptomatic when they try to walk. If the stenosis is severe, they may be able to walk for only five minutes or less than a block before having to stop. After resting for five minutes they are often able to walk the same distance again. This constellation of symptoms is called claudication.

Another orthopedic surgeon referred an 80+-year-old woman with lumbar spinal stenosis to me for surgery. This patient was unable to walk more than five minutes without stopping to rest. Her MRI showed severe narrowing of the lumbar spinal canal. After careful evaluation, I scheduled surgery to open up her spinal canal in order to relieve the narrowing of her spinal canal. When I met this patient in the pre-op area for her pre-op check, three of her daughters were present. I had not met them before. We chatted pleasantly. The anesthesiologist and operating room nurse wheeled the patient away, heading to the operating room. After the patient disappeared on her way to the operating room, the three daughters descended on me like harpies.

"You shouldn't be operating on Mom. She is constantly faking symptoms."

Patients with lumbar spinal stenosis do not have any obvious abnormality on physical exam. They do not know why they cannot walk far. They only know that they cannot walk long or far. Their symptoms are often vague and diffuse. I showed the severe stenosis (narrowing) on the MRI to the daughters. I told them that I was listening to them but that now was not the right time to express their concerns. I explained that the decision-making was between their mother and me. I told them that I hoped I was right. Post-op, this patient did superbly well with marked improvement in walking ability.

Lumbar spinal stenosis is a medical problem which is easy for doctors and orthopedic surgeons to miss. You have to actively look for it. You have to specifically ask the patient if she has difficulty walking for distance or time. You have to ask specific questions such as: "When you drive to the store, do you have to park near to the store, or can you park some distance away?" or "When you go to the supermarket do you have to hold on to the grocery cart?" or "When you go to the shopping mall, do you have to sit down frequently?" I have, on occasion, asked patients to walk rapidly for ten minutes and then come back to my office.

Sometimes I see them staggering down the hall as they try to keep walking. Questions like those listed above should be part of every annual physical exam.

How a Practice Grows

Six months into building up my private practice in hand surgery and orthopedic surgery, an elderly woman came into my office to see me. She started the office visit saying she was thrilled that I had space in my busy schedule to see her. She told me that she had heard so much about me. Recalling my review of that morning's schedule with the many open slots, I asked her who had told her about me. I noted that she lived in a small town an hour to the north. She told me that Mrs. A and Mrs. B had told her that I was a wonderful doctor. All three ladies lived in the same small town. Epiphany. In the first six months of my practice, I was becoming the go-to orthopedic surgeon for the elderly ladies in this small town. So builds a practice.

A year or two into my practice, I saw a teenage girl with a painful extra bone on the inside of her foot. This is called an accessory navicular. A minor operation to remove the extra bone cured her foot pain. Do recall, there is really no such thing as minor surgery. There are, however, minor surgeons. About three months later another teenage girl came into my office with the same problem. She was a close friend of the first patient. She came home from school one day and told her parents, "I want to see Sally's doctor." Sally is a pseudonym. She did well after the same surgery. So builds a practice.

Car-Jacking Patient

Wee hours of the morning. A woman stops at a stoplight. A man opens the driver's door, points a gun, tells her to move over, gets into the driver's seat, drives off. Within a few blocks, she opens the door and bails out of the moving car. Chance. There is a police car right behind her. High-speed car chase. High-speed car crash. Front end into tree. Airbags deploy. Hours of search. Police dogs. Police find suspect with open fracture of his arm. A little later, 4 a.m., there I am in the operating room doing my best to fix him up so that he will be good enough to do this again.

Weird.

The Wonderful, Wild and Wacky Ways People Injure Themselves

One of the things you discover as an orthopedic and hand surgeon is the myriad of wild, wonderful and wacky ways that people injure themselves. First example that pops into my mind is the man who took three Viagra tablets along with multiple alcoholic drinks. Then he stood up, fainted and crashed through a glass coffee table, suffering severe lacerations. The night did not turn out the way he planned. Then, there was the Sunday coed baseball game of 40+-year-old players. The testosterone blood levels in the men were stratospheric. The men were showing off. Three fractures from one game alone. Two came from one play. The male catcher, who was blocking home plate, was determined that no runner was getting by him, thank you very much. The male runner, who was racing to get to home plate, was determined to get there, no matter what, thank you very much. I forget the third injury. The collision between the runner and the catcher caused two of the fractures.

Tibia fractures from deliberate kicking of shins in soccer in simple pick-up games. Fractures of the upper arm bone (humerus) from being hit by a baseball bat. Two—one week apart—both happened in Germantown, Maryland. I don't know if it was the same attacker. Two fractures of the humerus, long spiral fractures from arm wrestling. One woman climbing a tree while drunk and wearing high heels. She fell out and suffered a fracture. Handcuffed man in police car tells officers he needs to pee. They ignore him. He pees in car. In anger, the police officers pull him out of the car and push him down. He falls, hits his head and fractures his neck.

My Personal Experience with the Patient Side of Medical Care

I am bothered that the practice of medicine that I have personally experienced from the patient side has seemed so ordinary. Perhaps I am asking too much of my physicians. Perhaps average and ordinary is exactly what it says it is. Average and ordinary is what occurs most often. Perhaps it is just my arrogance talking. Just before I started second-year medical school, my father traveled to Dallas, Texas, for open-heart surgery by Dr. Denton Cooley. I was in the hospital room when Dr. Cooley came in for the preoperative visit. He spent less than five minutes in the room. He was truly running a factory. He listened to my father's heart with a stethoscope through his shirt, truly perfunctory. Just going through the motions. My brother-in-law, an internist, was there. No effort to engage with the patient or family. No effort to comfort the family. No discussion. We could as easily have been pictures on the wall.

Two days after surgery my father's blood pressure crashed. He developed a blood infection, septicemia and acute renal failure (kidney stopped working). It was the weekend. No one in the family could find an attending (i.e., staff doctor) who would say, "I am in charge of this man's care." Truly, there was no chain of "command" in which there was a specific doctor designated as "responsible." While my father survived, his brain was damaged. He was never the same.

One week later, as a medical student back in Boston, I watched with strong disapproval as an attending physician with a group of medical students and residents rounded on a patient. The attending physician never entered the patient's room. He never addressed the patient. He never acknowledged the patient as a human being. Not all doctors are like that. However, too many are.

More on my experiences with ordinary medical care. As a child, I had an undescended testicle, which required two surgeries to correct. The older you are before corrective surgery, the greater the risk of testicular cancer. Throughout my childhood, young adulthood and not-so-young adulthood, no physician ever advised me that I should perform regular testicular self-examinations. No physician, that I recall, performed an extra careful testicular examination,

157

given my past history. No physician counseled me about my increased risk of testicular cancer. There was no discussion of routine ultrasound examinations looking for early detection of cancer. Is that "ordinary?" If that is ordinary, then ordinary is "bad" medicine.

One day in my 40s, I noted an irregularity in my right testicle. I was certain it was cancer. Next day: consultation with a urologist, who agreed. Next day: ultrasound exam, which confirmed the diagnosis. Next day: orchiectomy (i.e., ball in the bucket or removal of the testicle). The phrase "ball in the bucket" was used by my urologist when talking to me. Don't you love the empathy? Pathology: seminoma, which is a "milder" form of cancer. Allow the wound to heal, then 2600 rads of radiation therapy to the abdominal and pelvic lymph nodes.

The previous paragraph was written in a pleasant, low-key style. It does not reflect my whirlwind of emotion. I think they talk about the eight stages of grief. Far too simplified. For weeks, stunned, staggering shock was my overwhelming reaction. I had a few things going for me. I knew the success rate for treatment of seminoma was about 95%. Now, let's discuss my subsequent treatment.

After my surgery, my urologist discharged me. My "surgical" part was done. Never a question regarding how I was doing, other than strictly the surgery. Not one question. Nothing to do with the whole person. No follow up with him. Oh, and the radiation therapist. She had the emotional range of Rosa Kleb, a cold and villainous character in the James Bond film "From Russia With Love." Again, never a question about how are you doing? Do you need any counseling? Any help? Nada!

For the radiation therapy, the radiation therapist put tattoo dots on my abdomen and pelvis for aligning the radiation. Every—and I mean every—time I looked in the mirror, for years, there was a reminder of the cancer and the radiation. I finally had the tattoos removed.

I only missed a few days of work as a result of the surgery. I was able to schedule the radiation therapy for the late afternoon, so that the nausea side effects occurred in the evening. Three weeks after the surgery, I am sitting in the nurses' station of Holy Cross Hospital in Silver Spring, Maryland, when a doctor acquaintance of mine says to me across the nurses' station in a loud voice something to the effect of, "How are you doing, Frank? I hear you had your testicle removed for cancer." True story! Wrong on so many levels. One partner of my urologist gossiped to other doctor friends about me. The doctor at the nurses' station clearly did not recognize how inappropriate his behavior was, to announce this private information across a crowded nursing station. Such has been my personal experience with the "ordinary" practice of medicine.

Years later my internist detected an inguinal hernia on the side opposite from where I had the orchiectomy and referred me to a general surgeon. The general surgeon recommended laparoscopic hernia repair. I asked the general surgeon, who knew my past history (I had just told him), whether the 2600 rads of radiation therapy to the abdominal and pelvic lymph nodes was a contraindication to laparoscopy due to the possibility of increased scarring and adhesions within the abdomen. He said yes and changed his mind and scheduled open surgery. Again: ordinary. He should have thought of that, not me. Is my writing about this and judging this, being arrogant? I report; you decide.

Some years later, I spent two years with intermittent muscle aches and pains in my arms and legs with no specific diagnosis. Finally, my wife suggested from her online research that this might be a side effect of a blood pressure medicine I was taking. I went off the medicine and the aches and pains went away. My wife diagnosed and "treated' me for the intermittent muscle aches and pains; not my personal physician. In his defense, it is possible I did not complain about my symptoms sufficiently. However, he did not specifically ask me about possible side effects of the medicine.

The wife of a friend of mine was suffering from severe heartburn. Acid-reducing medication was minimally helpful. Endoscopy did not show any serious abnormality. Finally, her husband noted that she was taking cranberry extract for urinary tract infection prophylaxis. He suggested a trial of stopping the cranberry extract. The heartburn went away. A more thorough history by the gastroenterologist would have picked this up, should have picked this up. Had this been picked up early, the endoscopy would have been avoided. We, doctors, need to spend more time asking our patients what supplements they are taking. Detailed questioning regarding supplement intake should be a part of every annual evaluation.

As I read over the last few pages, I realize that I have really been negative about the quality of medical and surgical care I have received. I think that is a shame. I may have overstated the case. Medicine and surgery are incredibly complex and really hard to do well all the time. Many physicians are hardworking, serious and dedicated. Some may be going through ugly divorces. Some may have been up half the night, etc. I was privileged to train with some truly outstanding physicians and surgeons during my training years. I saw many of my primary training surgeons make at least one major surgical error during my time with them. These errors were not due to laziness, sloppiness, carelessness or being cavalier. They were, if you will, honest errors. If honest errors can occur to surgeons of that caliber, then honest errors can occur to anyone. It is humbling.

There are doctors who seem to always rush out of the exam room and leave patients little time for discussion. Two possible solutions to this. One: find another doctor. Two: while talking to the doctor casually stroll over to the door then lean against the door preventing the doctor from leaving the room. Only leave the door and allow the doctor out after all of your questions have been answered.

I have recently become acquainted with "Sturgeon's Law." Sturgeon's Law states, "90% of everything is crud." Theodore Sturgeon was a science fiction writer in the mid-20th century. In an interview he was asked why so much science fiction is poor quality. He replied, "90% of science fiction is crud. 90% of everything is crud." The last sentence is the one most often quoted. I do not think that Sturgeon's Law applies to modern medical care as I have seen it.

Long-Term Follow Up After Treatment

Here are two vignettes concerning patient gratitude or the lack thereof. A patient, perhaps 16 years old, came to me years ago with a fracture of the tibia (large lower leg bone), which had failed to heal (non-union) and was angulated.

He had previously had reconstructive surgeries at three different major medical centers trying to heal this non-union with unsuccessful results.

After careful evaluation with X-rays and CT scans, I operated. I opened the bony canal at the level of the knee. Using fluoroscopic guidance, I threaded a penetrating device down the bony canal to the level of the non-union. The end of the penetrating device was like a tapered screw. I, then, slowly rotated the penetrating device. Under fluoroscopic control, I carefully passed the penetrator through the tissue of the non-union. Through a small incision I loosened up the peripheral non-union scar tissue. After reaming, I was able to pass a metal rod down the shaft of the straightened tibia fixing the non-union. He healed.

I mention this case, specifically, because he never thanked me. Given that I had healed a non-union which the patient had for years, I guess I expected some verbal acknowledgement of appreciation. For years, he was my archetypical case of the saying, often repeated, that the patients you do the most for are the least grateful and the patients you do the least for are the most grateful. I often used this case as a classic example of this saying. Now, fast forward, perhaps, 25 years. He returns to see me for another problem. He is now in his early 40s. Surprise! He remembers clearly the events of those many years ago. He is profoundly grateful. He thanks me. His family had moved out west shortly after his surgery, so there had been only a short period of follow up after his surgery. He is doing well. How much we assume in life that is wrong. How much we assume about people that is wrong. Humbling!

Next vignette about gratitude. A six-year-old boy falls down the stairs and breaks his arm. The forearm is angulated about 45 degrees. I see him in the hospital emergency room with his father. I talk to him about what is going on and what I am going to do. Using local anesthesia and mild sedation, I manipulate the fracture back in place. With the sedation he does not feel any pain. He heals well. I discharge him from care.

Six months later, he falls down the same stairs, again. He stands up, holding the same arm with his other hand. His forearm is again angulated about 45 degrees. He looks up at his father and says, "If I'm not crying, it can't be broken, right?" He knows exactly what has happened. He comes into the emergency room. Happenstance. I happen to be on call that night. I talk to him. I treat him the same way. He does well.

Fast forward 30 years. Two men come into my office, one as a patient with his father. One of them says, "Do you remember …." I say, "Stop." I recognize them 30 years later. We reminisce. He still remembers clearly the events of age six. Most gratifying for me, he remembers my treatment positively.

"You Think Your Leg Hurts Now? Take That!"

One winter day in Boston in the 1970s, the temperature dropped about 30 degrees in a few hours to below freezing. The wind rose to over 30 miles per hour. The entire city became glazed with ice. The wind seemed to be blowing everybody over. In a 24-hour period over 70 fractures were seen at Mass General Hospital and over 30 fractures were seen at Peter Bent Brigham Hospital. We, orthopedic residents, were busy operating night and day, for several days, to care for all of these patients.

One fracture from this 24-hour period was not admitted to the hospital until three days later. The day of the ice storm, a woman walked down the front stairs from her apartment. She slipped and fell, hurting her leg. Her roommates carried her into their apartment and placed her on the couch. For three days, she complained of severe pain in her leg. Finally, her boyfriend got tired of her complaints. We were told that the boyfriend said something to the effect of, "You think your leg hurts now? Well, take that." Then he shot her in the leg, converting a closed fracture of the tibia (lower leg bone) into an open fracture with the bullet. We operated on her. She needed a new boyfriend, I think.

When Should You Get a Second Opinion?

Friends of ours had a son who, by age 18 months, had a second toe which was elevating and beginning to cross over the big toe. There was a family history of this deformity. His father had a second toe completely overlapping the big toe, causing difficulty with the fitting of shoes. They had seen the chief of pediatric surgery at a major medical center. He had recommended surgery to release a ligament and realign a tendon to the toe. This advice seemed extreme to me for an 18-month-old baby. I recommended they take their child to Dr. Michael Ehrlich, then chief of pediatric orthopedic surgery at Mass General. Dr. Ehrlich recommended taping the toes at night with a band-aid. With the sticky side up, under the third toe, over the second toe, gently pushing the second toe down, and then under the big toe, sticky side up. He recommended doing this for six months at night. Then resume taping only if the problem recurred. This simple recommendation solved the problem. Surgery was not necessary. Second opinions are often worthwhile, even for seemingly minor problems, even if the first opinion is from a world-renowned physician.

CHAPTER TWELVE

Complications; Problems; Difficulties: How Long Should Surgical Training Last?

Let me revisit the question: "How long should medical and surgical training last?" How much time should a trainee surgeon spend in the hospital? When things go well, surgery is often easy. Not really easy, but straightforward and simple for arguable definitions of straightforward and simple. There is a saying, "There is no such thing as simple surgery. There are, however, simple surgeons." Only rarely do things go badly, but when they do go badly, they often go badly quickly. Training needs to be long enough that a trainee has seen experienced surgeons get into trouble and then watched and learned how to respond to and treat the trouble. This does not happen often. These experiences cannot be programmed. If it happens in the operating room, you have to figure out what to do, then and there. There is no time to relax, have a beer and surf the web for information.

Murphy's Law is well known, "If something can go wrong, it will." This law is true in life and in surgery. One morning in my general surgical internship, I was away from the hospital for my military draft physical. That morning during a cholecystectomy (removal of gallbladder) under the direction of Dr. Francis D. Moore (have I mentioned him before?), the operating intern accidently cut the right hepatic artery of the patient they were operating on. This artery gives blood supply to the right half of the liver. What to do? Once again, the question "What to do?"

Dr. Moore decided to repair the right hepatic artery with small sutures. Then, in order to determine if the repair was patent (open and working), he placed a needle into the common hepatic artery and injected dye, while taking an X-ray to see if the dye passed through the repair of the right hepatic artery. Unfortunately, the tip of the needle was not in the lumen (opening; cavity) of the common hepatic artery, but in the wall of that artery. The injection of the dye dissected through the wall of the common hepatic artery closing it off completely. At this point the common hepatic artery was blocked. There was no blood supply to any part of the liver. This situation is not survivable if not successfully repaired. After many hours of surgery, vascular surgeons repaired the common hepatic artery. The patient survived.

This case was discussed at our weekly death and complications rounds. Dr. Moore spoke in detail about the mistakes he personally made in this operation. If the right hepatic artery is cut, it can be tied off. You can survive easily with half a liver. Removal of half of the liver is now done routinely when living patients donate half of their liver for transplantation. I repeat our surgical saying, "The enemy of good is better." Know when to accept what you have. You can always make things worse. A decision to repair the right hepatic artery was not "bad." It did not increase risk to the patient, but—repeat, but! Repeat, but!—having repaired the artery and taken out the gallbladder, stop! The decision to put dye into the common hepatic artery to see if the repair was patent was faulty. As stated above, even if the repair was not patent, this situation was survivable. The damage done to the common hepatic artery was not survivable unless repaired successfully. The decision to inject the dye was the bad one. Dr. Moore took full personal blame for that error in front of everyone. Admirable. Educational. Rare. I found it terrifying that someone with his extraordinary knowledge, skill and judgement could make such a mistake.

I returned to the hospital after my military physical, but before this case was finished. I was with Dr. Moore when he went out to talk to the family. He discussed everything in exhaustive detail. He explained his mistake. He explained his error in decision-making without the slightest excuse. He omitted nothing. Again: Admirable. Educational. Rare. I mention frequently the vagaries, the randomness, the idiosyncrasies of surgical training. A situation like this was a once-in-a-training lifetime situation. Most trainee surgeons probably never see a similar situation. Dr. Moore's integrity was astonishing.

An acquaintance of mine told me of a case of a chief of spine surgery in another hospital in another city who was demonstrating the insertion of Harrington Rod hooks for scoliosis surgery to a group of residents watching. In demonstrating the insertion of the hooks, the chief of spine surgery pulled up and down on the hook really hard, multiple times, to demonstrate how strong the attachment of the hook was. Post-operatively, this patient had a partial spinal cord injury at the level of this hook, called a Brown-Sequard syndrome. At the complication conference at this other institution, the chief of spine surgery did not admit to any possibility of his surgical error.

This story brings up another issue. When you are operating alone without an audience, you are more careful. When you have an audience, some of your attention is spent on entertaining or educating the audience and you are not as careful. I am reminded of an event years ago in which the crew of an American submarine was giving a "tour" to political donors. Due to the distraction, the captain and crew of the submarine were not as careful as they would otherwise have been. They rapidly surfaced directly under a Japanese fishing boat with loss of life.

Here are some other examples of "trouble" I have encountered during the course of my training and my practice. Since I am an orthopedic surgeon, these problems are orthopedic in nature. We orthopedic surgeons are extraordinarily dependent on the equipment we use and the design and manufacture of the prostheses we implant. Many of the problems I have encountered demonstrate this dependency.

I am doing a routine (as I have stated, no surgery is ever really routine) knee arthroscopy. To examine and work in the lateral or outside compartment of the knee, one technique used involves crossing the patient's leg with the patient's knee bent 90 degrees. The weight of the leg and the position of the knee puts stress on the knee that opens up the lateral side a bit. This position makes it easier to see and manipulate instruments on this side. I am using a cautery type instrument to ablate (remove) torn meniscus tissue. Suddenly, I see a piece of plastic or resin used to seal the end of the instrument, about a sixth of the circumference of a circle, break off of the instrument and float free. Having seen this type of situation before, I immediately turn off the flow of irrigating fluid. Fluid is kept flowing through the knee during arthroscopy to aid visualization by washing away any bleeding. Turning off the fluid often prevents the foreign body from washing away out of sight.

As I watch the image on the monitor, the fragment of plastic floats slowly downward through the water. It slides under the meniscus (joint cartilage), which sticks out from the edge of the knee. The fragment then slides down into a sulcus under the meniscus and moves out of sight. The arthroscope I am using is too large to slide under the meniscus. If I cannot see the plastic fragment, I cannot remove it. What to do? I freeze everything in place. I know I need help. There is no emergent rush, but I need another pair of educated eyes and hands. I call one of my partners to leave office and come to the operating room. After about a half hour wait, my partner comes in and dons gown and gloves. While waiting, I have asked the operating room nurses to prepare a smaller ankle arthroscope with a 70-degree angle lens for use. This small arthroscope with a 70-degree angle lens is designed for looking around corners in small spaces.

Under my direction, my partner makes a small puncture incision in the side of the knee and inserts the ankle arthroscope. Using the larger knee arthroscopic images, we direct the smaller ankle scope under the meniscus and turn it to look down into the sulcus. Now, we can see the plastic fragment on the monitor connected to the smaller scope. The plastic fragment has rotated so that the broken edges are facing into the soft tissue. Multiple times, we try to grasp the fragment with angled-grasping instruments and fail. Finally, we use a small rotary shaver (think of a small lawn mower attached to a vacuum cleaner with different shapes and sizes available) to gobble it up. No long-term harm to the patient. The procedure took an hour longer than it otherwise would have. Patient fully informed.

Another example of intraoperative arthroscopic trouble. I am doing a shoulder arthroscopy using a plastic, one-time use, cannula (tube). These cannulas have a rubber stopper with a small hole which allows the insertion of an instrument but prevents water from leaking out. Just after inserting the plastic cannula and inserting an instrument, I see a perfectly round, thin structure float across the monitor, which is showing me images of the inside of the joint. Nothing physiologic is perfectly round. This object is clearly a foreign body, which in some way, has been introduced into the shoulder.

As before, I immediately turn off the fluid inflow to try to prevent the object from being washed away out of sight. Unfortunately, this time, the object does drift out of sight. I use the arthroscope to look all around the shoulder joint searching for this object, but I cannot find it. I try really hard to find it. There are many nooks, crannies, crevices and folds of tissue in the shoulder joint. After 20 minutes of careful searching, I cannot find it. What to do? There will likely be little harm in leaving it. But that is an unknown. There is no experience or knowledge regarding what happens over 50 years if you leave something like that in a shoulder. But I can't find it. So, still the question, "What to do?"

I decide to ignore it for the moment. I really don't have any other choice. I still have an arthroscopic procedure to do. So, I go ahead and begin the procedure. Serendipitously, about a half hour into the procedure, the object reappears on the screen, floating in the water. I love the word "serendipity." It is the art of finding something good when you are not looking for it. I again immediately stop the fluid inflow, and this time the smooth round object stays in sight. It is then easy to insert a grasping instrument, grab the round object and remove it. Looking at the round piece of plastic, it was clearly one of the plastic washers from one of the plastic cannulas.

I examined all of the cannulas after the operation. All the ones I used had intact washers. I assume that in the manufacture of the cannulas, an extra washer ended up sitting loosely in the tube of one of the cannulas. I assume this extra loose washer was pushed into the joint the first time I inserted an instrument through that cannula. As surgeons, we are profoundly dependent on the quality of manufacture of the equipment we use. To be sure, I examined every cannula I ever used again with great care before use after that. Patient fully informed.

Another example of trouble in the operating room. I am doing a lumbar laminectomy. I make a small incision in the middle of a patient's back, split the muscles, which go down the center of the back, nibble away a small amount of bone and enter the spinal canal. This surgery is performed to remove bulging or herniated discs. I make a small incision in the tissue at the back of the disc space directly over the bulging disc. I then insert a long, thin instrument, called a pituitary rongeur, with small biting jaws into the disc space. The typical procedure usually involves multiple insertions of this instrument to safely take and remove small bites of disc tissue. In this way, I gradually remove enough of the disc contents to relieve the bulge, which is pressing on a nerve.

Usually the operation proceeds without excitement. This time, the first time I insert the pituitary rongeur and close it to take a bite, there is a snapping sound and the handle of the instrument goes slack. I lift the rongeur up and note that one of the jaws is missing. The jaw has broken off inside of the disc space. The opening to the disc space is only a two-millimeter puncture. I cannot see the broken jaw. It obviously is hidden inside of the disc space.

Again, the question, "What to do?" Breaking of a jaw of a pituitary rongeur has actually happened to me twice! The first time, I increased the size of the opening into the disc space but still could not see the broken jaw. I decided to continue the operation as if the instrument had not broken. I widened the opening into the disc space some more. My plan was to look for the broken jaw after removal of the disc material. I inserted a new pituitary rongeur. Luck! On the first insertion of the new pituitary rongeur, I grasped the broken jaw and retrieved it. I then went on with the operation. Patient fully informed.

The second time I was not successful with the next bite of a new pituitary rongeur, I again continued the operation. Repetitively, I inserted another pituitary rongeur, took small bites of disc material and removed them. After I had removed the disc material, I needed to know where the jaw of the rongeur was located within the disc space. I brought in a small ankle arthroscope and carefully inserted it into the disc space. On the monitor, I located the broken fragment. Knowing where it was, I was able to grasp it and remove it. Patient fully informed.

What went wrong and caused the jaws of the two pituitary rongeurs to break? As mentioned earlier, anything that is repetitively bent, even a little, will eventually break. This phenomenon is called metal fatigue, if the object is metal. More generally, it is called material fatigue. Airplane wings and jet engine fan blades are replaced on a regular schedule to try to prevent catastrophic breakage from metal fatigue.

Pituitary rongeurs are probably used for years without replacement. Eventually they will break, although it does not happen often. I recommended regular replacement of these instruments to the equipment personnel in the operating rooms I worked in after my first case of breakage. I did not get a positive response. The use of surgical equipment does not have an industry standard similar to the aviation industry for discarding equipment after a certain amount of use. Perhaps it should.

More operating room trouble. In the early days of total knee replacements, the prosthesis company provided a trial prosthesis of the size and shape of the prosthesis you planned on using. With an oscillating saw, you then shaved and trimmed the bones of the ends of the femur and tibia so that the trial prosthesis fit. Until this point in the surgery the real prosthesis was kept in its original sterile packaging. The packaging of the real prosthesis was then opened and the real prosthesis was cemented in place using bone cement. Specific jigs to align saw cuts have been used for a long time. They were not available then.

One time, my attending orthopedic surgeon and I carefully shaved the bone of the distal end of the femur (thigh bone) until it was a perfect fit for the trial prosthesis. The real prosthesis was then unwrapped and brought onto the operating field. We did not unwrap the prosthesis prior to this since once you open the package, you have bought the prosthesis. In this operation, the real prosthesis did not fit. It was a different shape and size than the trial prosthesis. We, my supervising attending surgeon and I, then retrimmed the bone to make it fit the real prosthesis and made it work.

Further investigation after the operation was over disclosed that the manufacturer had brought out a new series of prostheses with different shapes and sizes but had not provided the hospital with the trials for the new shapes and sizes. Another recurrent theme in my discussions: "Who can you trust?" My imagination reels that a company would, could allow such an oversight. It is not the only time such an oversight has led to difficulties in the operating room for me.

Another vignette. At one point in the development of total hip replacements, manufacturers began to put metal on the back of the plastic cups. I had a total hip replacement scheduled for a small patient who required the smallest sized cup. The new metal-backed cups had just been released. I was one of the first to schedule a patient to use it for one company. I am proceeding through the operation and have reamed the cup portion of the patient's hip to the correct size. A certain degree of obsessive-compulsive disorder is important to being a good surgeon. Let me rephrase that. A *considerable* degree of obsessive-compulsive disorder is important to being a good surgeon.

Once you mix the cement used to fix the cup in its socket, the clock is ticking and you only have a couple of minutes to get the prosthesis set in its proper position before the cement hardens. Thus, I always, always, always perform a dry run of putting the prosthesis onto the inserter and preparing to place it in the cup portion of the hip joint before mixing the cement. This time, I am going through my usual boring dry run. The scrub nurse hands me the inserter. I pick up the prosthesis. I put the prosthesis on the inserter. Rather, I try to put the prosthesis on the inserter. It does not fit!

After further investigation, I switched to a non-metal–backed prosthesis, which fit the inserter, and finished the operation using a non-metal–backed prosthesis. Further inquiry after the operation disclosed that for the two smallest metal-backed prostheses, the manufacturer had to make the plastic smaller. The smaller plastic required a smaller inserter. The manufacturer had neglected to supply the correct, smaller inserter when they shipped the new small metal-backed prosthesis for my operation. Again, my mind reels. How can a company allow such an error? Murphy's Law again. If something can go wrong, it will. Again, the question, "Who can you trust?" Again, the need for a considerable degree of obsessive-compulsive disorder in any competent surgeon. You have to be looking for potential problems constantly. Patient fully informed.

One hospital I worked in had a series of infections following simple pediatric hernia operations. The infection rate for this operation should be really, really low. There was clearly contamination from somewhere. One possibility was contamination of a specific suture from a specific company. I was told the hospital sent the remaining unopened, unused sutures back to the manufacturer for testing. The manufacturer reported that they had cultured all of the unopened suture packs and they were all sterile. Clearly the infection problem was "with the hospital" and "not the manufacturer!"

Except! I was told that the hospital only sent back half of the unopened sutures to the manufacturer without telling the manufacturer. The hospital cultured the other half of the unopened suture packs on its own and some of the suture packs grew out the specific bacteria that was causing the infections. Thus, the problem was contaminated suture from the manufacturer. Clearly a manufacturing problem. Clearly, you cannot trust a manufacturer to test itself. Again, the question, "Who can you trust?"

Yet another example of trouble in the operating room. It is the middle of the night. I am operating on a patient with a severely displaced, comminuted (many fragments) fracture of the wrist. I often treat this type of fracture with 20 pounds of traction straight down using gravity, massage the fracture fragments into better position and then insert an external fixator. The application of an external fixator involves placing two pins through the skin into one bone in the hand and likewise two pins into one of the forearm bones. Clamps are then fixed to the pins that are in the bones. These clamps are attached to each other with rods to make a rigid construct, which holds the fractured bones in place while they heal. An expensive and well-designed adult "Erector" set.

I place the patient's arm in 20 pounds of traction. I manipulate the bones back in place. I check the X-rays to ensure the fracture is in acceptable position. I am now ready to apply the external fixator. I open the external fixator tray kept at the hospital. I find that the set is incomplete. Clearly, the last time it was used, the nurse in charge of orthopedic surgical equipment forgot to replace the used parts. No problem. No problem. The hospital keeps a second external fixation set from another manufacturer. I request that set. I open the second set. Surprise. Surprise. The second set is also incomplete. Again, someone, perhaps the same person, forgot to replace previously used parts. We, orthopedic surgeons, are truly dependent on our equipment and our assistants.

Middle of the night. The two sets are not compatible, since the pins, screws and rods from the two sets are manufactured with different diameters. Neither set has enough parts to make a complete construct. I spend about 20 minutes at the sterile back table fiddling with the two sets. I finally find a way to use parts from each set and make it work. It was a funny looking external fixator construct, but it worked just fine. Patient fully informed. In orthopedics, we are equipment dependent and have to be prepared to adapt when we have equipment problems. We are also personnel dependent. Personnel had neglected to restock the external fixator sets. Later, a company began to manufacture a sterile, complete set of equipment for each external fixation application. I switched to using that company's set.

Let me revisit my discussion of how to train doctors and surgeons. Let me review the benefits and risks associated with that training. I rotated on to the thoracic surgery service as a junior resident in my second year of general surgical training at Peter Bent. As junior resident, I responded initially to all thoracic surgery consults from all over the hospital. On my first day or two on that service, we received a consult from the medical service to tap (aspirate, stick in a needle and draw out fluid) a collection of fluid from a patient's lung. In today's world, these patients are aspirated by interventional radiologists under computer tomographic (CT) control.

I studied the AP (anteroposterior; front to back) and lateral (side to side) X-rays of the patient and formed a three-dimensional image in my mind of where in the chest cavity this loculation (collection) of fluid was located. I pictured in my mind the exact location where I thought I should insert the needle.

I then went down to the medical ward to do the consult and perform the aspiration, if I thought I could do it. Understand, I had aspirated a chest only once before as a medical student, under supervision. That was the extent of my previous training. When I arrived on the medical ward, to my surprise, there was an audience waiting to watch a "thoracic surgeon" perform the aspiration. The audience included medical students on the internal medicine service, medical interns, medical residents of different levels of training and the attending internist. As near as I could tell, most of them had already tried to aspirate this fluid collection. As I examined the back and side of this patient's chest, I saw approximately 15 puncture wounds from previous attempts to aspirate this fluid. Interestingly, the only area of the back and side of the chest that did not have a puncture wound, was the area where I thought the fluid collection was located.

Here, again, arises the ethical question I have discussed previously regarding medical and surgical training. When do you perform a procedure for the first time by yourself? When do you call for supervision? The attending internal medicine physician and possibly the senior medical residents had more experience than I in aspirating chests. Should I back off and call for the attending thoracic surgeon to do the aspiration? Was it all right—that is, ethical—for me to go ahead and try? You need a certain degree of assertiveness to gain more experience. Otherwise, you will get to do little and will therefore learn less. I decided to proceed.

I numbed up skin and tissue around the rib at my planned needle insertion site. There are arteries running along the bottom of each rib. The safe way to do this procedure is to push the needle in gently and deliberately touch the bone of the rib with the tip of the needle. Then, you slide the needle over the top of the rib, on the side away from the artery. You then push the needle into the lung. I inserted the needle, as I have just described. I immediately hit the pocket of fluid and withdrew the fluid the medical doctors needed for diagnosis. They never knew I was doing only my second lung aspiration.

Why was I successful when so many of them failed? It was not because of the "technique" of performing the aspiration. The "technique" is actually quite simple. It was a "failure" to prepare; a failure to think about the procedure; a failure to form a proper three-dimensional image of the lung and the location of the fluid loculation.

In my second six months of orthopedic training, I was assigned at times to the orthopedic room of the Massachusetts General Hospital emergency room. There was sufficient business for an orthopedic resident to be assigned there full time, around the clock. A textbook by Rockwood and Green, "Fractures and Dislocations" had just been published in its first edition. After evaluating a patient every resident drew the curtain around the patient and then went over and sat down and read the pertinent section of Rockwood and Green. We then followed its advice. It was our bible. We were expected to be as independent as we thought appropriate. There were many treatments we did for the first time alone using our bible. I certainly remember reducing my first dislocated elbow by myself. The patient was an attorney.

Often in hospital settings you need to make decisions in a split second, without time to consider options and without time to seek advice. Here is a story told to me by a friend, which happened in another city, in another hospital. My friend, a general surgery intern, was early in his internship. He walked into the ICU he was covering and glanced into one of his patients' rooms. A respiratory fellow was at the bedside of a patient with a tracheostomy. The respiratory fellow seemed to be making some frantic motions. So, my friend walked into the room to investigate. A tracheostomy tube is a breathing tube which is placed into the front of the throat directly into the trachea (the breathing tube) to allow air or oxygen to go directly into the lung. A tracheostomy is used for patients who need long-term breathing assistance or who have suffered damage to the larynx above. The respiratory fellow had just removed the tracheostomy tube, planning on changing it. Changing the tracheostomy tube is proper, after a period of time, after the tracheostomy tube tunnel has healed. It is dangerous if done early before the tracheostomy tube tunnel has healed.

In this unfortunate situation, the respiratory fellow had removed the tube too early and the tracheostomy tube tunnel had collapsed within 30 seconds of my friend walking into the room. Another of those "What to do?" questions. The respiratory fellow had four to five more years of training than my friend. But! The respiratory fellow was not a surgeon. The patient was "my friend's patient." You have heard me use the phrase "my patient" before. We really take that responsibility seriously. My friend yelled over his shoulder to the nurses, "Call a STAT" and "Get a trach set STAT." My friend decided to give the respiratory fellow 60 seconds to try to reestablish the airway, while my friend was putting on sterile gloves. Then my friend pushed the respiratory fellow out of the way and tried to reinsert the trach tube himself. The throat area was swollen with air that had been blown into the soft tissues by previous attempts by the respiratory fellow.

Within minutes, multiple other doctors arrived, but the patient died. The principle error was the respiratory fellow's decision to remove the tracheostomy tube too early, without permission, without consultation with superiors. The surgery department demanded that in the future, no one was to touch their patients without their express permission. A serious judgement error by one trainee physician. I have discussed previously the question of when a trainee doctor should take initiative and do something on his own and when he should consult with superiors. This unfortunate case exemplifies the real risk of bad judgement inherent in this quandary.

Yet another complication. Before 1980, when Robert Breck Brigham Hospital merged with other hospitals into the Brigham and Women's Hospital, it was a free-standing institution, part of the Harvard Hospital System. It stood all alone on the top of Mission Hill. It was solely devoted to treating immunologic and arthritic diseases. It was not a full-service hospital and did not have an emergency room or an intensive care unit. Its clinics were staffed with both rheumatologists (medical arthritis doctors) and orthopedic surgeons who specialized in the surgical treatment of arthritic problems. It was a wonder to see the rheumatologists and orthopedic surgeons working together as a team.

Most orthopedic patients admitted to the hospital were surgical patients who were scheduled for total hip replacement, total knee replacement, total elbow replacement or hand surgery. There was only one orthopedic resident on call at night or over the weekend. Work when on call there tended to be quiet. For weekends on call, after an hour or two of rounds, there was nothing to do. Weekends when I was on call, I could not leave the hospital grounds. So, my wife and daughter came and visited for the day. We picnicked outside and played outside of the hospital on the hospital grounds.

One day, at Robert Breck Brigham, we performed a total knee replacement on a man known to have a bleeding disorder. He lacked a certain factor necessary for proper bleeding control. His bleeding factor was high enough that minor wounds clotted without difficulty. It was known that he needed special treatment to prepare for this big orthopedic operation. We consulted with our hematologists (internal medical doctors specializing in blood disorders). The hematologists gave us specific instructions. When people donate blood, the blood can be fractionated with a centrifuge to separate the red blood cells from the non-red cell fluid called plasma. We were instructed to administer, by IV, a certain amount of fresh frozen plasma, which contained the active clotting factor needed. We followed the instructions precisely. As part of the surgery, a drainage tube was left in the wound to allow post-operative bleeding to flow out of the wound to minimize the collection of blood in the wound. Standard procedure at that time.

We performed the total knee replacement in the afternoon; in my memory, it was a Friday. I know that I was on call that night. Around four to six hours after the surgery was completed, in the evening, when I was the only doctor in the entire hospital, the patient began to bleed, I mean bleed. I mean really, really bleed. There was uncontrollable bleeding coming out of the drainage tube. I called the orthopedic surgeon in charge of the case. He did not come into the hospital. Instead he allowed me to handle the problem. I began extensive blood transfusions to replace lost blood and extensive fresh frozen plasma infusions to replace the clotting factors needed by the patient. For hours the bleeding continued unabated. I finally pulled the hemovac (the drainage tube) and wrapped the leg tightly with multiple ace bandages. After some 20 units of blood (perhaps four times a normal blood volume) and some 25 units of fresh frozen plasma, the bleeding stopped. Surprising to me, the patient did well. I saw him in clinic six months later with a normal looking leg and knee, which worked well.

A few ideas spring to mind as I recall this evening. First, for a sleepy, little hospital, how did the blood bank personnel obtain, cross match and provide all of the blood products I needed when I needed them. I never recall a moment when the blood products I needed were not available. As doctors, we are totally dependent on the help of numerous assistants. We are also dependent on a complex system organized to provide us help. How did the blood bank employee—I suspect there was only one—manage to put out the call for help and supplies that were not in hospital? How the personnel in the system responded amazes me. I regret that I never investigated to find out who they were and thank them personally. At the time I simply took them for granted.

Second, I obviously was able to manage this crisis successfully. My two years of general surgical training, which I have highlighted in multiple vignettes described previously, certainly prepared me for handling this emergency. Handling this situation was excellent further training for me. However, the behavior of my superior seems cavalier at best. There was no guarantee that there would be a good outcome. Being placed in situations like this is excellent training for the trainee surgeon involved, but there seems increased risk to the patient. Different residents have differing levels of ability. As I have discussed before, the ethics in surgical training are complex. If you are never allowed to shoulder responsibility while in training, then when you become a practicing surgeon you will be woefully unprepared. In retrospect, I think this patient should have been transferred to Peter Bent Brigham Hospital immediately since it was an acute care hospital. I do not believe my supervision was proper. I believe I was left on my own to sink or swim.

Third, my attending orthopedic surgeon and I were convinced that the standard hematology recommendations for total knee replacements in patients with this clotting factor deficiency were incorrect. We wrote a paper for a journal discussing our concern. The reviewers of our paper informed us that our hematologists had given us incorrect advice. The fact that the problem occurred was due to incorrect advice from our own hematologists. Wow! Really! Incorrect advice from Harvard hematologists! Once again, the question: "Who can you trust?" The paper was not published because it did not provide useful information. If you can't trust your experts at a Harvard hospital, who can you trust? That was part of my training that led to part of my motto, listed at the beginning of this book, "Question everything!"

More about what can go wrong and situations in which the "What to do?" question arises. Christmas Eve. Thoracic surgery service has a late afternoon Christmas party for employees and residents. The pump team, who are the technicians, who run the cardiac bypass machine, are also present. Low-key party. No alcohol for anyone on call. I am on call. No alcohol for me. Half an hour after everyone has left the party, a young woman is rushed into the emergency room, barely alive, barely breathing, lips truly blue from lack of oxygenation of the blood. She has suffered a massive pulmonary embolism. A large blood clot has travelled from the legs or the pelvis up the inferior vena cava, through the right atrium and ventricle and into the pulmonary artery, which pumps blood into the lungs. There the clot has stuck, severely limiting blood flow to the lungs and therefore severely limiting the circulation of blood through the entire body.

Massive pulmonary embolism is a not uncommon cause of sudden death. Smaller clots are treated with blood thinners. This young woman's situation requires emergency surgery to try to clean out enough clot to allow the blood to flow into the lungs. Treatment for this requires open heart surgery in which the blood that flows to and from the heart will be shunted into the cardiac bypass machine for oxygenation and pumping while the heart is temporarily stopped. The pump team is paged. We rush the patient to the operating room. The pump team does not answer the page. We have no pump team. What to do?

General anesthesia. Split the sternum. Open the chest. The pulmonary artery, which carries blood from the heart to the lungs, is engorged. We can see the heart straining to push blood into it. The thoracic surgeon in charge places two cloth bands around the superior and inferior vena cavas. These are the two big veins that funnel blood back to the heart. I am in charge of the cloth band around the inferior vena cava. Another resident has the one around the superior vena cava. On command, we compress the bands and stop all blood return to the heart. On this command, a stopwatch on the wall is started and each second is counted out loud by a nurse. Longitudinal incision made in the pulmonary artery. Large amount of clot is seen. Suction tip is placed into the artery and for 60 seconds moved up and down the artery to remove as much clot as possible. At 60 seconds, a curved clamp is place over the incision in the artery, leaving at least half of the artery patent. Cloth bands loosened. Blood flows into the heart, then into the lungs, then through the rest of the body. Success without the pump team. Pump team fired.

Another night. Another vignette. We had another patient who underwent emergency surgery for a dissecting aortic aneurysm. Blood is dissecting through the wall of the aorta. It is about to rupture and cause massive internal bleeding. The affected portion of the aorta is removed and a prosthetic aorta sutured in place. The patient's tissue is poor quality, like soft cheese. The sutures do not hold. The repair leaks. Hour after hour after hour, the surgeon removes more aorta, trying to find a level with good tissue which will hold sutures. Six hours go by. Unable to achieve a repair that works. Unable to achieve a repair that does not leak. Finally, the surgeon gives up and orders the bypass pump turned off allowing the patient to die peacefully. Frustrating. An impossible case.

While in training, I had a patient scheduled for a straightforward hand operation. After the patient was positioned, I went out to wash my hands. The anesthesiologist began anesthesia. Many anesthesiologists begin anesthesia by injecting only a small amount of anesthetic initially to see how the patient reacts before giving the full dose of the initial anesthetic. Following this whiff of anesthesia, my patient's heart stopped beating effectively. There was electrical activity, but no useful heart contraction. This clinical situation is called pulseless electrical activity. We began immediate resuscitation. For about three hours, the patient's heartbeat temporarily became effective and then faded out again. Finally, he stabilized with a good stable heart rhythm.

Rapid, further evaluation showed that he had three heart arteries with major blockages. He underwent emergency coronary artery bypass graft surgery and did well. This kind of heart blockage often results in people dropping dead on the street. This patient was lucky, in a sense. The whiff of anesthesia demonstrated how fragile his heart was. If you are going to "drop dead," there is no better place to do it than an operating room. With the event occurring in the operating room, with multiple doctors nearby, with all resuscitation equipment present, we were able to save him.

I am going to spend some time looking at additional vignettes that involve issues with decision-making. I have already discussed many of them. One was the seminar with Dr. Millender and the gunshot wound to the hand. Another was the "zugzwang" situation in the plastic surgery case. Decision-making in medicine, in surgery and in life can be complex.

When I was in medical school, we admitted a patient with a straightforward diagnosis of appendicitis. Nausea, vomiting and pain and tenderness in the right lower quadrant of the abdomen. The complicating factor in this case was a diagnosis of hemophilia, which is the lack of a specific clotting factor (Factor VIII). Operating without treating the lack of clotting factors would result in the patient bleeding to death. Normally, we gave these patients infusions of the clotting factor and then operated.

Complicating this case further: this patient had had many previous infusions of Factor VIII and had high levels of antibodies to Factor VIII. These antibodies bind to the Factor VIII molecules and prevent clotting. The hematologists told us that they could guarantee to control bleeding for six hours after surgery. They could not guarantee that they could prevent severe bleeding after that elapsed time. No surgery was performed. The patient was treated with antibiotics. The appendix ruptured and formed an abscess. At this point the patient was able to tolerate a simple small incision and drainage of the abscess and survived. From my reading it seems that the treatment of uncomplicated appendicitis with antibiotics is now being evaluated.

Another decision-making vignette. There is a common problem with the kneecap (patella) that often begins in the teenage years. It occurs far more often in girls than boys and is called recurrent dislocation (displacement) of the kneecap (patella). When this happens, the patella shifts toward the outside (lateral side) of the knee. If the dislocation or subluxation (slipping out part way) occurs frequently, it can be disabling.

Physical therapy may help some mild cases but is ineffective for more severe cases. There are a number of operations described to treat this problem. As a general principle, if there are multiple operations used to treat a specific problem, then no one operation has provable "best" results. Otherwise, it would be simple and easy to demonstrate the superiority of that one operation.

If you straighten your leg completely and look at it carefully, you will see that your leg is not straight. In most people, the thigh tends to angle slightly inwards and the lower leg tends to angle slightly outwards. There is an angle at the knee with the apex of the angle pointed inwards. Contraction of the quadriceps muscle, the muscle on the front of the thigh, which straightens the knee, tends to pull the patella (kneecap) outwards (laterally). Normally this lateral pull is resisted by a groove at the end of the femur (thigh bone) and by restraining ligaments. When the groove is shallow and/or the restraining ligaments have been torn and are incompetent, recurrent slipping out occurs.

One common operation involves taking a plug of bone with the attachment of the distal end of the patellar tendon (the tendon the quadriceps uses to straighten the leg) and move it inwards (medially.) Shifting the plug of bone medially counteracts the lateral pull of the quadriceps tendon. Another operation splits the patellar tendon. The lateral (outside) half of the patellar tendon is shifted inwards (medially) to counteract the lateral pull. At the same time the inside (medial) side of the quadriceps tendon is advanced (tightened) to provide greater medial pull to further counteract the lateral pull. The latter operation was the one I used the most in training and in practice. I had good results using it and continued to use it. There are, of course, other operations for this problem.

A young woman came to my office complaining of subluxation and dislocation of her kneecap medially. That is, her kneecap was slipping out in the opposite direction from which most kneecaps dislocate. She had previously developed the typical lateral subluxation and dislocation of her kneecap. She then underwent the bone plug shifting operation by another orthopedic surgeon in a different area of the country. Unfortunately, she was overcorrected and began slipping out medially. She had consulted several other orthopedic surgeons. Patellectomy (complete surgical removal of the patella) was recommended by all. She had just moved to Maryland. She opened her first office visit with me, stating, "I'm here to have my kneecap removed." Good historian. Got right to the point.

I took a detailed history. My examination showed clear medial instability of the kneecap. I discussed the problem with her. I told her I was willing to remove her kneecap, but I recommended instead trying to correct the medial instability by opening her knee and trying to adjust the patellar tendon and quadriceps tendon to a straighter pull. I explained that surgical removal of the kneecap weakens the knee. If you ever develop osteoarthritis of the knee and need a total knee replacement, the results after total knee replacement in patients without kneecaps are not nearly as good as in patients with kneecaps. I told her I was willing to take out her kneecap, but I really wanted to try to salvage her kneecap. I told her that she had an unusual problem. No one had much experience trying to solve the problem of overcorrection following the bone plug shifting operation. She could always have the kneecap removal operation later if necessary. She was young. I did not want to give up on her. I wanted to give her a chance at keeping her kneecap. Obviously, I could not guarantee results. We had a long chat.

She agreed to let me try. At surgery, I split the patellar tendon and performed the reverse of the typical operation I usually do. I also advanced the lateral side of the quadriceps for more lateral pull. At this point in the operation, I spent about a half an hour trying different combinations of the degree of lateral translation of the medial half of the patellar tendon and different amounts of advancement of the lateral side of the quadriceps. With each combination, I flexed and extended the knee and also manipulated the patella medially and laterally, looking for an "ideal" balance. After finding what I thought was the optimal configuration, I put in the permanent sutures and closed. She had an excellent result and did not suffer a recurrence of patellar subluxation over the next few years that I followed her.

So, what worked here? A willingness to listen to her problem. An unwillingness to be led by the recommendations of other orthopedic surgeons. The knowledge of and experience with an operation that I knew to be adjustable. I had to be comfortable with judgement and decision-making in a non-standard situation. If I recall correctly, I was the fourth opinion she sought. Occasionally, multiple opinions are worthwhile.

Another vignette. What do you do when things don't go well and unusual decision-making is required? Early in my training, a relatively young man in his early 40s took a hard fall skiing onto glare ice, fracturing his hip. In those days, one of the devices used to fix a fractured hip was a fixed angle Jewett nail. The attending orthopedic surgeon and I measured carefully to determine which length of nail to use. Fluoroscopy was not available in the operating room at this time. Each X-ray took 20 minutes, so you tried to limit the number of X-rays you needed to take. The nail that was put in was just a little too long. It was protruding into the hip joint by one millimeter. Even a little protrusion is not acceptable. If the joint is allowed to move, the protruding corner will scrape and damage the joint. No problem. Remove the nail and put in a shorter one.

The problem in this case was the fact that the patient was young and had strong bone. The bone seized on the nail. The Jewett nail came with specific extractor devices. We broke two extractor devices trying to remove the nail. We grasped the nail with locking pliers and used sledgehammers to try to release the nail. It would not budge. The attending decided to close the wound. Then he put the patient at bed rest and traction for five days. Bone is living tissue. The bone that is right next to metal will actually melt away a little by the activity of bone-resorbing cells. The attending took advantage of the bone's reactivity. Five days later we took the patient back to the operating room. The nail came out without difficulty and we replaced the nail with a slightly shorter one. The patient did well. I have discussed before the randomness and vagaries of training. Situations like this one are rare. Watching a good attending deal properly with a difficult situation is a valuable part of training.

Patients sometimes do weird things which result in the need for creative decision-making. I helped treat a patient with a segmental fracture of the femur (thigh bone). A segmental fracture means the bone is broken in more than one place. In those days we sometimes treated these fractures in traction. Now almost all are treated with surgery. His treatment included placing a long pin crosswise across the distal femur with weights attached to a rope running through pulleys. The traction pulled the fracture straight, so that it would heal straight. We were working in the days of open wards with 30 patients. Every morning when we residents came by on rounds, the patient was out of traction. The leg was lying on the bed in a zigzag configuration. Every night, our patient asked his fellow patients to take him out of traction, which they did. Why did this patient behave this way? Don't ask. I don't know. Cases like this require creative thinking.

There is a known technique, usually used in primitive settings, for treating patients with unstable fractures. It is called the pins-in-plaster method. It involves putting at least two large diameter pins into each fracture fragment and leaving one end of each pin sticking out of the skin. This technique is similar to the external fixation technique I mentioned earlier for certain wrist fractures. For this patient, we inserted the pins under general anesthesia. Two large pins into the proximal fragment. Two large pins into the middle fragment. Two large pins into the distal fragment. The fracture was pulled straight into good alignment. Then a cylindrical cast was applied around the thigh, incorporating the pins into the plaster cast. We utilized this technique on this uncooperative patient. The fracture healed in good position. I was a junior resident watching a senior resident solve an unusual problem with out-of-the-box thinking. Great training.

Yet another vignette. One with multiple complications. A woman suffered an open fracture of her leg when a cow stepped on her foot and pushed her over. Following her first surgery, the wound becomes infected. Take her back to the operating room to wash out the wound and pack it open. First swabs, for gram stain and culture, show an easily treated bacteria. At first, she seems to respond to treatment. Then, two days later the wound suddenly looks much worse.

Immediately take her back to the operating room to wash out the wound again. This time, I see air bubbles tracking up the tissue planes. Bad! Bad! Bad! Air bubbles tracking up tissue planes is one finding in infections with "flesh eating bacteria." Also called necrotizing fasciitis. In the past also called Melaney's synergistic gangrene. At least two bacteria growing in concert enabling each other to grow and spread with amazing rapidity.

I have seen a few of these patients in my career. One was a stab wound to the abdomen. Day one, infection spread several inches in the abdominal wall. Debridement of infected tissue with an inch of normal tissue. Day two, further spread of infection in abdominal wall, with extensive debridement of much of the abdominal wall. Day three, dead. Despite antibiotics and full support. I had another patient with a necrotizing fasciitis infection in the lower leg stopped after the first extensive debridement and antibiotics. A fourth patient, a diabetic, with a small skin break and infection in the lower buttock area: dead in two days. As you can tell by my limited clinical experience, necrotizing fasciitis is a terrifying infection which is rare, spreads rapidly and kills often.

Back to the leg fracture patient. I see air bubbles in the tissue planes. I immediately call for another orthopedic surgeon to come into the operating room to help me. Never be afraid to ask for help. Hours of careful extensive debridement. Multiple powerful antibiotics. As we are packing the wound open, the anesthesiologist informs us (the two surgeons) that the patient's blood pressure has dropped and urine output has stopped. Seriously ill patients have a catheter placed in their bladder to monitor urine output.

The patient has developed gram negative shock, that is, a severe decrease in blood pressure from toxins secreted into the bloodstream by live bacteria growing in the bloodstream (septicemia). Eighty percent short-term mortality at that time. A general surgeon comes in to help and inserts a central line into the right subclavian vein to monitor central venous pressure and give us a central line for medications. More antibiotics. Steroids. Fluids. Half an hour later, the blood pressure finally increases to normal and urine output resumes. We have successfully resuscitated our patient from gram negative shock. We think we are out of the woods.

We are still in the operating room. A good place to be with a seriously ill patient. Any equipment you need is available. The patient has remained awake throughout this treatment. She begins to complain of right-sided chest pain. Blood pressure again drops; urine output again stops. EKG is normal. Heart sounds are normmal. We get a chest X-ray, which shows massive fluid in the right chest cavity pressing on the heart and lungs. We insert a chest tube and blood spurts out of the chest tube with enough force to splatter the wall of the operating room. The bleeding from the chest tube then stops. Blood pressure comes up; urine output resumes. We have just treated tension hemothorax shock with the insertion of the chest tube. Tension hemothorax is high pressure in the chest cavity from bleeding within the chest cavity. This pressure prevents the heart from beating well. No further bleeding. We watch and wait. Clearly the bleeding is coming from the subclavian vein stick performed by the general surgeon. He must have hit the subclavian artery by mistake. Bleeding has momentarily stopped.

Suddenly, blood begins to pour out of the chest tube. Blood pressure drops; urine output stops, again. We are now treating blood loss hypotension or shock (low blood pressure.) We transfuse the patient. We have previously called in a thoracic surgeon for assistance. He opens the chest and finds a laceration in the subclavian artery which occurred when the central line was inserted by the general surgeon who was helping us. The thoracic surgeon sutures the subclavian artery. Patient stabilizes and survives, having been resuscitated from gram negative shock, tension hemothorax shock and acute blood loss shock, all in the course of a few hours.

Let's move on to another type of problem, a communication problem. Junior resident. Children's Hospital. Pre-op patients are routinely admitted the day before surgery. We residents see each patient to perform the routine pre-op history and physical. I am going through my list of patients, doing the routine histories and physicals. I walk into a hospital room and meet a 13-year-old girl still prepubertal, as terrified as any patient I have ever met. She doesn't know why she is in the hospital. She knows she is going to have an operation. She doesn't know what the operation is going to be. She just knows that there is something terribly, terribly wrong with her; so terribly wrong that no one will tell her what it is. Not her doctors. Not her parents. No mention of clergy. Her exam is normal except for an inguinal scar. I leave her, shaken and confused. I mean, I am shaken and confused. I have already described her terror. No one has given me a "heads up" concerning this patient. I don't know what her problem is. I don't know what the operation will be. So, I can't even talk to her. I am just given her name to perform her "routine" history and physical.

I seek out the attending, which is what the doctors on staff at teaching hospitals are called. In a small hospital in the Midwest, this patient had been operated on for a lump in her groin, thought to be a hernia. The surgeon found an undescended testicle in this patient. He sewed her up and referred her to the big medical center. The problem is testicular feminization. The patient is genetically XY, that is, the patient is a chromosomal male. But, due to a genetic mutation, the body either does not make testosterone, the male hormone, or makes testosterone, but the target organs cannot recognize the testosterone. Thus, her body developed looking female. Issues of gender "differences" are front page news now. Talked about frequently. Recognized. Accepted. At least partially understood. Back then, it was a taboo subject. Not talked about. Not accepted. Not understood. Families with these children often changed their names and moved to another city far, far away.

So, this poor child only knew there was something horribly wrong with her, so horrible no one would tell her. I am unable to imagine what her life was like. Add to that, the callousness of my attending in not preparing me for this encounter. Sometimes our learning comes from watching the behavior of other doctors and saying to ourselves, "That is wrong; so wrong. I will not behave that way in the future." I fault my attending for callous disregard for both the patient and me.

Some years ago, I treated an elderly woman with a long, oblique or spiral fracture of the humerus or upper arm bone. She had severe osteoporosis. Osteoporosis is loss of bone density or mass that severely weakens bone. When the bones are severely weakened, a minor fall that will cause nothing more than a bruise in a younger person will result in a severe fracture in an osteoporotic patient. At surgery, osteoporotic bone is much thinner than normal bone. Not only is it weak, but due to the marked thinness, surgical screws have less pull out strength. The bones are really fragile. Long spiral fractures are often treated with a plate and screws. I had successfully reduced (put back in place) the fracture and had put on a fixation plate and all but one screw. I was tightening the uppermost screw with what we call "two-finger tightness," the amount of force two fingers can exert. The purpose of two-finger tightening is to try to avoid excessive tightening of screws, which can cause fracturing of the bone. As I was finishing the tightening of this last screw with only two fingers, I heard a cracking sound loud enough to be heard across the operating room. With the sound, I saw the fracture propagate (spread) three inches up the bone. One of those "moments" in the operating room. I stood there and thought, "I have two choices. I can get really upset. Alternatively, I can appreciate this really interesting surgical challenge. I think I'll choose the latter." I applied a second plate to cover the elongation of the fracture. She did well. Patient fully informed.

More on osteoporosis. Common problem. Easily diagnosed by a quantitative X-ray study of the hip and spine. A quantitative X-ray accurately measures the amount of X-radiaton which passes through a specific bone. Normal X-rays are used for taking pictures of the body. Often the first symptom of osteoporosis is a fracture following a fall. Any adult who suffers a wrist, hip or ankle fracture that does not result from high energy trauma should be tested for osteoporosis. Anyone who suffers multiple fractures including multiple fractured ribs following a fall should be tested. Anyone who suffers a spontaneous compression fracture of the spine should be tested. Many physicians including orthopedic surgeons are not aware of this need for testing. They do not test for osteoporosis as often as they should when treating patients with fractures. This lack of testing is unfortunate. There are good medical treatments available. Fractures of the hips, spine and wrists are common causes of significant disability in older patients. I am told by internists that testing for osteoporosis is not advised until age 50. I think testing should be performed at a much younger age so that you can pick up the severe cases earlier and begin treatment earlier.

In high school, college and medical school, we doctors are accustomed to doing well in our studies pretty much all of the time. So, it comes as a shock when we have patients that don't do well. A few years into my practice, a well-respected local physician came to me with a fracture of both bones of his ankle. It was a "straightforward" fracture to the extent that anything in medicine or surgery is "straightforward." I operated on him, fixing one fracture with plates and screws and the other with screws as was appropriate and standard. I gave him the standard, strict instruction of no weight-bearing activity on that ankle for six weeks. I saw him at Weeks 1 and 2 post-op and everything looked fine. He returned at Week 3 and everything had pulled out and displaced.

Ugh! Eeek! Ack! Ouch! I showed him the X-rays and apologized profusely. I told him I really didn't know why the fractures had displaced; that I needed to reoperate. He laughed and told me that it was all his fault. He told me that he had completely ignored my advice. He had been walking on the ankle full weight bearing ever since the surgery. He took full responsibility for the complication. Whew! Only ankle fracture I ever had that displaced like that. Doctors can really be difficult patients. For that matter, from what I read, they are terrible pilots. They have an awful safety record with high accident rates.

Yet another "problem" vignette. As a junior orthopedic resident, I rotated onto the ward service and inherited a large group of inpatients. One patient had been in an automobile accident and had broken his lower leg bone, the tibia. I reviewed his X-rays. The first X-ray showed a displaced fracture of the tibia. The second set of X-rays showed good reduction of the tibial fracture fragments. The patient was in a long leg cast. Knowing that I was now responsible for this patient, I ordered new X-rays to determine the position of the fracture fragments as of my assuming responsibility for his care. The new X-rays did not show a fracture of the tibia. How can this be? What to do? I asked the patient if he was having leg pain. He said, "No." I removed his cast. His leg was not tender. There was no swelling or bruising.

Further investigation disclosed that two men, both in their mid-30s, with exactly the same name, were involved in separate automobile accidents and came to the Mass General ER within 30 minutes of each other. The radiology department technicians mixed their X-rays together. The orthopedic surgery resident in the ER thought both patients had broken their tibias and placed both in casts. In retrospect, a "careful" examination by the ER orthopedic resident would have disclosed an absence of tenderness in the leg of my patient, which would have raised a red flag. My patient was the one without a fracture. So many ways for errors to occur. Fortunately, in this case, no harm done.

Let's look at some examples of poor decision-making in orthopedic surgery. A woman fell down and suffered a displaced fracture of her wrist. This fracture was of the distal end of the forearm bone called the radius, a common fracture. Doctor Number 1 (an orthopedic surgeon) treated this fracture with a closed reduction (injection of numbing medicine and manipulation; standard treatment) and application of a cast. The fracture shifted position and healed with 45 degrees of angulation. Generally, less than ten degrees of angulation is considered ideal. The older the patient the more angulation you are likely to accept. This patient was in her 40s. There was little emphasis on motion of her fingers during the six weeks in the cast. Occasionally, a fracture can shift position between the second and third week of treatment and then get sticky quickly.

The patient then consulted a hand surgeon, Doctor Number 2, for a second opinion. Doctor Number 2 saw the X-rays with the 45-degree angulation of the healed fracture and immediately scheduled surgery to straighten the angulated radius. The postoperative X-rays were superb. Remarkable carpentry. Two months after the second surgery, the patient came to me for a third opinion because she had only flickers of motion in her fingers. After multiple months of therapy with Lynne, she regained partial use of her hand, perhaps 50 percent of finger motion.

Where could her treatment decision-making have been better? First, more emphasis on movement of her fingers by the first doctor. I did not see the first cast. Many orthopedic surgeons continue to apply casts that extend too far toward the fingers on the palm side and limit the flexion of fingers unnecessarily. I don't know if the cast prevented full finger flexion but it happens frequently and is either poor decision-making or poor craftsmanship. It is lack of pride. It is failure to self-criticize. It is failure to be self-aware. It is failure to self-police. Enough said. In summary, for the first six weeks of her fracture treatment, there was no awareness or concern by Doctor Number 1 that there was limitation of motion of the fingers.

Now comes the really poor decision-making in this case and my reason for discussing this case. The second doctor, a hand surgeon, looked at the X-rays and with a kneejerk reaction, treated the malunion (fracture healed in a bad position) with immediate surgery. Taking the broad view, the most important problem this patient had at the first visit with the second doctor was poor motion of the fingers, hand and wrist. The second doctor did not recognize the poor finger motion; did not examine for finger motion; did not focus on finger motion; was not aware of the importance of finger motion. Lack of the big picture. I have mentioned before the importance of early motion and therapy early and often. This patient did poorly because she did not receive attention to early motion and early therapy.

This patient should have been sent to hand therapy immediately by the second doctor. Only after she reached maximum motion should she have undergone the bone angulation correction surgery. There was no need to rush into the surgical correction. That surgery could wait six months without long-term harm.

Years ago, a young employee physician of mine asked me to assist on an operation for a malunion of a distal radius fracture similar to the case above. My young associate also wanted to operate on a non-union of a small avulsion fragment on the little finger side of the wrist seen on X-ray. I asked my associate if the patient was having any pain or tenderness on the little finger side of the wrist. My associate said he didn't know. He hadn't asked the patient. I asked if the patient was tender at the location of the avulsion fragment. My associate did not know. He had not palpated the area on his physical exam. Poor decision-making. My approach was: No pain; no tenderness; no proper evaluation; no reason to operate there. I refused to help him if he was going to operate there. He decided not to operate at that location. For this problem and other judgement issues, he was not asked to join our orthopedic group as partner.

Yet another problem vignette. I saw a college student with a displaced fracture of a finger. The fracture was unstable and required surgery to hold the bone fragments in place. I used a common technique in which two crossing small steel pins are drilled through the two fragments, like shish kebab, in order to hold the fragments in place while the bone heals. Complicating his post-operative care was the fact that he was due to leave for Australia in three days' time for a semester abroad. I normally like to follow my patients for six weeks for therapy and for wound evaluation. The pins are usually removed at six weeks. Against my advice the college student flew to Australia three days after surgery. I strenuously and stridently advised follow up with a hand surgeon in Australia. I urged the patient to keep the finger dry, dry, dry, dry, dry.

Five days later his mother called me. My patient, her son, went scuba diving at the Great Barrier Reef with pins sticking out of the skin! EEK! He was now in a small hospital in northeastern Australia with a severe infection in the finger. I urged immediate discharge from that hospital, immediate drive to a major medical center and urgent consultation with a hand surgeon. Sometimes patients do not follow up the way we would like.

CHAPTER THIRTEEN

The Art of History Taking

- Evaluation of a Child with Scurvy
- Evaluation of a Child with Heavy Metal Poisoning
- Evaluation of a Patient with Hip Pain
- Look for Multiple Diagnoses
- Are the Medications Any Good?

Let's shift topics. How do you obtain information from a patient? Taking a history from a patient or parent is not always a simple, straightforward process. Taking a history means talking to the patient and/or parent and/or family member to gain information about the problem the patient is complaining about. In an office setting, doctors often begin with an open-ended question, such as: "Why are you here?" or "What brings you here today?" or "What seems to be the problem?" or in the case of trauma, "What happened?" Often figuring out the problem is easy and straightforward. Sometimes exasperatingly difficult. Common things occur commonly, so statistically the patient will most likely have a common problem or more than one common problem. But, if you see enough patients, the statistics suggest you eventually will see rare problems as well. Thus, you always should be on the lookout for the obscure zebra. Why the word zebra? From the saying, "When you hear hoofbeats, don't look for zebras." I suspect this saying is not often used in Africa.

As doctors take a history from a patient, we form a list of probable diagnoses in our head with the most likely diagnosis at the top of the list. This mental list is called the differential diagnosis. We then ask further questions designed to help us sort through the differential diagnosis list. As we progress to the physical exam and laboratory studies we further refine and rearrange our list of probable diagnoses. It is important to figure out what questions to ask. Figuring out the right questions can be difficult.

When faced with a patient with unusual symptoms, making an accurate diagnosis is difficult. As medical students we were advised to run down a mental list of types of diagnoses as a mental aide. The list of types of diagnoses includes vascular, infectious, traumatic, endocrine, degenerative, congenital, genetic, neurologic, immune system abnormalities and cancer. Examples of vascular include heart attacks and strokes; infectious: pneumonia and abscesses; traumatic: broken bones and repetitive trauma; endocrine: diabetes and hyperthyroidism, etc.

Evaluation of a Child with Scurvy

My father was a pediatrician who trained in the 1920s. He was born in 1901 and was old enough to be my grandfather. He was 45 when I was born. I remember two stories he told me which illustrate the need to keep asking questions until you find the right question. These stories probably date to the 1930s. He had a young patient with typical symptoms of scurvy. Scurvy is caused by a lack of Vitamin C. Multiple times, my father asked the patient's mother, if she was giving her child orange juice, which contains Vitamin C. Each time the child's mother replied that she was.

Finally, my father thought to ask the mother for more detail about what she was doing when she gave her child orange juice. She replied she was boiling it to sterilize it. Now, boiling orange juice sounds insane to you, I know. But, remember, this was happening in the 1930s. The patient's family lived on a farm and they boiled the milk they got from their cows to sterilize it. This is called pasteurization and it is done to all the milk we drink today. The parents were simply doing the same thing to the orange juice. The boiling destroyed the Vitamin C. Some of the orange juice you drink today is pasteurized. The producers add Vitamin C after the pasteurization. If you don't figure out the right questions to ask, if you don't make the correct diagnosis, you will not figure out the proper treatment. In this instance, the proper "treatment" was the advice, "Don't boil the orange juice."

Evaluation of a Child with Heavy Metal Poisoning

Another patient, a young toddler, came to my father in Cincinnati from Fort Campbell, Kentucky, with symptoms of heavy metal poisoning. The child was admitted to the hospital and got better. Despite intense investigation the source of the heavy metal poisoning was not found. The child recovered, went home and then returned a few months later with the same symptoms. Further detailed questioning finally disclosed that the child's father was an artillery officer in the army. He was bringing home spent shell casings for the child to play with. Putting these in his mouth was the source of the heavy metal poisoning. If you don't ask the right questions, if you don't figure out which questions to ask, if you don't keep asking questions, then you can't figure out what is going on, and you won't be able to solve obscure medical problems.

Evaluation of a Patient with Hip Pain

In evaluating a patient's complaints, the patient's age is of prime importance. For example, consider a patient who comes to the office complaining of the spontaneous onset of hip pain. In a child between the ages of four and six bacterial infections in the hip need to be considered. A young, non-verbal child with a spontaneous limp should be evaluated by watching her walk on her feet and on her knees. If she limps when walking on her knees as well as on her feet, the pain is in the thigh or hip. If he limps when walking on his feet but not his knees, then the pain is coming from the lower leg or foot.

In a child between the ages of four and ten, a common diagnosis is transient synovitis of the hip, also called toxic synovitis of the hip. Basically, the hip hurts for a few weeks and then spontaneously improves and nobody is sure why. Whenever doctors don't know the cause of something, they say it could be a virus. Maybe it is.

In an adolescent between the ages of 10 and 15, slippage of the top of the ball portion of the femur (thigh bone) away from its position on top of the rest of the femur is an occasional cause of hip pain. This problem is called slipped capital femoral epiphysis, which is a separation through the growth plate of the proximal femur. More common in boys than girls. More common in obese or tall adolescents. Pain and aching may develop slowly and insidiously. The pain may be more in the thigh or knee. If diagnosed early, it can be treated with surgical pinning to stabilize the slippage. If undiagnosed, the slippage can be severe and lead to long-term hip disability. I have seen several cases in my career in which the pediatrician or primary care physician failed to be sensitive to an adolescent's early complaints of hip, thigh or knee pain. In these cases, a few weeks was all it took for severe slippage to occur. In a patient this age with knee pain it is important to X-ray the hip to look for slippage. Hip problems can present with complaints of knee pain.

Hip pain in patients in their 20s through 50s is less common. Bursitis is one common cause. Occasionally patients develop early degenerative arthritis. In the 50s and beyond degenerative arthritis is a common cause of spontaneous hip pain.

Look for Multiple Diagnoses

When patients visit a doctor, the doctor usually tries to diagnose the problem. My approach to evaluating patients is to try to diagnose the problems. Notice my emphasis on the plural problems. When I was in medical school one of the teaching exercises was the clinicopathologic conference. A patient was presented to the students with multiple system complaints. The intellectual teaching exercise led us to try to find the one diagnosis which explained all of the symptoms.

The diagnosis might be extremely rare. I found that when I was in practice, I often found two, three or even four new independent diagnoses when evaluating a new patient. Thus, for example, I was never surprised to find new diagnoses of trigger fingers, carpal tunnel syndrome and cubital tunnel syndrome in one new patient office visit. I recall one new patient in whom I made five new diagnoses: a rotator cuff tear of one shoulder, a torn meniscus in one knee, right carpal tunnel syndrome, left carpal tunnel syndrome and a trigger finger. Five new diagnoses in my first evaluation. Thus, I always approach new patients with the idea, "How many diagnoses can I find?" rather than trying to pack all of the symptoms into one package. I think the emphasis of the clinicopathologic conferences was wrong. It is far more likely to find three, four or five new common diagnoses, rather than one obscure diagnosis. Nonetheless, it still is important to look out for that occasional rare diagnosis.

Are the Medications Any Good?

Some years ago, I evaluated a patient for joint pain with a history of gout. In gout there is too much of a chemical called uric acid in the blood. The uric acid may crystallize out in a joint or in the soft tissue, causing severe pain. This patient was not getting better. His uric acid level remained high despite being on medication. He swore that he was taking the medication. Again, the issue of finding the right question or questions to ask. Finally, I think to ask, "Where are you getting your gout medicine from?" Answer. "Honduras. Very cheap." Whatever he was taking, it was not the proper gout medicine. Treatment. Switch his source of medication. Gout improved. Another situation in which it is important to find the right question to ask. Another situation in which my best treatment may simply be advice.

CHAPTER FOURTEEN

Humor; Embarrassment; The Unexpected

Sometimes the practice of medicine is pure comedy. Not so much laughing at patients as laughing with them. There is comedy at times even within the tragedies. Shakespeare deftly shows us the comedic within his tragedies. Here are some examples.

As first-year medical students we were encouraged to participate in the examination and treatment of patients at a free clinic in Cambridge and at the Harvard Radcliffe student infirmary. A few months into medical school I came to dinner to find a friend of mine looking a bit dazed. I asked what was going on. He told me he had gone to the Harvard Radcliffe infirmary to work with the doctors there. He had taken a history from a Radcliffe student. He then started to say "I need to examine you. Please undress behind that curtain and put on a gown." He did not get beyond the word "undress" when the student stood up, slipped off her dress and stood there naked without underwear. He rapidly stammered that she should go behind the curtain and put on a gown. Such was his "initiation" into the power of the white coat.

I am working in an emergency room in one of the suburbs of Boston. Moonlighting. At a time before there was the specialty of emergency room physician. It's 3:30 a.m. and quiet. A young man comes in for emergency treatment of genital crabs. Basically, lice in the pubic hair. Not an emergency, in the proper use of the word "emergency". But for him it was an emergency. His girlfriend wouldn't sleep with him until he got treated. The question was never raised whether the girlfriend was concerned about when and where he caught the lice, since it obviously was not from her.

A fellow resident of mine described a situation when she was in medical school on a rotation in a psychiatric ward. A six-foot six-inch wrestler, during a psychotic episode, lifted a petite nurse up in the air. With the nurse sitting in the palm of his hand, the psychotic patient was running all over the ward holding the nurse high in the air. The psychiatric resident managed to talk the patient down and the patient put the nurse down without harm. I wish I could give you follow up on the nurse's later career plans.

Another emergency room. Another 2 a.m. I am working in a suburban emergency room. It is quiet. I am writing in a chart. This hospital has a psychiatric ward. Patients often come in to talk to the psychiatric nurse. As the doctor on call, I do a brief history and physical exam before these patients are seen by the psychiatric nurse. The psych room has deep pile carpeting with a couch, coffee table, lamp and chair designed to help these patients feel comfortable. A new patient comes in asking to speak to the psychiatric nurse. The nurse I am working with walks by me with a cup of coffee, which she is taking to the new patient. My nurse tells me the patient will be ready for my history and physical exam in a moment. All is quiet. I am not needed. I continue writing in another patient's chart.

From down the hall I hear the nurse yell "You're getting it all over the rug!" I alert! But! The nurse hasn't called for me. It doesn't sound like an emergency. If it were an emergency, the nurse would call for me. It doesn't sound like I am needed, yet. I am not sure what is going on. I have worked with this nurse before. She is experienced. She does not get excited easily. Whatever is going on, she is handling it. If she needs me, she will call me. A moment later, the nurse walks calmly back into the doctor's room, still holding the patient's cup of coffee. Now, I am intrigued. Why hasn't she given the patient her coffee?

The patient came into the emergency room with a book and a razor blade hidden inside of the book. While in the psychiatric room, the patient cut her wrists, fortunately not deeply. The nurse, as I have said, an experienced nurse and a good nurse, walked into the room and saw the patient sitting there, dripping blood onto the carpet. With a fine set of priorities, the nurse said what I quoted above. She then took a waste basket and placed it under the patient's wrists so that the blood would not drip further onto the carpet. The nurse obviously felt the patient did not deserve the coffee or that drinking the coffee would splash more blood around. I sewed up the patient's wrists. She spoke with the psych nurse. She was admitted to the hospital.

More humor in medicine. A male resident friend of mine described a resuscitation scene in an ICU (intensive care unit). My friend was standing at the bedside rounding on a patient with a group of interns and residents when a female patient arrested and became unconscious. My friend immediately jumped up on the bed, straddling the patient and began chest compression. The first compression restarted this patient's heartbeat. She immediately woke up from her arrest. Seeing a man straddling her, she began screaming, "Rape!" A quick save!

I once had a post-op hand surgery patient come to his first post-op visit late one October with his hand hidden under his jacket. He carried on and on about how terrible his hand looked and how worried he was. After suitably stroking my anxiety, he brought out his hand inside of a Halloween monster costume hand. After a good laugh, I walked him through my crowded waiting room with his hand on display. Loud enough for everyone to hear, I assured him this was a normal post-op appearance of a hand following my surgery.

Yet more humor in medicine. When I was a junior resident at the VA Hospital, we performed our own arthrograms. We did not have a radiologist in the hospital to do them. This technique involves injecting a dye that shows up on X-ray into the knee joint to look for evidence of a torn meniscus. We were working in the days before MRIs. The senior resident and I had two patients scheduled for knee arthrograms one afternoon. We brought the first patient into the X-ray room and prepped his knee. We then took a small needle and were ready to push it gently into the skin to begin injecting a Novocain-like medicine.

The needle was small and usually is barely felt. The moment the needle touched his skin this patient leapt off of the table slamming into the wall while emitting a loud shriek. He then ran around the room screaming loudly. Naturally we aborted the procedure. When we went out into the hall to call for the second patient he had disappeared. We never saw him again. He never returned to our clinic. Having heard the shrieking and screaming coming from the room, who knows what he must have thought was going on in there?

One time, we were treating a patient who had had surgery at another hospital several years before. The clinical course over the past few years was inconsistent with the pathology report from the previous hospital. We wrote a letter to the hospital asking for the slides and the pathology specimen, so that our pathologist could perform an independent evaluation. We received the most humorous letter back from the hospital pathology department stating that the specimen had been lost, but they would be more than happy to send us a specimen from another patient with the same diagnosis. I'm not sure that they understood exactly how stupid their letter was.

Another pathology report we laughed about was a liver biopsy pathology report which stated, "barium with colonic mucosa." When the biopsy needle was inserted, they missed the liver completely and speared the large colon, which had recently had a barium enema. I was not treating this patient. I do not know if surgery was required for the complication.

More humor from the training trenches. A young man was involved in a severe automobile accident three weeks after his marriage and suffered severe fractures to both legs. He was treated in traction for both legs, standard treatment at that time. When his wife came in to visit him each day, she closed the door to his hospital room. The nurses, all good Catholic nurses as I recall, immediately rushed in whenever the door was closed. The couple appealed to me for help. They simply wanted some private time in the midst of this busy public hospital. I spoke to the nurses. The nurses said, "Do you know what they are doing in there?" I replied that I most certainly did and that I was happy for them. Speaking to the nurses did not work. They continued to barge into the room. I was forced to write a formal and official order in the chart, that the nurses should leave the door shut. That worked.

Back to early medical school clinical training. During one early physical diagnosis rotation, I was getting comfortable examining the heart and lungs and felt ready to expand to the neurologic exam. I was performing a physical exam on an otherwise healthy 22-year-old athletic male with an inguinal hernia in preparation for his surgery. In your own physical exams, you may have had a doctor stroke the bottom of your foot. It feels weird, ticklish and a bit uncomfortable. Your foot arches and your big toe flexes down. This test is called a Babinski test. When the big toe goes down this is normal. In certain neurological conditions the big toe flares upwards rather than the usual downward direction. When this happens, the test is abnormal.

I had never done a Babinski test on a patient before. I was slowly working up my confidence to expand my examination repertoire. I figured now was as good a time as any to begin the neurological exam. I took the sharper end of the reflex hammer, often used for this test, and stroked the bottom of his foot. Whoops. Rather than the gentle stroking required for this test, I probably took off several cell layers of skin, hurting him.

Picture this now. He leaps up out of bed screaming at me. I get up, apologizing, grabbing my doctor's bag and walking fast out of the room. The patient follows me down the hall, screaming insults. I keep walking fast, head bowed, listening to the insults, agreeing silently that they are probably deserved. I envision Charlie Chaplin or Buster Keaton playing my role in a silent movie to near perfection. Embarrassment is a common accompaniment to early life in medical training.

There was a sense of a "cult" within the neurology departments in Boston at that time that you should only perform the Babinski test with a Yale key. Don't ask! Like so many things, don't ask why. Herd mentality, I guess. Many of us obtained Yale keys and carried them around with us to use in performing this test. I threw away my Yale key long ago. I switched to using the back of my thumb nail. Works well and you never leave home without it.

In my many years of practice in a non-neurology field, I continued to do the Babinski test routinely. Only one time did it prove useful. A man got out of a chair, fell down unexpectedly and suffered a herniated disc in his low back. His Babinski test was clearly and classically positive. This test is not positive in patients with herniated discs. I ordered an MRI of the entire spinal cord and made the diagnosis of multiple sclerosis. This diagnosis explained the reason for the unexpected fall and the reason for the abnormal Babinski test. This vignette further emphasizes the importance of following a detailed protocol for every physical examination. If I had not performed the Babinski test on this routine back pain patient, I would have missed the diagnosis of multiple sclerosis. This is also another example of finding more than one diagnosis in a new patient evaluation.

My embarrassment with the Babinski episode was not my only embarrassment in training. There is a technique in using a dissecting scissors or suture scissors in which you use it in the normal way, but when you are temporarily finished, you flip your hand to rotate the pointed end back into your palm. This technique is handy when done right. You do not need to put the scissors down and pick them up again. You free up your thumb, index and middle fingers to continue using them. Then, when you need the scissors, you flip your hand and rotate the scissors back to its normal cutting position. The scissors rotate on the ring finger. Done well, the maneuver is efficient. I used it throughout my career. Done poorly, well....

In my learning phase of this use of the scissors, I had two mishaps. Once, they flew out of my hand backwards and hit the wall behind me. No harm, but embarrassing. Another time occurred during a neurosurgical operation on the brain. At that time the neurosurgeons used glass test tubes to hold the cautery tip and the suction tip when they were not being used. One unfortunate time— unfortunate for me, that is—I flipped the scissors forward to cut suture. The tip of the scissors hit one of the glass test tubes. The glass test tube shattered, spreading glass fragments across the sterile field of instruments. No glass fragments went into the brain. Fortunately!

The solution was to clear away the sterile field and bring in a whole new set of instruments. Fortunately, no harm to the patient. As I look back on this sad and sorry episode, I recall that the neurosurgeon I was working with did not get upset or angry. Now why should this be? Was he someone with remarkable equanimity? Or did he have such a low opinion of me that he was not surprised by my action? Was I simply meeting his low expectations? I still wonder. Again, epiphany time. These episodes are marvelous teaching moments. You learn how easy it is to screw up. In a moment. In a heartbeat. Thus, you learn care and caution. You learn that the most trivial-seeming activity can be problematic. I learned. I still feel that I deserved greater criticism than I received. Maybe, just maybe, the neurosurgeon had done something similar in his early training and was doing everything he could to keep from bursting out laughing. I think I'll go with that scenario.

Yet another embarrassing vignette. I am operating through the chest for one of Dr. Hall's scoliosis procedures. Normally, we harvest a portion of a rib for bone graft material. Normally, one end of the rib is clamped and held before the rib is cut off with a bone cutter. Still young and fearless, I cut off the rib before it is clamped. The rib flies up end over end into the air and lands on the floor. Oops! Epiphany time once again. This episode was the last and final incident which chastened me and matured me into a serious and cautious surgeon. The rib was autoclaved to sterilize it and was used without complication. Once again, I don't recall anger or criticism by my attending. Now why should this be? There is a long learning curve in the training of a good surgeon.

More humor in medicine. I was once STAT-paged to a patient's room. The patient was in the midst of treatment for delirium tremens (alcohol withdrawal). He had become violent and had been placed in four-point restraints, restrained by both legs and both arms. When I got to the patient's room, security had already arrived. Somehow this patient, restrained by both arms and both legs, had managed to get out of bed. He was still restrained by all four limbs to the bed. But! He was standing on his feet and the heavy hospital bed was on its side behind him, all while still in four-point restraints. The security team was slowly inching around the edge of the room trying to decide how to proceed. I think I'll go with Mel Brooks as the director to film this scene for a movie.

More comedy. Beth Israel Hospital. I am on the dermatology rotation. There is an overweight woman with an unusual whole-body rash. Picture this please. She is lying on an examination table with pubic area and breasts barely covered. The teaching dermatologist is teaching. Gathered around the patient are eight dermatology residents, internal medicine residents and medical students. All eight of us have compound magnifying lenses to look at the rash. All eight are leaning over this patient at the same time carefully examining this rash on different parts of her body. The patient is "gushing" "You are all such nice Jewish doctors." I think I will leave the image in your mind as only Woody Allen might direct it. Only three of us were Jewish.

More on the wondrous ways people sustain injuries. I will let you decide if this vignette is comedic. While I was in the army, one of the self-defense instructors was in a bar with three or four of his students. The inebriated verbal discussion veered into the territory of whether the instructor could defend himself against the entire group of students. The non-verbal portion of the discussion progressed to broken beer bottles. The instructor "won" but suffered two transverse lacerations on the back of his hand, which also lacerated tendons on the back of his hand. I operated to repair the lacerated tendons.

In the unarmed defense against short sharp weapons such as knives and broken beer bottles, it is important to keep the back of your hands facing outwards towards the sharp weapon. You have to expect to get cut. Lacerations on the back of the hand are not incapacitating injuries and do not prevent you from continuing to defend yourself. This instructor knew his stuff. What he failed to practice was how to avoid the physical confrontation itself, sometimes called verbal jujitsu.

Early in my training, I was suturing a scalp laceration on a child's head. I allowed the family in the room in order to comfort the child. As I was suturing the child's laceration, the father fainted, falling backwards like a log. He hit his head on the corner of a machine, lacerating his head. I sutured the father next. In my experience women never seem to faint, whereas men do far more frequently. So different from descriptions of Victorian times. Following my experience with the father fainting, all men who wanted to remain in a room were required by me to sit. Sitting seemed to cure the male fainting problem.

I was taught that, "You cannot faint lying down." I was taught this maxim as an absolute. "You cannot faint if you are lying down." Thus, anyone who feels like they are going to faint should lie down. If you see someone who is about to faint, lie them down quickly. Do not keep them upright. I had never had a patient faint once they were laying down. Years ago, I had a woman in my office suddenly say to me, "I feel faint; I feel faint; I feel faint." I quickly laid her down on the floor and elevated her feet on a chair. Even after I laid the patient down, she continued complaining of feeling faint. Then. Suddenly. Her eyes shot upwards. She became unconscious. Whoa! What is happening? "You can't faint lying down." Yet, she had just fainted lying down. What is happening? What to do? Yet another "What to do?" situation. I take hold of her wrist. She has a good, normal pulse. She is breathing normally. What to do? So many times, I have been faced with that question. I am convinced that you cannot faint lying down, but I have just seen it happen in front of me. I continue to watch her breathing and continue to take her pulse. I decide I will wait three minutes before calling 911 for an ambulance. I can wait the three minutes because of the normal breathing and the normal heart rate. After about a minute, her eyelids flicker. She wakes up. She looks at me. She says, "I must have had a seizure." She had a history of petit mal seizures. Petit mal seizures are "small" seizures which may have little or no obvious seizure movements. So, she had not fainted. Whew!

Another patient of mine had petit mal seizures. His symptoms were subtle. He might be walking along and then he would stop and freeze for five seconds. Then, he would recover and continue walking. People who did not know his problem simply thought he was strange. He was cured by neurosurgical removal of a small part of the brain that was causing the seizures.

In my general surgery internship, we evaluated a patient with abdominal pain. We obtained an X-ray as part of his evaluation. The X-ray showed a paperclip overlying the right lower quadrant of his abdomen. We initially assumed that the paperclip was in a pocket of his clothes which the X-ray technician had mistakenly left in the field of the X-ray. We carefully checked that there were no paper clips overlying his abdomen and retook the X-ray. The paper clip was still there. The patient denied swallowing a paperclip. We questioned our patient further. As a boy of 14, he was living in northern Italy in 1944, behind German lines. He developed appendicitis and underwent surgery, which was successful. The paper clip was in the area of the appendix. As near as we could figure, the surgeon, in Italy, in 1944, lacked sterile suture, due to war shortage. He must have used a sterilized paper clip to seal off the appendiceal stump. The paper clip was not the cause of his abdominal pain.

I have mentioned a few successful resuscitations from cardiac arrest. The critical issue with success is the immediate recognition of the arrest and the immediate start of the resuscitation. One of our legends described a successful resuscitation outside of the hospital, which could only have happened in Brookline, Massachusetts. Brookline is a neighborhood near to three of the large Harvard hospitals. According to the legend, a man stopped his car at a stoplight in Brookline. The light turned green. The man collapsed unconscious over his steering wheel in cardiac arrest. According to the legend, there was a cardiologist in the car behind him. There was a second cardiologist in the car behind the first cardiologist. There was, yet, a third cardiologist in a car coming the other way. Immediate resuscitation by three Harvard cardiologists. He survived. A wonder the three cardiologists did not get in each other's way. A neighbor of mine was at a beach on Cape Cod, when he arrested. A cardiologist was on the blanket next to him. Another successful resuscitation. Ah, the element of luck in life, both good and bad.

More humor in medicine. A new anesthesiologist was working for the first time with a general surgeon. This general surgeon was reputed to be the fastest (not necessarily the best, but the fastest) surgeon in the hospital. Normally, anesthesiologists keep their anesthetized patients under light anesthesia until just before the surgery starts. The new anesthesiologist was carrying the patient light. When he looked up, the general surgeon was beginning his incision in the abdomen as the sterile drapes were still settling. The anesthesiologist pushed more anesthesia medicine quickly into the IV. The patient tensed for 10 or 20 seconds and then relaxed as the anesthesia took effect. On rounds the next morning, the anesthesiologist asked the patient how he had tolerated the anesthesia. The patient replied fine. However, he mentioned that he had the strangest dream during the surgery. He said he dreamt that someone took a hot sword across his chest. The anesthesiologist replied that indeed that was a strange dream.

When my son was about age ten, he began walking around with his shoelaces untied. Naturally, I began to nag him about his shoelaces. In his precise and analytical manner, he said, "Dad, you're an orthopedic surgeon, right?" To which I replied, "Yes." He followed with, "You treat patients who fall and break bones, right?" Again, I replied, "Yes." Then, my son asked, "Have you ever treated a patient who injured himself because of untied shoelaces?" My honest reply was, "No." My son followed with, "So, please, stop bugging me." And, I did. Eventually he started tying his shoelaces. Probably 20 years later, I saw my first and only patient who tripped and fell over untied shoelaces breaking something, I forget what. I called my son immediately.

The next few vignettes fall under the heading of "fun with the newbie." I worked in emergency rooms frequently during my training and while in the military to earn extra money. A common, non-serious but quite painful injury is a crush injury to the tip of the finger. The bone breaks and the bleeding is trapped under the fingernail causing significant pain. I had not seen a patient with this problem in my training before. It is a common injury, which does not come to a teaching hospital often. The nurse I was working with told me to take a paperclip, partially straighten it, heat it in a flame until it was glowing red hot and then touch the red-hot tip of the paperclip to the nail above the subungual hematoma (collection of blood under the fingernail). I was convinced she was making fun of the newbie. I required considerable encouragement and convincing. Eventually, I tried it. Worked like a charm. The paper clip has to be red hot. If so, it just melts through the nail and relieves the pressure of the bleeding. Immediate decrease in pain. No anesthesia needed.

As a medical student on general surgery I frequently scrubbed in on surgery cases. During one case the surgeon took my gloved hand and placed it in the lower pelvis so that I could feel a firm, round anatomic structure approximately two centimeters in diameter. He then asked me to identify the anatomic structure. The only round structure I could think of was the prostate, but this patient was a woman and I didn't think you could palpate the prostate from the inside of the abdomen anyway. After admitting that I was stumped, the surgeon informed me that I was palpating the inflated balloon of the patient's Foley catheter.

More fun with the newbie. I rotated onto a total hip replacement service, which used a special room to try to reduce the risk of postoperative infection. There was a strong laminar flow of air across the room. All operating personnel wore "space suits" with helmets and body-covering suits. There was air inflow by hose and outflow by hose to keep us cool. My first time scrubbed in there, I found myself getting hotter and hotter and hotter. Sweat was dripping off my face. I could not understand how anyone could work in this environment. Then, one of the surgeons I was working with took his foot off of my air outflow and I cooled down immediately. The surgeons hazed every new resident in this manner. Don't you just love human nature, which has to behave this way? Naturally, I continued the tradition with the next newbie. Of course.

More on the hazing that occurs with growing up. As a first-year boy scout at a camporee, I remember two of us were sent out to the other troops in the camporee. One of us was sent to get a "sky hook" and the other to get some "shoreline" to tie to it. How gullible and naive we were. The other scoutmasters, recognizing the "fun," told us they did not have any, but the next troop might. Gradually, of course, we figured it out. So much to learn as we grow.

I occasionally did something similar in the operating room. When I was in the army, as I was starting an operation, I once told a new nurse that I had the kit but I needed the kaboodle. I needed the kit and the kaboodle. She ran out of the operating room to the control desk of the operating suite and told the head nurse that I needed the kaboodle. Recognizing what was going on, the head nurse told her to go to the sterilizing department, that they might have the kaboodle. The head nurse then called ahead and alerted them to expect the new nurse.

I continued with my operation, forgetting about my joking request, assuming it had been forgotten. About a half hour later, the new nurse came back to the operating room, having been run all over our small hospital. With an exasperated voice, she said, "Dr. Seinsheimer, there is no such thing as a kaboodle." I had no idea what I had started. To the nurse, if you read this book, I apologize.

The classic joke is for the orthopedic surgeon to ask for the Otis elevator. In orthopedic surgery an elevator is an instrument used to elevate tissue off of bone. I did use the Otis elevator a few times, but it was too well known.

Early in my career, I was performing an open operation for overgrowth of the undersurface of the bone, which forms the point of the shoulder (the acromion). In this operation, I used an oscillating saw to trim the undersurface of the acromion. I then used a hand bone rasp to smooth the cut surface of the bone. Deciding to have some fun, I asked for the power rasp, knowing there was no such thing. The circulating nurse immediately ran out of the operating room. As I was laughing to myself, she returned with a power reciprocating rasp tool, which I had never seen before. I loved it and used it in all of my future surgeries of this type. The joke was on me this time. But, with a useful result.

One of my medical school friends was on his general surgery rotation when a patient was seen with right lower quadrant abdominal pain. With abdominal pain and tenderness, the key treatment concern is deciding when and whether to operate. There are always numerous possible diagnoses. Predicting the diagnosis is not only difficult, it is often impossible. The key is determining who needs immediate surgery. The attending, elder statesman general surgeon told my friend that this patient clearly had a case of acute appendicitis inside of a strangulated hernia.

A hernia is a weakness or opening in the abdominal wall. Occasionally bowel can bulge through this opening without complication. If the bowel twists and blood supply to the bowel is cut off, this is called a strangulated hernia. It requires immediate surgery to remove the dead portion of bowel and connect the healthy ends of bowel together. My friend's mentor surgeon was predicting that not only did this patient have a strangulated hernia, but that within the hernia was the appendix that had acute appendicitis. A ridiculous prediction.

They took this patient to the operating room. To my friend's amazement, the attending surgeon's diagnosis was exactly correct. There was acute appendicitis in a strangulated hernia. After the operation, in the surgeons' locker room, my friend in total and utter amazement stammered out the question, "How did you make that diagnosis? It's incredible." The attending surgeon laughed and told my friend, he had been making that diagnosis as a joke since he was a resident. He was as surprised as my friend. First time he had ever been right.

Another vignette. The first fiberglass casting material was pale yellow in color. Some years later a fiberglass casting material salesman brought colored fiberglass casting material to our office. One of the first times I used it, I put a bright blue short leg cast on a woman patient. She returned to my office the following week for a check. She told me that she had traveled up to a small town in Pennsylvania that weekend. While in a grocery store an unknown "strange" man walked up to her. He then went on his hands and knees crawling around her looking at the cast uttering, "Oohs" and "Aahs" as he crawled around. He then stood up and introduced himself. He was the local orthopedic surgeon. He had never seen a colored fiberglass cast before and was thrilled to see it. The colored fiberglass casting material was first delivered to the big cities.

CHAPTER FIFTEEN

Protocols

- Sponge Count Protocol
- How Do You Declare A Patient Dead?
- Quick Rule of Thumb in the Evaluation of a New Patient Entering the Emergency Room

Sponge Count Protocol

I have talked a lot about protocols. One of the protocols in surgery is the sponge count. Each sponge has a radio-opaque (shows up on X-ray) string woven into it, which shows up on X-ray. Most of the time, sponge counts are routine. Every now and then they are vitally important. When doing spine surgery, I was always careful to leave an end of each sponge outside of the wound in an attempt to prevent leaving a sponge behind. Once, in a spine case, I had a sponge count which was incorrect, missing one sponge. I could not find it. X-rays showed it in the upper corner of the open wound. I removed it. Thank you scrub nurse! Saved by the sponge count protocol!

At Children's Hospital there was an incorrect sponge count in a case I was not scrubbed on. They were missing one sponge. The case involved a long incision in a spine operation for scoliosis (curvature of the spine). The surgeon took X-rays, which showed the entire Harrington Rod which had been inserted for treatment of the scoliosis. The X-rays did not show the sponge. Assuming that the incorrect sponge count was incorrect, the operating surgeon closed the wound. In these patients, after they were rolled onto a specific post-op bed, additional X-rays were obtained to ensure that the hooks had not displaced. These X-rays showed the missing sponge above the Harrington Rod at the top of the wound. The patient was taken back to the operating room and the sponge was removed.

This case was discussed at complications rounds. Why did one X-ray show the sponge and one did not? The first X-ray showed the entire Harrington Rod. But— I repeat; but, I repeat; but, I repeat; but— the first X-ray did not show the entire scope of the surgical dissection. If you are going to leave a sponge in a spine case, it will likely be in a corner at the extreme end of the surgical dissection. The second X-ray happened to cover more area than the first. Epiphany! If you take an X-ray to look for a possible missing sponge, make sure the X-ray covers the entire scope of the surgical dissection, not just the surgical implant. I only ever saw this mistake happen once. That was all it took for me to be extra careful throughout my career. Many trainee surgeons will never see this error happen and thus will never learn this lesson. Again, I emphasize the randomness and idiosyncrasy of medical and surgical training. I also emphasize how easy it is for good surgeons to make mistakes. It seems strange that this lesson was not taught didactically at some point in training to ensure everyone was aware of the potential for this error. I repeat for emphasis: If you take an X-ray to look for a possible missing sponge, make sure the X-ray covers the entire scope of the surgical dissection, not just the surgical implant.

Once I had an incorrect sponge count that showed an extra sponge. As we examined the sponges, we found one "unmarked" sponge. An "unmarked" sponge is one without an X-ray marker. They are NEVER allowed on the operating field. Where did it come from? We never could figure it out. My best guess is a manufacturing error, with an extra sponge in a pack of ten and the scrub nurse only counting the blue X-ray marked sponges at the beginning of the case.

I once had an incorrect sponge count, missing a sponge. It was a small hand case. Hard to hide a sponge in the wound. X-rays did not show the sponge. Good, experienced nurses. After the patient left the operating room, none of us was satisfied with the "Mystery of the Missing Sponge." We searched for half an hour. Finally, in a trash bin, just outside of the operating room, rolled up inside a discarded glove, we found the missing sponge. We never figured out who violated protocol by removing the sponge from the operating room.

How Do You Declare A Patient Dead?

If a patient is rushed into an emergency room and appears dead, when and how do you "declare" that patient dead. This issue was never discussed or taught while I was in medical school or in my training. One patient, rushed into the ER by ambulance when I was moonlighting, was cold and rigid with rigor mortis. That one was easy. A doctor at one of the ERs I worked at pronounced a patient dead one night. The patient did not appear to be breathing and this doctor did not hear a heartbeat. After he spoke with the family, the patient was noted by nurses to still be alive, although he died a few days later.

I was never taught a protocol for this scenario. I presume there are protocols in place now. If not, there should be. Having heard the story above, I usually waited 15 minutes and also took an EKG to confirm the lack of electrical activity in the heart. So many things to learn. So many practical things that were not taught during my training.

Quick Rule of Thumb in Evaluating the Severity of Illness of a New Patient Entering the Emergency Room

I am not certain this vignette qualifies as a "protocol" vignette, but I found it useful when covering the emergency room. How do you perform a rapid evaluation of the severity of illness or injury as a new patient is wheeled into the emergency room on a stretcher? One quick rule of thumb: The patients who are yelling and screaming loudly are the least likely to be seriously ill. It takes significant heart, lung and brain function to yell and scream loudly. The patients who are lying quietly and not moving are usually of much greater concern.

CHAPTER SIXTEEN

Malpractice Issues; Complaints; Liability

- Malpractice Issues
- Complaints
- Evaluation of Injured Patients with Third Party Liability
- When Should You Order Expensive Diagnostic Tests?
- An "Administrative" Complaint

Malpractice Issues

Why have I placed the discussion of the specter of potential malpractice legal liability in the middle of my book? Quite simply because the specter of potential malpractice liability exists in the midst of every interaction between a physician and a patient. Overall, I wish to reflect on my surgical career, somehow, in a pure, unalloyed fashion without dealing with the influence of potential malpractice legal liability. However, no discussion of my surgical career would be complete without evaluating the influence of potential malpractice liability. To repeat, I do not want to color my discussions with my concerns and fears regarding the risk of malpractice lawsuits. Unfortunately, the risk of such lawsuits overhangs every interaction between a patient and a physician. Here goes.

So, what was my experience with malpractice lawsuits like? Some years ago, I treated a woman with a non-displaced spinal fracture suffered in an automobile accident. Due to persistent pain, I ordered a myelogram to image the spine for possible herniated discs. I was involved in this case before the advent of MRIs. A myelogram is performed by a radiologist and involves inserting a needle into the spinal canal and injecting radiologic dye into the spinal canal. X-rays are then taken of the dye in the spinal canal.

For reasons that were never clear, the patient developed permanent weakness in both of her legs with dysfunction of her bowel and bladder following the myelogram. I first learned of this complication when one of my partners made rounds on her the next morning. Rare complications following myelograms had been reported elsewhere. Just under three years later, a malpractice lawsuit was filed against the company which made the myelogram dye, the hospital in which the procedure was performed, the radiologist who performed the procedure and me, the doctor who ordered the procedure. The lawsuit demanded payment of more than 50 million dollars.

Being sued for over 50 million dollars early in my career grabbed my attention quickly and powerfully. Major epiphany: There is no such thing as a "trivial" interaction with a patient. The most minor, seemingly benign action, such as ordering a diagnostic test, can result in a lawsuit which, if successful, will pauperize me. I was told by my malpractice defense attorney that there had never been a successful lawsuit in the United States against a physician for the simple act of ordering a diagnostic test. This malpractice case dragged on for six years. Each year the case was open cost me $10,000 in extra malpractice insurance cost.

In preparing my response to the lawsuit, I reviewed the hospital chart carefully. I was surprised to find that the radiologist had recognized that there was a problem the evening after the procedure. The hospital chart showed multiple notes written by him that evening. Then, in one of his notes, partially written over his signature, was a statement that he had called me and spoken with me that night. He had not called me. So much wrong with the radiologist's behavior that night. He recognized a complication and did not call me, the treating physician. Then he wrote a note in the chart lying about having called me.

When I went into my deposition for the lawsuit, six years had passed since it had been filed. I had already given a deposition in the automobile accident case which caused the fracture and had nothing to add. I was advised, "You don't remember, you don't recall, you have no opinion." I was dropped from the case immediately after my deposition. The lawsuit (related to the complication of the myelogram) against me was a nuisance lawsuit, solely designed to force my testimony, which was of no value to the plaintiff.

Another case. I operated on a woman for carpal tunnel release. The next day she returned an evaluation postcard to the surgery center checking excellent for every parameter of treatment. She was discharged from my care in a few weeks, having done well. She returned to see me about four months later complaining of problems in the same arm. Examination showed severe atrophy of multiple muscles in her upper arm and forearm. In essence, her arm was wasting away for some reason. Carpal tunnel syndrome never presents with these findings. I elicited a past history of breast cancer on the same side. I felt that the breast cancer was likely growing into the nerves of the brachial plexus on the same side. My diagnosis was Pancoast Syndrome, mentioned earlier in my discussion of my interview for general surgery internship at Mass General. I ordered diagnostic studies on this patient. She did not return for follow up.

A year later, I received notice of a lawsuit claiming that I had cut two nerves in her hand at the time of my surgery. Their allegation that I had cut two nerves in the hand did not explain the atrophy of muscles higher up in her arm. How the plaintiff's attorney came to this conclusion escapes me. The patient died of her cancer one month later. The case was dropped.

A man developed an infection following surgery for an ankle fracture. I treated this complication initially with surgical drainage and antibiotics. The infection recurred and I then referred him to a university medical center for additional care. Three years later, I was sued for this complication without clear mention of exactly what I was alleged to have done wrong. Then, nothing was done by the plaintiff's attorney for three years. The case was then denied "without prejudice" because of the lack of activity by the plaintiff's attorney. The phrase "without prejudice" means that the attorney can sue me again, which he did. Then, three more years passed without the plaintiff's attorney acting to push the case along.

Additional information. Initially the plaintiff's attorney hired as his expert witness an orthopedic surgeon who was the first orthopedic surgeon censured by the American Academy of Orthopedic Surgery for fraudulent legal testimony. During the long delay, this expert witness died of natural causes. His office had possession of all of my X-rays. After the expert witness's death, his office contacted the plaintiff's attorney to pick up my X-rays. He did not pick up the X-rays and the X-rays were destroyed due to the attorney's lack of action.

At this point, we are approximately nine years after the incident in question. The infectious disease doctor who I had called in to consult on this case, nine years earlier, had destroyed his records. During their depositions, the patient and his family "remembered" the events of nine years earlier in exquisite detail.

The judge threw the case out without trial. The judge was not a judge who threw out cases often. The loss of the X-rays and the inability to obtain the infectious disease doctor's records due to the profound ineptitude of the plaintiff's attorney led the judge to determine that the lack of records would seriously hamper my ability to defend myself. He also commented, tongue in cheek, that the memories of my patient and his family were so incredibly "clear" that there was no way my memories could "compete" with theirs.

One of my orthopedic surgery friends had a lawsuit in which a patient sued because she could not move her elbow following treatment for a fracture. During the trial, the patient "forgot" that she could not move her elbow. She "allowed" her elbow to straighten out and rest on the table straight. All of the members of the jury saw her elbow straighten. Needless to say, my friend won the case.

My friend had another case in which, following total hip replacement surgery, his patient ended up with a five eighths inch leg discrepancy. Patient sued because of the leg length difference. At trial, the defending attorney asked the orthopedic surgeon expert for the plaintiff how much discrepancy is acceptable. Where is the border between standard of care and malpractice? The expert replied one half inch. With one question the defense attorney established that they were arguing over one eighth of an inch.

The defense attorney then asked the plaintiff's expert if the acceptable leg length changed, depending on the height of the patient. "Can you accept more leg length discrepancy in taller patients and less in shorter patients?" The plaintiff's expert could have argued either way. He answered the question, "Yes. It could be greater for a taller patient." The defense attorney then asked the plaintiff's expert, "How tall is the plaintiff?" In preparing for the trial testimony, the plaintiff's expert had not noted the plaintiff's height. He guessed five feet and six inches. The hospital chart said five feet and nine inches. That suggested that the extra three inches in height could account for the extra one eighth of an inch leg length discrepancy.

For research purposes, there is a hip-rating scale called the Harris Hip Scale. The defending attorney took the plaintiff's expert through the rating of this patient's post-op grade. The post-op grade was 99 out of 100. Leg length discrepancy only accounts for one point in this rating. Thus, the defending attorney pointed out to the jury that the suit was filed because the plaintiff got a 99 score rather than a 100 score. My friend won the case.

During my career I never settled a lawsuit. Nor did I have a lawsuit reach trial. During my career I paid between $20,000 and $45,000 each year for malpractice insurance coverage. Over 37 ½ years of private practice, I estimate I paid approximately one million dollars for malpractice insurance. All the while never having a successful lawsuit brought against me.

Complaints

The most frequent operation I performed in practice was carpal tunnel release. One day I received a letter from the Maryland Commission on Medical Discipline stating that a complaint had been filed stating that I had cut a nerve in the wrist of a patient I had operated on. Up to that time, I was not aware of a dissatisfied patient. So, I read this complaint with obvious surprise. I pulled the patient's chart. The notes documented a successful carpal tunnel release. The patient sent a survey form back to the surgery center, the day after surgery, with all positive comments. Four months following the carpal release surgery, the patient had returned to see me with complaints of a different type of arm pain. My workup, including an MRI of her neck, showed significant degenerative disc disease in her neck, with bulging discs pinching multiple nerves in her neck. The chart also showed that prior to her carpal tunnel release, she had developed severe atrophy (wasting) of the muscle at the base of the thumb due to preoperative nerve damage. Following my workup of her neck, she left my care.

She then consulted a neurosurgeon. The neurosurgeon apparently saw the atrophy of the muscle at the base of the thumb. Based on that observation— based on that observation alone; without reviewing my records; without obtaining new electromyographic studies—the neurosurgeon told my patient that I had cut the nerve to the muscle at the base of the thumb. Recall, that muscle had severe atrophy prior to my surgery. The neurosurgeon then operated on this patient's hand. The neurosurgeon told this patient that he found the nerve cut and that he repaired the nerve. As a result of this information, the patient filed a formal complaint against me.

In researching my response to the complaint, I reviewed the hospital records for this patient. I found that six months after the neurosurgeon operated on the patient's wrist, he finally focused on her neck and then operated on her neck. As part of his evaluation of her neck, he obtained electromyography (EMG) studies, which included studies of the nerves and muscles of the hand in question.

Without going into the electrophysiological details, the EMGs showed, unequivocally, that the nerve in question had never been cut. There are electrical changes that never completely go away if a nerve is cut and later repaired. I sent this information to the Commission and received back a letter stating I had provided standard of care treatment. That is, they confirmed that I had not cut the nerve.

In my letter to the Commission I stated something to the effect, "One wonders what the neurosurgeon thought he was doing during that operation, since he stated he thought he had repaired the nerve and clearly had not." Obviously, it was either fraud on the part of the neurosurgeon, in that he was lying in his operative report, or the neurosurgeon was totally "at sea" and thought he was repairing a nerve when he wasn't.

I called the Commission's investigator and asked if the Commission was going to follow up on my letter, since it was so clear there was a problem with the neurosurgeon. The investigator said, "No." He said the Commission only responded to letters of complaint. Even when they had an obvious problem in front of them, they would not follow up. I would have to write a specific letter of complaint.

I brought this issue to my partners for discussion. The consensus was to let the matter drop. The feeling was that in any mud fight, mud gets on everyone. How difficult it is to oversee physicians. I am able to write about this whole sorry saga now only because the neurosurgeon is deceased.

I was extraordinarily fortunate that there was EMG evidence readily available to exonerate me. Otherwise, it would have been his word against mine. He would have been believed. Here the Commission on Medical Discipline had clear evidence of a problem with the neurosurgeon but did not follow up. Why?

One evening in an emergency room, I was reducing a fracture in a child. I injected numbing medicine and placed the patient in 20 pounds of traction, as I have described before. I called for portable X-ray. After a long delay, the X-ray tech came with her machine. I took the X-ray cassette to position it the way I wanted. The X-ray tech got upset and said that she wanted to place the cassette the way that she wanted to. I told her that I would take full responsibility for the positioning of the cassette, since I knew what angulation of the X-ray I wanted. She took the X-ray. I reviewed the X-ray after it was developed. Mini C-arm fluoroscopy with immediate imaging was not yet available. The fracture was not fully reduced. I manipulated the fracture again and requested another portable X-ray. The X-ray tech then refused to take another X-ray. Meanwhile, my patient had been in traction for a long time and was having increasingly severe pain. It took me half an hour to get a different X-ray tech, who was not assigned to the ER, to take the X-ray. The patient's mother was upset about the X-ray tech's behavior. I should have formally complained about the X-ray tech. I didn't because of past experience with such complaints being useless. I did however write a contemporaneous memorandum to myself describing the events of that evening.

Fast forward maybe four months. I receive a letter from the president of the hospital staff threatening loss of privileges at the hospital because of my behavior toward the radiology employee. I call the president of the hospital staff to inquire. It turns out that the X-ray tech formally complained about my behavior. There apparently then followed multiple committee meetings "discussing" my behavior. No one on the hospital staff and none of these committees thought it appropriate to ask me for my side of the story. The complaint actually reached the board of directors of the hospital without anyone contacting me.

I asked the patient's mother to write a letter describing the X-ray tech's attitude and behavior. I forwarded my contemporaneous memorandum and the mother's letter to the president of the hospital staff and threatened legal action if my record was not cleared. The president of the hospital staff, then and only then, decided to investigate further. It turned out that the nurse helping me that night was so upset that she independently filed a formal complaint about the X-ray tech. Her complaint was ignored at that time but was easily discovered when they bothered to look. It also turned out that there had been multiple similar complaints about this X-ray tech in the past.

Why am I writing about this episode? The hospital did not follow protocol in evaluating the initial complaint about me. Normal protocol allows an accused person to respond to a complaint. The X-ray technician's complaint about me went through several levels of decision-making up to the board of directors without anyone raising the question of due process. Without anyone suggesting that I be given a chance to respond to the complaint. Without any modicum of an investigation. The X-ray technician's complaint was simply taken at face value. A rush to judgement. A lack of due process. I was fortunate that I had the testimony of the nurse and mother, who witnessed the entire interaction between me and the X-ray technician. Otherwise, I would have been engaged in a "he said, she said" situation and I would have lost.

Some years ago, I treated a child with a severe fracture of the elbow. At that time, treatment for this fracture involved placing a surgical pin across one of the elbow bones and then pulling upwards with traction using weights and pulleys. I did this procedure in the evening, carefully adjusting the traction and carefully manipulating the fracture fragments into good alignment. When I came by to make rounds in the morning, the child's mother asked me if hospital personnel were supposed to take down the traction when they moved the patient in his bed back to the ward. I said, "No! They were not supposed to do that." New X-rays showed that the fracture had displaced. I took the child back to the operating room for a second anesthesia and second manipulation.

I went to the hospital administration to alert them to the problem. Over the next few weeks several hospital employees spontaneously came up to me and informed me that the hospital administration was interviewing employees asking specific questions to try to put the blame for the problem on me. Child did well. Mom never initiated any legal action. Do you think I ever warned the hospital administration about any problem again?

More on patient complaints. While I was in the army, a patient filed a complaint against me with the US Army Inspector General's office. The soldier, who was a patient of mine, stated that in a conversation with him, I said there was an operation that I only performed on officers, not on enlisted soldiers. He named a nurse who was witness to our discussion. I did indeed recall a conversation with this soldier on one of the hospital wards. I also recalled the nurse being present. I know that I never made a statement like that. The nurse stated that I had never said that. So, what happened?

I see two possibilities. One, the soldier was simply trying to make trouble for me. He was doing a poor job of it since he named a witness who did not support his complaint. The other possibility is the one I think most likely. He must have misinterpreted something that I said. He must have believed this interpretation sufficiently to file his formal complaint. Fortunately, I had a witness to back me up. Otherwise, it would have become a "he said, he said" situation.

Evaluation of Injured Patients with Third-Party Liability

At times, we are called on to evaluate patients for legal reasons. We are asked to determine if the patient is injured, how badly injured, etc. Part of the evaluation is trying to determine if the patient has real symptoms. I remember the first patient I saw in the orthopedic clinic when I entered the army. The sergeant in charge of the clinic told me this patient was a malingerer. He had been hanging around the orthopedic clinic for six months saying he could not work driving a truck because of continued hand pain. The history was of an automobile accident in his role as a truck driver in the army. The patient had hit his hand on the steering wheel in the accident. Allegedly his hand continued to hurt six months later, preventing him from driving a truck. Previous examinations by two other orthopedic surgeons found nothing. I examined him. I found nothing. I dismissed him from the clinic.

As he was walking out the door, I suddenly realized that there was one diagnosis I had not examined for. I realized I had failed to perform my usual complete hand examination. I had failed to follow my personal protocol for hand and wrist examinations. I called the patient back to the exam room. I pressed on a place in the palm where one of the small bones in the hand is located. A protrusion of this bone is called the hook of the hamate. I pressed there and the patient was tender. Further workup with a CT scan showed an unhealed (non-union) fracture of the hook of the hamate. Six weeks in a cast. He healed. Returned to work. If you fail to consider the diagnosis of fracture of or non-union of fracture of the hook of the hamate or if you fail to palpate the hook of the hamate, you will not make the diagnosis.

The hook of the hamate is so well "hidden" that the fracture does not show up on routine X-rays of the hand. The fracture requires a CT scan or an MRI scan to confirm the diagnosis. As stated before, his fracture had been missed by the previous orthopedic surgeons who had examined him before I arrived. I almost, almost, almost missed it. The fact that the sergeant in charge told me that the patient was a malingerer pushed me toward not taking him seriously. Thus, my initial incomplete examination. Fortunately, I was able to resist that push sufficiently to perform a thorough exam. I initially violated my protocol by omitting one part of my standard hand and wrist exam. If your examination protocol for the wrist and hand does not include palpation of the hook of the hamate, you will miss fractures and non-unions of the hook of the hamate.

Another vignette. Another time. I was referred a patient for review by a workers' compensation insurance company. The patient had a heavy weight fall on the back of his hand. He developed persistent pain and had not worked for six months due to his hand pain. The patient was referred to me with his medical record and covert video surveillance. The video showed him helping a friend move objects onto a truck. At one point on the video, the patient stops and shakes his hand for 30 seconds. He then resumes helping his friend move. The use of covert surveillance indicated that the insurance company was sure the patient was faking. Careful palpation of the back of the hand near the middle finger disclosed a subtle, barely perceptible, vibratory, rubbing sensation as the patient opened and closed his fist. His treating physicians had found nothing. I felt he had a small mass pushing on the extensor (straightening) tendon from inside. After receiving my report, the insurance company referred the patient to me for treatment. I operated, found a benign mass and removed it. Having been out of work for over six months, the patient was back at work three weeks after my surgery.

Another patient was sent to me by a workers' compensation insurance company for evaluation of her shoulder. A heavy object had fallen onto the top of her shoulder while she was at work. She claimed she was unable to work due to continuing pain and weakness in her left shoulder. Her treating orthopedic surgeon was requesting permission for arthroscopic surgery of the shoulder. As part of my routine examination of the shoulder, I have a patient lift the affected arm up in front of her body and push against my hand. Meanwhile, I am palpating the scapula (wing bone) at the back of the shoulder with my other hand. Normally, there is a muscle called the serratus anterior (names are unimportant here) which is attached to the side of the chest wall and pulls the scapula forward. This muscle holds the scapula against the chest wall when the arm is elevated. Contraction of the serratus anterior helps to stabilize the shoulder. In this patient, the scapula winged out backwards with this maneuver. The serratus anterior muscle was paralyzed and unable to hold the scapula against the chest wall. The weakness was caused by damage to the nerve, which innervates this muscle, called the long thoracic nerve. This injury is often caused by a heavy weight falling on the shoulder.

The treating doctor had failed to do a sufficiently thorough exam to pick this up. It is not a common injury. Arthroscopic surgery was not indicated. Arthroscopic surgery would not address the injured nerve. Wrong diagnosis by the treating doctor. Why was I able to make the diagnosis? My personal protocol for examining the shoulder is sufficiently detailed that it will pick up this abnormality. I am willing to perform this maneuver as part of my routine examination for each and every shoulder exam, even though I have found this abnormality only three times in my career. Issues of how rushed is the doctor, how careful is the doctor, how compassionate is the doctor are present in every interaction between patient and doctor.

I have seen numerous patients referred for evaluation with undiagnosed or incorrectly diagnosed hand pain. These patients were tender to palpation on the palm side of the hand at the base of a finger. There is a tight tendon tunnel, called the A1 pulley, in this area. Slight swelling of the tendon can cause rubbing, pain and/or locking. Treatment involves cortisone shots or surgical release of the A1 pulley. The treating doctors had failed to palpate this area for tenderness. If you do not think of a diagnosis, you will not examine for that diagnosis and you will miss that diagnosis. If your examination protocol is insufficiently thorough, you will miss diagnoses. Again, the issue is how careful and thorough is your doctor?

I have seen, of course, patients exaggerating their symptoms. Patients who stagger down the hall when asked to walk, but when I watch them outside walking to their car, walk normally. There are also patients whose examinations were not physiologic. For example, patterns of loss of feeling or loss of muscle strength that do not match any anatomic pattern. A pattern of loss of sensation called stocking glove anesthesia is not physiologic and does not follow the pathway of any specific nerve.

When Should You Order Expensive Diagnostic Tests?

Some years ago, a woman came to my office complaining of neck pain. She was a nurse at one of the hospitals I worked at. X-rays of her neck were normal. I treated her with standard medication, physical therapy and exercises. For three months her neck pain persisted. It did not get better or worse. Finally, I ordered an MRI of her neck to look for a reason her neck pain was not improving. She returned to my office with the MRI. The MRI showed that an unknown cancer had spread to four bones in her neck.

As I stood there looking at the MRI, I felt two overwhelming emotions. First, utter horror at the diagnosis, particularly in a patient I knew and worked with. My second emotion was relief that I had ordered the MRI and made the diagnosis. Had the patient left my care the week before I ordered the MRI, I might later have been sued for failure to make the diagnosis. There is no clear guidance or protocol regarding how long to follow a patient with "routine" neck pain, before ordering an MRI. Going forward, I ordered MRIs quicker.

An "Administrative" Complaint

Once, when I was on call in the emergency room at Mass General, a woman, who was on welfare, called an ambulance and came to the ER by ambulance for routine post-op suture removal. The ambulance crew handed me a form to sign authorizing the ambulance ride. I refused. It cost the state $125 for the ambulance ride back then. Now, look at it from the patient's point of view. A bus ride or subway would cost a few dollars. A taxi more. A bus, subway or taxi would be less convenient. For this patient, the ambulance ride was free and convenient. You can understand why she called for the ambulance.

As the result of my refusal to sign this sheet of paper, the social service department of the hospital made a formal complaint about my behavior to Dr. Henry Mankin, my chief of service. Dr. Mankin was not particularly upset. It staggered me, though, to think that the social service department felt that it was appropriate behavior for a patient on welfare to call for an ambulance to come in for routine suture removal. The Massachusetts state bureaucracy was allowing this misuse of emergency personnel without auditing or control.

When my first child was born, my wife and I bought a used crib from friends. We knew of at least four other babies who had been raised in the crib previously. We also knew it was used before that. We had no idea how many children had been raised in this crib. The hinges and catches on one side were broken. That side was tied up with rope. After raising our two children in it, we sold it to other friends. However, if you were on welfare in Massachusetts in 1975, you were given a new crib for each new child.

CHAPTER SEVENTEEN

A Cornucopia of Vignettes

- Regarding Diet and Supplement Intake
- Severity of X-ray Findings Do Not Correlate Well with Severity of Symptoms
- Stainless Steel vs Titanium Plates
- The Placebo Effect
- Treatment of Knee Osteoarthritis
- The Treatment You Are Offered by a Doctor May Depend on Which Doctor You See
- Wrong Site and Wrong Side Surgery
- Percutaneous Lumbar Discectomy
- Basal Thumb Arthritis
- Certificate for Added Qualification for Surgery of the Hand
- Lyme Disease: Orthopedic Presentation
- Patients' Expectations
- Terminal Illness and Dying
- Deep Pain; The Use of Computer Mice
- Regarding Education
- Banning an Artificial Sweetener
- We Don't Know What We Don't Know

- Medicare and the Law of
  Unintended Consequences
- Thoughts Regarding Nursing Staffing in Hospitals
- Airbags
- When to Use a New Surgical Technique
- Treatment of Jehovah's Witness Patients
- Incidence of Errors in Reading X-Rays
- When to Order a Diagnostic Test
- When Abortions Were Illegal

began this book with a series of exciting vignettes which occurred early in my training and remain indelibly etched into my memories. They were an early part of the steep learning curve of my early clinical training. I then followed with a chronological approach to my training years. The past few chapters have contained vignettes which were easy to group together. This chapter contains a variety of vignettes all of which I find interesting and educational. I did not find an easy way to group them. They are discussed in no specific order.

Regarding Diet and Supplement Intake

Earlier, I discussed the McCash technique for operating on Dupuytren's contracture. Dupuytren's contracture occurs when tough, abnormal scar-like tissue forms in the palm and pulls the fingers into the palm. In the McCash technique a transverse wound is left open in the distal palm after surgery. This wound always heals completely in about three weeks. That is, of course, except when it doesn't. A few years and a lot of Dupuytren's surgeries later, I suddenly was confronted with a patient who, at three weeks after surgery, showed only minimal healing changes. At three weeks, it looked like a three-day old wound. Clearly, something was not right; not standard; outside my comfort boundary.

This case is an example of the need to constantly evaluate how your patients are doing. It is an example of the need to constantly look for problems and to constantly be proactive when you see them. This case is also another example of the need to figure out what questions to ask. Further questioning disclosed the following. The patient was a strict vegetarian who was also taking multiple different vitamin supplements. He also was not careful about eating a sufficient amount of protein. He was not careful about ingesting sufficient amounts of the essential amino acids. An essential amino acid is one your body cannot synthesize. You need to obtain it from food or you get sick because you don't have enough of it. To summarize: this patient had a combined problem of general protein deficiency and/or deficiency of specific essential amino acids and/or excessive overdosing of one or more vitamins. The vitamin overdose was subclinical vitamin poisoning. (Subclinical means without clear symptoms until stressed, in this case, stressed to heal a "simple" surgical wound.) I instructed my patient to eat a palm-sized amount of meat, including chicken or fish, each day as medicine and to stop the vitamins. He complied. He healed within two weeks.

Since then I have seen multiple patients with wound healing problems or fracture healing problems from one or more of three different reasons: general protein deficiency and/or essential amino acid deficiency; vitamin deficiency; excessive vitamin intake of one or multiple vitamins. The general protein or essential amino acid deficiency group includes patients who were strict vegans or vegetarians and were not careful about total protein and/or essential amino acid intake. These patients often ate only salad and pasta. The vitamin deficiency patients often ate meat but they did not eat any fruits or vegetables and did not take vitamin supplements. The excessive vitamin intake patients often took multiple supplements, sometimes not knowing what was in them. Sometimes they were taking a large number of different vitamins. Often, they were just taking large doses of Vitamin C alone.

Here are some specific examples. One of my partners had a young patient with a soft tissue injury to his leg about two inches in diameter, which had failed to heal over one month. My partner admitted the patient to the hospital and called for a plastic surgery consult. I came to see the patient on rounds the next day. Seeing the delayed healing of a simple soft tissue wound in a young patient with good blood supply, I took a dietary and vitamin intake history.

His dietary history was perfect. He did not take too many vitamins. I told him that it was unusual for a simple soft tissue wound in a young patient with good blood supply to fail to heal. I told him that I did not understand why he was not healing. I was concerned that if he could not heal this normal wound that he could not heal a plastic surgery incision wound either. I said goodbye and walked toward the door. As I reached the door of his hospital room he called, "Doc. Come back. I haven't eaten anything but Doritos for three months." I prescribed him a palm-sized portion of meat per day as medicine and a one multivitamin per day regimen. He healed quickly. Diagnosis: mixed protein, essential amino acid and vitamin deficiency.

I was not taught anything in medical school or during my surgical training regarding the prevalence and importance of being aware of a patient's dietary and vitamin intake behavior. I only became aware of the influence of diet and supplement intake because of my experience with the healing of McCash open palm technique wounds. I knew from experience how these wounds were supposed to heal. Thus, I was fertile ground for recognizing that there was a clear, specific problem when I encountered my first patient who was not healing properly. I do not think that the abnormal diet and vitamin intake problem is sufficiently recognized within the medical and surgical community.

Another example. I operated on a patient for a spontaneous rupture of a tendon in his hand and performed a tendon transfer. In a tendon transfer operation, you shift the attachment of a tendon so that its muscle does a different job, the job of the ruptured tendon. Our brains are remarkably plastic. By plastic, I do not mean the stuff used in manufacturing, I mean adaptable and change-able. Within days to weeks the brain learns how to use the transferred tendon correctly. This adaptation of the use of the tendon occurs almost automatically.

Following surgery, stitches are often left in arms and hands for seven to ten days. My tendon transfer patient was out of town and did not return for suture removal for three weeks. He called me the next day to tell me the wound had split open. I told him to come right over to the office. It looked like a three-day old wound. I took my usual dietary and vitamin intake history. He said he took Vitamin C all the time. "I pop them like candy." Diagnosis: Hypervitaminosis C or subclinical Vitamin C poisoning, or just too much Vitamin C. Call it whatever you want. I told him to stop the Vitamin C. He healed within the week. I do not know if the excess Vitamin C intake increased his risk of the spontaneous tendon rupture.

I was at a wedding years ago. Late in the evening, actually, early in the morning, as I was walking out, a woman stopped me. Four months previously, she had had a minor fracture of the bone on the outside of the ankle, which was non-displaced. This fracture, essentially, always heals. I never had a patient fail to heal this specific fracture. As I say, they all heal except when they don't. Now, four months later, the fracture had failed to heal. This woman was scheduled by her orthopedic surgeon for reconstructive surgery. Dressed in my tux, having enjoyed the champagne, I took my usual dietary and vitamin intake history. Everything sounded normal. I told her it was unusual for this fracture to fail to heal. Then, her husband spoke up and said to his wife that what she told me was not true. She kept an open bottle of Vitamin C on her kitchen counter and was taking them all the time. I recommended she stop the Vitamin C, cancel the surgery and give it another month or two to heal, which it did.

One theme evident in the vignettes I described above: patients do not always tell the truth, particularly if the subject concerns something that embarrasses them. We physicians may know the right questions to ask. We may not get truthful answers.

Another patient suffered a stab wound to the calf with a small box cutter type knife. Normally a small stab wound heals without difficulty, the only concern being possible infection. However, within hours, the stabbed muscle compartment swelled severely due to uncontrolled bleeding. The patient came to the emergency room complaining of severe calf pain. I was called; came in immediately; diagnosed a compartment syndrome. If there is too much bleeding within a tight muscle compartment or too much tissue swelling within a tight muscle compartment, the pressure within that compartment rises. Blood circulation cannot push through the increased pressure. The muscles within that compartment die.

It was late at night. Often there is a delay while the night operating team is called in. We were lucky. The operating team was already in the hospital. They had just finished a previous case. So, with minimal delay, I got the patient into the operating room, opened the compartment and released the pressure on the muscle. The muscle looked pink and healthy. I left the wound open, which is standard procedure to allow for swelling while ensuring the pressure remains released. I brought the patient back to the operating room for a standard second look two days later. The muscles in the compartment were completely dead. An unusual finding, considering how quickly the compartment was released. I cleaned out the compartment and sutured it up. I left the sutures in for three weeks. Standard for legs is 10 to 14 days. Following the removal of sutures at three weeks the wound spontaneously opened up. Further history from a family member disclosed that for religious reasons, the patient was a strict vegetarian. He was not careful about protein intake and was mainly a salad and pasta eater. Diagnosis: Protein deficiency and/or essential amino acid deficiency.

Yet another example. A patient suffered a comminuted (many fragments) fracture of the patella (kneecap). When there are many fragments, treatment involves removal of all of the bone fragments of the fracture and repair of the soft tissues including the extensor (straightening) tendon. I have performed this operation frequently. This patient was the only patient of mine who ever suffered a dehiscence (splitting open of a wound) of the tendon repair. The repair pulled apart so that the patient could not straighten his leg. Reoperation was necessary. Given the unusual complication, I elicited a dietary and vitamin intake history. A salad and pasta eater. Minimal protein intake. I recommended my palm-sized amount of meat daily as medicine. He healed following the second surgery.

My patient chose to file a formal complaint about me to the Maryland State Commission on Medical Discipline. In his letter, he complained that I was not interested in his knee, but "wasted time" talking about diet and vitamins. My response to the board was that I was trying to be a complete physician. I investigated, trying to understand the cause of the complication; I found the cause of the complication; I gave advice to prevent the complication from recurring after the second operation. The board determined that I had acted properly.

One last diet, vitamin and supplement intake vignette. When I was on my pediatric rotation, a six-month-old child was admitted to the hospital with irritability and increased cerebral spinal fluid pressure. The fontanels (space between the bones of a baby's head) were bulging. Imaging was negative for tumor. Further questioning finally disclosed that the mother was feeding her child chicken liver. A lot of chicken liver! Why? Because it was "healthy." Liver has a high concentration of Vitamin A. Too much Vitamin A just as too much of anything is not healthy. Mother advised to stop the Vitamin A and the child recovered.

I was taught that in the early days of Arctic exploration, polar bear liver was considered a delicacy and was consumed by these explorers. I was taught that polar bear liver has the highest concentration of Vitamin A of any known source. I was taught that many of the journals of the early Arctic explorers record headaches and other symptoms characteristic of Vitamin A poisoning.

With multiple experiences with patients such as I have described above, I began to take dietary and vitamin intake histories on all my pre-operative patients. Poor diet and/or excessive supplement intake occurs surprisingly often. I think a detailed dietary, vitamin and supplement intake history should be part of every annual physical exam. It should be part of the preoperative evaluation for any big surgery. Really, it should be part of the pre-procedure evaluation for any surgery or procedure. I think it is a significant, unrecognized, serious health issue. I also think that many elderly people, especially those with mild cognitive deficits, suffer deterioration in the quality of their diets. I suspect that one factor in the high incidence of complications following surgery or trauma in the elderly is due to improper diet and/or vitamin intake.

I do not present myself as a knowledgeable or trained dietician. However, from a practical point of view, I have seen the results of strict vegetarianism without concern for total protein intake and/or essential amino acid intake. I have seen the effects on patients who did not eat fruits or vegetables and did not take vitamin supplements. I have seen the effects of taking too much Vitamin C or too much of many vitamins. The problem here is excess. The ancient Greeks had a motto, "Everything in moderation." Excessive behavior in avoidance of certain types of food or excessive intake of certain vitamins or supplements harms the body's metabolism. In my experience, as an orthopedic and hand surgeon, this behavior has manifested as failure to heal wounds and failure to heal fractures.

More on the supplement question. If you take supplements, you need to know, you want to know, you should know what it is that you are taking. A friend told me that his yoga teacher had been chronically ill for two years. The yoga teacher was taking a supplement from somewhere overseas; India, I think. One of her students, by happenstance, was a toxicologist, who asked for a sample of the supplement. Analysis showed it was loaded with live parasites.

Wow! This yoga teacher had been unknowingly dosing herself twice a day for years with live parasites. As I have discussed above, sometimes the trick is figuring out what questions to ask. I presume this yoga teacher had seen physicians for her symptoms. Her physicians had not thought to inquire into supplement intake or to look for foreign parasites. Doctors generally only look for parasites when there is a history of foreign travel. It took a yoga student toxicologist to thoughtfully ask the right question and then do the right diagnostic test. It is important to not only ask patients for their supplement intake but also to ask where the supplements come from. This investigates the "quality" of the supplement.

Further thoughts regarding nutrition and vitamin intake. I knew a 95-year-old World War II veteran who was in remarkably good health for years. The Veterans Administration gave him two free "Boosts" (a nutrition supplement) each day. I believe the protein and vitamin intake he received each day from this "treatment" played a role in his continued good health and longevity. I have seen many elderly patients lose their appetite and fail. I am convinced that part of the failure of some of my patients results from their poor diet, that is, their lack of protein and vitamin intake. The policy of the Veterans Administration of distributing two free Boosts a day to Veterans is brilliant. My only complaint: I am told that each year, the veteran gets to choose one flavor and one flavor only. Then he is stuck with the same flavor all year.

Severity of X-ray Findings Do Not Correlate Well with Severity of Symptoms

There is a remarkable lack of correlation between the severity of findings in an X-ray, CT or MRI image and the severity of symptoms in orthopedic patients. I find the lack of correlation particularly true with respect to changes in degenerative arthritis of joints and degenerative disc disease in the neck and low back. I recall a patient I saw when I served as an orthopedic surgeon in the US Army. A green beret special forces soldier in his late 30s came to my office complaining of knee pain if he ran more than five miles or hiked with a full pack more than 20 miles. Weight-bearing X-rays showed complete loss of articular cartilage in his knee. There was bone-on-bone arthritis with complete loss of joint space. I showed him the X-rays and told him that I was willing to restrict his activities. He said, "No! I'm having too much fun. I just wanted to know why it ached a little." Then there are patients with near normal X-rays of the knee who have a great deal of pain. Some of the difference may be differing levels of inflammatory molecules.

I have seen patients with massive large herniated discs who have no pain or other symptoms related to the bulging disc. I have seen patients with completely normal MRIs of the cervical and lumbar spine who have severe pain in the neck or lower back.

Stainless Steel vs Titanium Plates

Many fractures are treated with metal plates and screws to hold the fracture fragments in position while the fractures heal. The metal plates and screws are typically manufactured with a type of stainless steel which is resistant to rust and corrosion or made with titanium. Occasionally patients develop persistent pain in the location of a plate which does not go away with time. There is usually tenderness to palpation over the plate. If enough time has passed and if the pain remains sufficiently severe, then surgical removal of the plate is indicated. Usually the removal of plates and screws is routine but not always.

In removing an isolated screw, the head of the screw may break off if the rest of the screw is tightly bound to bone. Most operating rooms have "difficult screw sets" of equipment. These have hollow drills which allow you to drill the bone around the outside of a broken screw thread. If the broken screw protrudes a bit there are instruments for grasping the protruding screw so that you can rotate and unscrew it.

If a screw welds to a plate and cannot be turned, there are other choices. A stainless steel screw can be drilled out with a titanium drill bit. Titanium is stronger than steel. Most operating rooms have air turbine instruments that rotate a tip 60,000 rpm. These instruments are so powerful that orthopedic surgeons have to take a special course to learn how to use them. When I took the course, I saw how a cutting instrument could cut through a cow pelvic bone as easily as a hot knife through butter.

Titanium is a curious metal. It is light and strong. It is also soft. When trying to unscrew a titanium screw from a plate, the titanium screw may easily strip. The high-speed turbine instruments have a diamond wheel tip which can cut through the titanium plate. The titanium plates are so strong that you have to cut the plate on both sides of the stripped screw to remove the plate. Removing the protruding screw with the grasping instrument from the difficult screw set then is easy. Once, when trying to remove a titanium plate and screws with a stripped screw, I discovered that the operating room did not have a diamond wheel available. It had not been replaced after a previous surgery. Another "what to do?" situation. I closed the patient up and brought him back to the operating room a few weeks later after the operating room obtained another diamond wheel. Patient fully informed.

The Placebo Effect

There is the continuing question which occurs in medicine and surgery concerning whether a specific treatment actually works or whether the improved results seen are the placebo effect. The placebo effect is a real phenomenon. I was taught that there was a study of patients who underwent open hernia operations. These patients were asked if they were willing to try a new, powerful oral pain medication. If the new powerful pain medication did not work, the patients were allowed to ask for the regular narcotic pain medication. After agreeing to participate, the patients were then given sugar pills for their pain. Forty percent of the patients reported significant pain relief and required no further pain medication! Recall. They had just had an open hernia operation. They had just been cut open. That hurts! Forty percent of the patients were sufficiently suggestible that something physiologic happened in their brain and they truly felt less pain. It is not that they were faking pain and were fooled into faking less pain. They had just had an open operation. Forty percent of patients are sufficiently suggestible that if they think some medicine or other treatment is going to make them feel better, they will actually feel better.

Years ago, there was an operation for angina, which is chest pain from insufficient blood supply to the heart. The operation consisted of taking an artery from the inside of the chest wall, the internal mammary artery, and burrowing this artery into the heart muscle. This operation was used before microvascular surgery techniques had been developed. No arteries were sutured together. The surgery with implantation of the internal mammary artery was popular. The results were great. Large numbers of patients reported relief of chest pain.

Experimental surgery in dogs did not find any measurable increase in blood supply to the heart following this surgery, even when the dogs were followed for two years after the surgery. Finally, a thoracic surgeon performed a series of sham surgeries on human patients without implanting the internal mammary artery, with equally good results. This surgeon proved that all of the "good" results were actually "placebo" results. Surgeons stopped doing the operation. Distinguishing "real" results from "placebo" results is difficult and is the reason you read about "double blind" research studies. "Double blind" means that both the patient and the researcher are "blinded," as to who has been treated with medicine or real surgery and who has been treated with placebo, until the end of the trial.

Treatment of Knee Osteoarthritis

I treat many middle-aged patients with the spontaneous onset of knee pain with no history of significant injury. For these patients, my protocol is to try conservative therapy for six weeks. If significant pain persists beyond six weeks, then arthroscopic surgery is worth considering. I am not always sure of the diagnosis but I am at least 80% sure I will find something at arthroscopy that I can help. In patients over the age of 30, my workup beyond a detailed history and complete physical exam includes an X-ray series that includes standing AP (anteroposterior, which means front to back), lateral (side to side), tunnel (an angled view through the inside of the knee) and the sunrise patella (an angled view which show the kneecap-thigh bone joint). The standing or weight-bearing view is important. Front to back X-rays taken with the patient lying down can look normal. Yet, when taken with the patient standing or weight bearing, they can show complete loss of joint space.

Some years ago, I read two studies of thousands of patients who underwent arthroscopy for degenerative arthritis of the knee. On initial reading, the studies seemed well done and double blinded. The results of these studies suggested that arthroscopy did not help patients with degenerative arthritis of the knee. I was surprised by these two studies because I felt I was generally getting good results with "carefully selected" patients. Note please, my emphasis on the phrase "carefully selected."

I read these two studies carefully, trying to determine the severity of the arthritis of the individual patients who were treated. I was unable to do so. The authors did not report the results of weight-bearing X-ray studies for any of these patients. Thus, in reviewing these studies, I could not tell, how many patients had severe bone-on-bone arthritis. In my practice, any patient with severe bone-on-bone arthritis does not get sent for an MRI. An MRI will not give any information which will alter treatment decision-making. Any patient with bone-on-bone arthritis is not offered arthroscopic surgery. With bone-on-bone arthritis, there is nothing to do at arthroscopy which will help.

After non-steroidal anti-inflammatory medicine and physical therapy, my treatment algorithm is to evaluate the results of the weight-bearing X-rays. If the X-rays show bone-on-bone arthritis, I try injections of hyaluronic acid (large molecular weight-lubricating fluid; extract of rooster combs). If that does not work and the pain is bad enough, then total joint replacement is indicated. If the weight-bearing X-rays show joint space preservation, then I order an MRI. If the MRI shows a torn cartilage (meniscus), I try arthroscopy first. If the patient is not improved, I use hyaluronic acid injections. If the MRI does not show a torn cartilage, I try the hyaluronic acid injections first. If they do not help, then I recommend arthroscopic surgery. This decision pathway is the treatment algorithm I use for treating patients over the age of 30 with knee pain.

Many of these patients have varying degrees of degenerative arthritis of the knee. A few paragraphs above, I used the phrase "carefully selected patients." Only certain, carefully selected patients end up with my recommendation for arthroscopic surgery. My patients seem to do much better than those reported in the two studies I mentioned above. I assume that the patients in those two studies were not carefully culled. If a significant portion of those patients had bone-on-bone arthritis, then I am not surprised that the arthroscopic surgery did not help them. It seems the studies were either poorly designed or poorly reported, since I was unable to determine the severity of the arthritis of the patients treated in those studies.

The Treatment You Are Offered by a Doctor May Depend on Which Doctor You See

The treatment you are offered by a physician or surgeon may depend on that doctor's training and area of specialization. Osteoarthritis of the knee, as I have stated, is common. At a certain level of severity, there is some decrease in joint space on weight-bearing films, that is obvious, but not yet bone on bone. I often spend time with individual patients trying to decide whether to recommend arthroscopy, hyaluronic acid injections or total knee replacement first for treatment. There is no good data from studies to inform decision-making when dealing with these borderline patients.

Here is an interesting issue. Which doctor you are referred to, which doctor you happen to choose, will determine what options are offered to you. When should you seek a second opinion? When should you go to a major medical center? If you go to a major total joint replacement center, you will be offered a total joint replacement. If you go to an arthroscopic surgery center, you will be offered an arthroscopic procedure. Once at a national meeting, I asked one of the orthopedic surgery professors from Robert Breck Brigham Hospital (now part of Brigham and Women's Hospital) how he decided between arthroscopy and total joint replacement for these borderline patients. His reply? Priceless. Precious. Something to the effect of: "I don't do arthroscopy. Thus, any patient referred to me gets a total knee replacement." Second opinions are valuable.

In my description of the fracture conferences at Mass General, I describe how often well-trained physicians disagree regarding suggested treatment. These reasonable disagreements also occur frequently in the evaluation and treatment of other problems. For degenerative arthritis of the knee, there is no good and clear evidence regarding the level of severity for which arthroscopic surgery is best and the level of severity for which total knee replacement is best. The optimal treatment also varies with age. For older patients, it is often better to avoid big operations.

With older patients, the risks of surgical treatment are higher. General anesthesia can cause permanent alterations in mental function. When should an older patient refuse surgery? When accept? I have seen patients refuse surgical reconstructive surgery due to their age. Then over a few years, these patients develop additional problems. With too many problems, these patients become too debilitated to treat and they rapidly decompensate further. Choosing reconstructive surgery can allow a longer active life. This decision accepts the increased risks of operating on older patients. There is no clear right or wrong answer to this question. It often depends on the psychology of the patient. Some older patients are more passive and accepting of their gradual increasing senescence. Others fight it more aggressively.

Wrong Site and Wrong Side Surgery

The issue of wrong side and wrong site surgery is constantly in the news. Call me lucky, fortunate or careful, I have avoided wrong side surgery in my career. In the past, patients signed written consent forms for surgery prior to the operation before seeing the surgeon on the day of surgery. On four occasions in my career, I have come into a hospital, looked at the consent form and noticed that the consent form was written for the incorrect side and signed by the patient for the incorrect side. How easy it would have been to operate on the wrong side. Fortunately, I noted it each of those times. Currently, patients sign the consent form in front of the surgeon.

In my orthopedic residency, one of my mentors always wrote "No" on the incorrect side when he saw the patient in the pre-op area. Epiphany. A brilliant, simple method of decreasing the risk of wrong side surgery. I followed his example and began writing "No" on the incorrect side for all of my surgeries. My reason for wanting to mark the incorrect side is to stop someone from starting to wash and prep the incorrect side. Thus, I wrote "No" in large letters.

The current national protocol instructs each surgeon to write his or her initials at the site of the surgery. The national protocol does not call for anything to be written on the incorrect side. I personally disagree with the national protocol. I like a warning on the incorrect side. Since "No" can be confused with a person's initials, I switched to writing in large letters with indelible pen the words, "WRONG SIDE" on the incorrect side.

I am aware of a wrong-side surgery performed at one of the hospitals I previously worked at. I discussed the case at length with two of the nurses who were in the operating room when this wrong-side surgery occurred. The patient suffered from severe dementia. She had a displaced fracture of the ball portion of the hip joint, which required replacement of the bony ball of the hip joint with a prosthetic metal ball. To perform this surgery, the patient is rolled on her side, after anesthesia is induced. After prepping and draping, an incision is made and dissection is carried out down to the hip joint. Only after entering the hip joint does the operating surgeon see the fracture.

In this case, the operating orthopedic surgeon was diligent and careful. He put the X-rays up on the viewing screen to double check which side had the fracture. Having put the X-rays up on the viewing screen, the operating orthopedic surgeon pointed to the X-rays and announced out loud to all personnel in the operating room which side they were going to operate on. He, again, carefully noted the side of the fracture. He specifically noted that the patient was in the correct position with the side of the fracture up. The surgeon proceeded to operate. On opening the hip joint, he discovered an intact hip. He recognized that he had opened the incorrect side. He closed the wound, turned the patient over and proceeded to operate on the correct hip.

What happened? The X-ray technician in the X-ray department who took the original X-rays labelled the X-rays incorrectly. The sides were reversed. The patient suffered from severe dementia and was unable to tell the surgeon which side hurt. It was not obvious by looking at the patient which side was fractured.

Sometime, early in my career, I saw one of my attending orthopedic surgeons rotate each leg of a senile preoperative hip fracture patient. He was looking to see which side caused the patient to grimace when he rotated the leg. The side which was painful with rotation was the side which was fractured. Epiphany! What a simple, easy, obsessive-compulsive way of ensuring identification of the side of a hip fracture. Yes, it causes the patient a little extra pain, but YES, YES, YES, it prevents wrong-side surgery. Ethically, the advantage of confirming the side of the fracture outweighs the concern of causing the patient a moment of increased pain. The maneuver of rotating each leg to confirm the side of the hip fracture would have prevented the wrong-side surgery mentioned above. It is a maneuver I used for every hip fracture I operated on throughout my career. I continue to discuss the randomness of medical and surgical training. Clearly not everyone does a leg rolling maneuver to check the fracture side. I ask, why not? Shouldn't something like this be part of basic orthopedic training? I think so. But, obviously, it is not. You can never be too careful. Murphy's Law—that if something can go wrong, it will—is alive and well in medicine and surgery.

I once performed an unnecessary surgery as the result of incorrect and inaccurate information from a totally conscious, alert and "with it" patient. The patient quite simply did not give me an accurate history. My patient fell off the back of a truck, injuring his shoulder. X-rays showed that the shoulder was dislocated. I attempted to reduce (put back in place) the shoulder in the emergency room, which is something that I was almost always successful in doing. I only failed with occasional chronic alcoholics who did not respond to sedation medication. My attempted reduction was unsuccessful. After further discussion with the patient, I took him to the operating room to reduce it under general anesthesia, something I was always able to do. Under general anesthesia, I was unable to maneuver the ball portion of the shoulder back into the socket. Never happened to me before in the shoulder. Never since. There are other joints for which irreducible dislocations are more common. In cases in which we orthopedic surgeons are unable to maneuver a dislocated joint back into place, there is usually some anatomic structure which has slipped into the joint, preventing relocation, which requires open surgery. What to do? Once again, the "what to do?" question.

I made an incision, prepared to dissect down to the shoulder joint to effect reduction. I found a surprise. The ball of the shoulder joint was sitting in its own little sack of soft tissue in front of the shoulder joint with no bleeding or injured tissue. Just old scar. There was no connection to the shoulder joint. The shoulder joint itself was completely filled with old scar tissue. There was no shoulder joint space into which I could shift the ball portion of the shoulder joint. My patient clearly had an old, chronic anterior dislocation of the shoulder. I closed up the wound.

After the patient awoke from anesthesia, I explained what I had found at surgery, that he had an old, chronic problem which was not the result of the fall from the truck. Thus, there was nothing to do about it. The patient did not complain about the unnecessary surgery. He did not explain to me why he had failed to inform me about the previous injury to his shoulder. I still do not understand why he neglected to tell me he had an old problem with his shoulder. Perhaps, he never knew it was dislocated. Perhaps, he thought he had a bad shoulder from an old injury. Perhaps, he had never had it evaluated by a physician. Perhaps, he had never previously had an X-ray of the shoulder.

Another example of a patient failing to give me important information. One Sunday, I treated a woman who fell down the icy steps of her church. She suffered a displaced fracture of a bone in her hand, which required surgery to put the fracture back in place and then hold it in place. She was elderly. Among the many questions I asked her prior to her surgery, "Have you ever had a heart attack." She said, "No." I asked her "Have you ever had chest pain." She said, "No." She appeared to be in good health except for advanced age.

I took her to the operating room to fix the fracture. I used a technique called a Bier Block in which you fill the arm with Novocain-like numbing medicine. The Novocain-like medicine is kept in the arm by a tight pneumatic tourniquet around the upper arm. The patient does not feel any pain. In essence, the rest of the body does not even know it is having an operation. A safe way of performing arm and hand surgery on elderly patients.

During the procedure, my patient began to complain of severe chest pain. Her electrocardiogram showed changes called elevated STT segments, which are EKG changes for an acute myocardial infarction (heart attack). She remained stable. I finished the surgery. She was transferred to the coronary care unit for treatment of her heart attack.

The following morning, I came by to see her. I expressed my surprise that she had had an acute heart attack during the surgery. I told her I was surprised because she had told me that she never had chest pain before. She laughed and told me, "Oh doctor, I have been having chest pain for a week." Surprised and shocked, I asked her why she hadn't told me. She replied, "Oh doctor, I didn't want to worry you." Her response left me gasping. Fortunately, she did well and left the hospital in stable condition. We physicians may know the correct questions to ask. We may not obtain truthful answers. Who can you trust?

Percutaneous Lumbar Discectomy

In a herniated disc the shock-absorbing material between the vertebral bones in the spine degenerates and bulges backwards into the spinal canal, often pinching nerves. When the pain is severe enough, for long enough, treatment may include open surgical removal of the bulging disc material. Percutaneous lumbar discectomy was a popular technique some years ago. The technique of percutaneous lumbar discectomy involves placing a small tube through the skin into a lumbar spine disk space to suck out and remove disc material to treat herniated lumbar discs. I used this procedure myself, and many of my patients had good results. Otherwise, these patients would have required open back surgery to treat their back and leg pain. If the percutaneous discectomy failed to work, open surgery remained an option.

The developer of the percutaneous lumbar discectomy technique gave seminars on how to perform the technique. If I recall correctly, at the first seminar I attended, the developer quoted 88% excellent results. I did not believe these numbers. Way too high for the treatment of back and/or leg pain. Not believable. I still used the procedure because I was getting perhaps 60% good results without open surgery.

A couple of years later, I attended a second seminar in which the developer announced a new and "improved" method of performing percutaneous discectomy. If I recall correctly, he now claimed 92% good results. Again, I did not believe his reported results. I continued using the procedure, however, because I was getting what I thought were acceptably good results without open back surgery. A few years later, I went to a third seminar. He announced another new and "improved" method. If I recall correctly, he was now claiming 96% good results. Once again, I did not believe his claimed results. I said to myself, at his claim of 96% good results, you're going to have to retire soon because you can't claim any greater improvement in results. I think he retired a few years later. I don't think I had anything to do with his retirement. In my hands, it was an acceptably good technique but by no means perfect. I never believed his claimed results. Have I ever raised the question before of who should you trust?

Basal Thumb Arthritis

There is a common arthritis which affects only the joint at the base of the thumb called basal thumb arthritis or carpometacarpal arthritis of the thumb. It occurs more often in women than in men at a ratio of four or five to one. As apes and early hominids developed opposable thumbs, the joint at the base of the thumb became flatter and flatter, which resulted in the increased motion necessary for an opposable thumb. As a consequence of the flattening of the joint surfaces, there was decreased stability of the carpometacarpal joint. Basal thumb arthritis occurs frequently in the non-dominant thumb. Thus, its occurrence is more due to a "natural" process than due to overuse of the hand and thumb.

A hip joint has a deep socket. The ball side of the hip joint seats deep within the bony socket giving the hip joint excellent bony stability. With excellent bony stability, one can stand and walk with relatively little use of muscles. Consider that you can stand or walk for long periods of time without serious fatigue, whereas, if you place your arm straight out at your side parallel to the ground, your shoulder muscles will fatigue quickly. In contrast to the hip joint, the joint at the base of the thumb is shaped like two flat saddles facing each other. The saddles are so flat, there is minimal bony stability.

For many patients, the onset of basal thumb arthritis begins when the outer or distal bone starts to shift slowly out of joint. As the bone begins to slide out of joint, the use and contraction of the small muscles that control the base of the thumb actually have greater efficiency in pulling the bone further out of joint. The abnormal stress and wear on the joint surfaces cause loss of articular cartilage, the covering of the bone at the joint that allows smooth gliding.

Non-surgical treatment of this arthritis includes hand therapy, anti-inflammatory medicine by mouth or cortisone shots and splinting. When that fails, there are surgical reconstructions. With your hand lying flat on a table palm down, spread your index finger outward toward your thumb. Now spread your index finger outward toward your thumb against resistance. Now look at your thumb as you push your index finger outward. You will see your thumb stiffen and pull inward slightly. The muscle which pulls your index finger outward has a small attachment to the bone at the base of your thumb, which is the bone that slips outward in basal thumb arthritis. Strengthening this muscle is one of the hand therapy exercises used to help this arthritis.

The number of different operations described for the treatment of basal thumb arthritis is large. Some years ago, I was at a three-day conference on hand surgery devoted just to treatment of arthritis of the upper extremity. One entire morning was reserved for discussion of the treatment of basal arthritis of the thumb. I remember Doctor A got up and discussed his results with Operation A. He claimed 80% good results. The audience of some 200 hand surgeons applauded politely. Then, Doctor B got up and discussed his results with Operation B, claiming 80% good results. Again, the audience applauded politely. Then Doctor C got up and claimed 80% good results with Operation C. Again, the audience applauded politely.

No one claimed greater than 80% good results. I believed them. Why? Up to this point in my career, I had tried four different operations for basal thumb arthritis. My results were never better than 80% good results for any of the operations I tried. The entire audience believed Doctors A, B and C. Why? Everyone in the audience was trying different operations and none of us was getting better than 80% good results. Anyone claiming better results would have been laughed out of the room. These were real, honest presenters, unlike the unrealistically high results for percutaneous discectomy I discussed earlier. I used the term "good results" above. This is obviously a somewhat arbitrary classification but is often the best we can do in evaluating results following surgery in orthopedics and hand surgery.

There is a classic operation for basal thumb arthritis called the LRTI, which stands for ligament reconstruction, tendon interposition. In the LRTI procedure, no attempt is made to reconstruct the arthritic joint. The bone of the arthritic joint on one side of the joint is surgically removed. A tendon or portion of a tendon from the forearm is used to create a strong ligament to suspend the base of the thumb. The LRTI procedure provides, with a reasonably high degree of success, a pain-free, usable thumb. It does not restore normal pinch or grip strength. During the course of my career, as stated above, I utilized at least four different operations, finally settling on the LRTI. At the end of the morning presentations I described above, there was a panel discussion. The conclusion was that the LRTI remained the gold standard. For any new operation to become widely used, it would have to be clearly superior to the LRTI. So far, none have.

Some years ago, I interviewed a prospective hand surgeon for our practice. He was training with a group of three hand surgeons. I asked him which surgical technique for treating basal thumb arthritis his supervising hand surgeons were teaching him. The applicant told me that each of the three hand surgeons was using a different operation. Wow! Even within one small group of hand surgeons, there was no agreement on which operation for basal thumb arthritis was best. Another situation in which who you choose to operate on you determines which operation is chosen. You as a layman can't choose the operation. You can only choose your surgeon.

Early in my career, I utilized an older, now abandoned, technique to reconstruct basal thumb arthritis. This technique used a type of plastic, called silicone, as a spacer. I had good results with the silicone spacer technique a long time ago. It fell into disfavor because of a small incidence of inflammatory erosion of bone from silicone particles. There was a patient I performed the silicone spacer operation on in the early 1980s. The patient did well and was discharged from my care. Many years passed. My wife and I decided to build a water feature in our backyard. My wife hired a husband and wife team to do the work. The gentleman appeared to be in his 60s. I watched with awe as he, a

60+-year-old man, carried large cinder blocks with just his thumb and fingers, with the cinder blocks hanging down.

As I was writing the check to pay for his work, the man noted my last name and said, "Your father operated on my thumb many years ago." I said, "No. That was me." I then went on to say that given the operation I had performed it was "impossible!" for him to have the strength to carry cinder blocks as he had carried them. I asked him to come to my office for X-rays so that I could see what his thumb looked like. The X-rays showed that over time the silicone spacer had slipped out of position. The X-rays also showed that his body had somehow formed an entire new large joint at the base of the thumb with a wide new joint space. He was able to carry the cinder blocks because the silicone spacer was out in the soft tissue and he was using his "new" stable joint. If we could just figure out how to stimulate the body to form new joints like happened by chance to this one patient, it would be a major advance. I only ever saw a new joint form like happened to this patient one time.

First Examination for the Certificate of Added Qualification in Surgery of the Hand

In 1998, the first examination for obtaining the Certificate of Added Qualification in Surgery of the Hand was administered. It was like a subspecialty board examination, but for some reason they deliberately did not call this exam a subspecialty board exam. Prior to the exam, review courses in hand surgery were given. Just about everyone who was planning on taking the exam attended these review courses, even the professors. I took the exam, along with hundreds of other hand surgeons. I was fascinated to see all of the "gray hair" world famous hand surgeons sitting in the exam room along with me concentrating furiously on the exam. After the exam, everyone stood around asking each other which answers they chose for certain questions. Just like in high school, college and medical school. I stood outside of a circle of four or five of the world's more renowned hand surgeons. Just like kids, they were going through the questions, asking each other what their answers were.

For one question, the test showed a postoperative X-ray following the silicone spacer operation for basal thumb arthritis. The X-ray showed that the spacer had slipped out of position. The question on the test stated, "This happened because:" The multiple-choice answers included: the prosthesis was too big; the ligament reconstruction was insufficient; the cavity for the prosthesis was too small. I forget the two other choices. When I read the question while taking the exam, I thought that each of the three answers I mentioned above was correct. So, I randomly chose one. As I was standing outside of the group of "gray hairs," the silicone spacer question came up. As they went around the circle, each of them had chosen a different answer. So, what was the right answer? This test was written by a small group of hand surgeons. One of the themes of my book, highlighted in my description of the fracture conferences at Mass General, is the honest differences in opinions we orthopedic surgeons may have. Prior to the test, no specific "passing grade" was determined. When the results of the test were announced, the administrators of the test stated that they threw out any question which less than 80% of test takers got right. So, I think that question was probably one of the ones thrown out. There was no "right" answer.

The administrators of the test published a graph of the test scores. Normally, you would expect a graph that peaks at some point and slopes down on both sides. The results from this test showed a large peak near a high score, then a valley and a second peak near a lower score. It was as if there were two different populations of test takers. The administrators arbitrarily determined that the passing score was any score above the bottom of the valley in the graph. I think about 80% passed.

Lyme Disease: Orthopedic Presentation

The practice of any medical specialty varies depending on the geographical location of the doctor. For example, Lyme disease is endemic in Maryland, where I practice. The history of the discovery of Lyme disease is worth discussing. Juvenile rheumatoid arthritis is an uncommon disease. An epidemiologist noted that in a part of Lyme, Connecticut, ten percent of teenagers had been diagnosed with juvenile rheumatoid arthritis. His investigation showed that these teenagers were infected with an unknown organism which turned out to be the Lyme disease organism. Lyme disease is more common in Maryland than in Lyme, Connecticut. Diseases are often called by the geographical location where they were first discovered, rather than where they are most common. Lyme disease is spread by the bite of a specific tick. Rocky Mountain Spotted fever is much more common on Cape Cod but was first discovered in the Rocky Mountains.

Typical Lyme disease often presents with a bull's-eye type of rash which allows for a quick diagnosis in these patients. During my 37 years of practice in Maryland, I diagnosed approximately five or six new cases of Lyme disease each year. None of my patients reported a history of a rash or a history of a tick bite. Only one of my patients gave a history of walking in the woods. The presenting complaint for all of them was a swollen wrist, knee or ankle joint. As an orthopedic and hand surgeon, I obviously saw a specific subset of Lyme disease patients: those whose first symptom was only a swollen joint. Example: 10-year-old boy is running and hits his knee on a house. Comes in with a swollen knee with extra fluid in the knee joint. There is no abrasion or bruising of the knee joint. With no abrasion or bruising, it was highly unlikely the fluid in the knee joint was the result of hitting his knee. I order a Lyme titer test. One week later the test comes back positive for Lyme disease. I call his mother. She tells me the swelling has gone away. Her child is normal and asymptomatic. If I had not ordered the Lyme titer test at the first visit, there would have been a serious delay in making the diagnosis and in starting antibiotic treatment. A delay in the treatment of Lyme disease may result in serious permanent problems. In Maryland and anywhere that has a significant incidence of Lyme disease, ALL, repeat, ALL patients with a spontaneous swollen joint should get an immediate Lyme titer test. I repeat, only one of my patients reported walking in the woods. Thus, the absence of a history of walking in the woods should not decrease the concern for Lyme disease as the diagnosis.

Patients' Expectations of Treatment

Patients have certain expectations of the treatment they receive from their doctor. I have mentioned previously that I used to work in emergency rooms, moonlighting. I worked fee for service, which means I billed patients directly. I was not paid a salary. Patients sometimes came in with a simple puncture wound of their foot that had happened within the previous few hours. Most simple foot puncture wounds do not require treatment. Most heal without problem. Occasional puncture wounds become infected. Puncture wounds that occur through a sneaker have a higher risk of infection with pseudomonas, a difficult bacterium to treat. If a patient with a puncture wound of the foot develops an infection or an abscess, treatment with antibiotics and/or surgery is then indicated. Antibiotics are not indicated prophylactically for every simple puncture wound. No treatment is indicated for a small simple puncture wound on the sole of the foot that does not appear to have a retained foreign body.

Initially, I counseled patients with simple puncture wounds of the foot that nothing needed to be done, that the patient should return if the foot became infected. I charged a minimum emergency room fee. Many patients complained and refused to pay their bill because "I hadn't done anything." Evaluating, diagnosing and counseling wasn't considered "worthy" of payment. So, I learned. Henceforth, I carefully washed each foot with Betadine soap, an antibacterial solution. Then, I applied antibiotic ointment and applied a large bandage. I also gave the same counseling. The complaints disappeared. My bills were paid without question. Patients wanted "treatment," they could "see" and "feel," so I gave them "treatment," they could "see" and "feel."

Another vignette regarding patients' expectation of treatment. There are five "short'" long bones, or "long" short bones in the forefoot called metatarsals. A strong tendon glides down the lower leg and attaches to the base of the most lateral metatarsal. This tendon swings the foot laterally toward the outside. In a situation in which you stumble and your foot turns inward, the muscle which controls this tendon pulls really hard on the tendon to try to straighten the ankle. If the tendon pulls too hard, the proximal end of the bone, the fifth metatarsal, pulls off, causing a fracture of the proximal tip of the bone. A common fracture. In my entire career, all healed without long-term problems. I was taught in my training to treat these patients with "benign neglect." Weight bearing as tolerated. A soft wrap for a few days for comfort.

Early in my practice, two patients were upset, that I did not take their problem "seriously." They were upset that I did not provide sufficient "treatment." These two patients were so upset that they independently filed formal complaints about my treatment to the Commission on Medical Discipline for the State of Maryland. In their letters of complaint, they each stated they found a doctor who took them seriously and who put them in a short leg cast.

The Commission agreed my care was proper in both cases.

I note that a short leg cast is not without risk of complications. A short leg cast increases the risk of phlebitis, which is venous blood clots in the leg. These blood clots can break off, travel to the lung, block the blood vessels of the lungs and cause death. In fact, in 37 years of practice in an orthopedic group that has varied between three and eight orthopedic surgeons, we had one unfortunate patient in a short leg cast who died of a pulmonary embolism (blood clot to the lung). The risk is real. Our group has seen it. From my point of view, the treatment of the fracture mentioned above with a short leg cast, which the patients loved, was dangerous overtreatment.

A quick mnemonic on the difference between metacarpal and metatarsal. The metacarpal bone is in the hand. The metatarsal in the foot. Your catch a carp with your hands. Thus, metacarpal is in the hand. You walk on tar, thus the metatarsal is in the foot. While in medical school we frequently used mnemonics to help memorize anatomy. My favorite joke mnemonic was the TEON mnemonic. TEON stood for "Two Eyes; One Nose." In case you forgot. We also had the SEW mnemonic. SEW stood for "Shoulder, Elbow, Wrist", in case you forgot their order.

More on the metacarpals. The fourth and fifth metacarpal bones are frequently fractured. There are two common mechanisms which cause these fractures. First is the punch: either someone's jaw or a handy wall in anger. Take your hand and try to push and pull the distal ends of the second (index) and third (middle) metacarpal up and down. They do not move. The joints in the middle of the hand are rigid and allow little motion. If you try pushing the distal ends of the fourth (ring) and fifth (little) metacarpals up and down, you will find there is significantly more motion. When the distal end of the fourth or fifth metacarpal hits a hard object during a punch, the distal end moves downward. The forward motion of the hand then makes it easy to break the bone. These are called boxer's fractures.

Many orthopedic and hand surgeons try to reduce (put back in place) these fractures and then hold them in a snug splint or cast. During the course of my career, I saw few if any patients with late complications of untreated boxer's fractures which required treatment. Whereas I saw numerous patients with stiff fingers resulting from the treatment of these fractures. Fingers do not like immobilization! They scar and get sticky easily. Once stiff, obtaining good motion is difficult. I think these fractures are often overtreated.

Another type of metacarpal fracture is caused by sideways pressure on the partially flexed finger, which results in a long spiral fracture of the bone. If there is sufficient rotatory displacement of the metacarpal fracture, the attached finger will not flex into the palm normally. It will overlap or deviate from an adjacent finger, an abnormality commonly missed by emergency room physicians and physicians in walk-in clinics. These fractures require closed manipulation to correct the rotation deformity and buddy taping to a neighboring finger or open surgery if unstable. Buddy taping involves taping the injured finger to a neighboring finger with thin tape keeping the joints free of tape. The uninjured finger acts as a "moving splint" allowing the injured finger to move with flexion and extension while being protected from side to side or rotation stresses.

Terminal Illness and Dying

Another vignette. This time from the patient's family's point of view. Actually, from my point of view. I was travelling with my family in Bryce and Zion National Parks. When I returned to our motel one evening, I received a message that my mother had fallen, broken her hip and would be operated on the next morning. The following morning as I was making a reservation to fly to Cincinnati, I received a call that the surgery was over, but that my mother was unconscious and the treating physicians did not know why.

I arrived in Cincinnati later that day and found my mother in the ICU (intensive care unit) connected to multiple machines including an EEG (electroencephalogram) with EEG electrodes all over her head. She was suffering continual seizures, called status epilepticus. Status epilepticus is constant and continual seizures in the brain, a rare condition. These continual seizures rapidly damage the brain permanently if they are not stopped. Despite intensive medical treatment, days passed with the seizures continuing non-stop. No one is talking to me about what is happening to my mother. I am assuming that her brain has been severely and permanently damaged by the passage of time. No one is talking to me or giving me information, even though I am at the bedside all day, every day.

I read and reread my mother's advanced directives. The neurologist in this academic center makes rounds each day with a coterie of fellows, residents, interns and medical students. I am on the opposite side now. The patient's family's side. Day after day, this academic robot …. no, I shouldn't say that. It is unfair to humanoid robots to come. Anyway, neurology robot scarcely recognizes my existence. I misspeak. He does not recognize my existence. He walks right by me.

Days pass. I am there every day. All day. There has been no progress in stopping these continual seizures. Finally, I decide that it is time to make decisions regarding my mother's treatment. I don't know when in the day, "Neurology Robot" will arrive to make rounds. It is a different time each day. I don't want to miss him. I call him three times during the morning to inquire when he will round on my mother. I wish to make an appointment to see him. He does not respond.

From early morning through mid-afternoon, I do not take a bathroom break or go for lunch. I do not want to miss him. Finally, in the midafternoon, he struts in with his entourage. I interrupt him to get his attention. I ask him for information regarding the question of whether there has been permanent damage to my mother's brain. I ask whether there is any chance she may recover.

He gives me some weird answer, starting with the phrase, "From a legal point of view…." I do pull out of him, reluctantly, that yes there is permanent, severe damage. My mother will not recover. I regret that I did not turn to his coterie and use him as a teaching example of how "not" to behave with family. At the start of my book, I inserted a four-line motto. The first line, "Learn from everyone," applies here. Not the only time I learned from the negative behavior of others.

Prior to my experience with my mother's terminal illness, my wife and I had written our own personal advanced directives. Originally, we allowed for the withholding of food and water in terminal end-of-life situations. After discussion with friends, my wife and I changed our directives to prevent the withholding of food and water, thinking that was cruel. My mother had a long and remarkably healthy life up to age 87. The day she broke her hip, she played bridge with friends in the afternoon. While walking to her car to drive her friends to a restaurant, she fell swatting at a bee. As the only member of her group of friends still driving, she was popular. Her group of friends called themselves "The Saturday Night Club." You did not need to attend their Saturday night "meetings," but any members of the "club" who did not have other plans got together each Saturday night for cards and dinner.

Confronted with the information that our mother had suffered severe and permanent brain damage, my sister and I elected to withhold intravenous food and water. My mother died without suffering a few days later. Having lived through the decision regarding my mother's care, my wife and I immediately changed our advanced directives to allow the withholding of food and water. We doctors and sometimes family have the ability to prolong suffering in elderly patients for entirely too long.

Deep Pain; The Use of Computer Mice

I previously discussed learning how to properly position myself when performing microsurgery. The lessons I learned in performing microsurgery translate into many of our everyday tasks. For example, the use of a standard, ordinary, original, classic computer mouse requires the muscles on the back of the forearm to remain in constant contraction to hold the wrist up continually. In addition, the shoulder muscles are in constant use, moving the mouse around in frequent small motions. While many people tolerate prolonged computer mouse use without complaint, my office was filled with a constant stream of patients with vague complaints of aching in the neck, shoulders, upper arms, forearms, wrists and/or hands from extensive computer mouse use.

Deep pain is diffuse, achy, poorly localized, radiates a distance and is difficult to describe. It is important that a doctor take the time to find the correct questions to ask in order to make the correct diagnosis. The doctor has to find out how the patient is using her hand and arm in order to figure out whether the symptoms are coming from computer mouse usage.

There are "pointing" devices in which the hand rests comfortably, little finger side down in a groove. The thumb moves a trackball on top and the index and middle finger click buttons for left and right clicks. The shoulder muscles, upper arm muscles and forearm muscles remain totally relaxed. I have "sold" hundreds of these devices over the years, especially to graphic designers and people who spend more than 50% of their day using "mice."

For any job you perform it is important to be an educated "consumer." It is important to think about how you can do your job as safely and thoughtfully as possible. Some examples. When my wife and I lived in Boston we hired a local moving company. In those days my desk was two metal filing cabinets covered with a piece of plywood we had varnished. Our bookcase was cinder blocks with pieces of plywood we had varnished. The cinder blocks were sitting in a box. One of the movers picked up the extremely heavy box of cinder blocks by himself and carried it out. Smart would have been to use a two-wheeled cart.

If you have something heavy to carry, better that two of you share the burden than for one of you to carry it. Always use wheels when you can.

More on the radiation of deep pain. I recall being taught about a study performed in the mid-1900s. An orthopedic surgeon took test subjects and injected a salty solution into the ligaments at different levels of their lower backs. Regardless of which level of the lower back he injected, the test subjects experienced pain in the lower back and/or buttocks and/or posterior thigh. Thus, irritation of ligaments at any level of the lower back may cause pain in any of those areas. Conversely, the specific location of pain in the lower back and/or buttocks and/or posterior thigh gives no information regarding which level in the lower back the pain is coming from.

Pinched nerves in the lower two levels of the lower back may cause pain to radiate down the leg to the foot. Pinched nerves in the upper levels of the lower back may cause pain to radiate to the groin and/or anterior thigh. Similarly, pinched nerves in the neck may cause pain to radiate down into the hand. The location of pain from pinched nerves may provide specific information regarding the location of the pinched nerve.

Pain in low back, buttocks and posterior thigh is not specific with respect to site of origin. Many patients with pain in their buttocks think that their pain is coming from the sacroiliac joint. The sacroiliac joint is a large, stable joint. I doubt it often causes pain. More likely pain in the buttock area is referred from the low back.

Regarding Education

One year early in my practice, I entered an examining room to see a new patient. I had a number of information sheets on different topics that I routinely handed out to patients. My new patient was reading these sheets. He looked up and smiled. Before I even said, "Hello," the patient said, "I have been reading these. I give them a D+ grade." I smiled and said, "I wrote them." We had a good laugh. At the end of the office visit, he offered to edit them for me. He was a professor of English at a local university and taught non-fiction writing. Fortunately, he responded well to treatment.

Some years later, he called me. He was organizing a course on science writing and asked for my suggestions. I told him of my experience at Boston City Hospital, discussed earlier. I discussed that if you want to write, for example, about volcanoes, write one article for fourth graders, one for tenth graders and one for *Scientific American*. Not only does the information presented have to change, but the complexity of words and concepts also have to change, depending on the audience. My patient thanked me and told me later that he had used these suggestions for the course he taught. Sounds like a good science writing course. This course was in college. Surely, this kind of teaching should be presented to students far earlier.

Banning an Artificial Sweetener

While at medical school the head of HEW (Health, Education and Welfare) spoke at Harvard. He was asked about the recent ban by the government of an artificial sweetener. He explained that he was against the ban. However, there was a law passed by Congress that any substance reported to cause cancer in laboratory animals, no matter how mild an effect, had to be banned. Researchers had fed enormous amounts of the artificial sweetener to rats. A mild increase in cancers was noted. The head of HEW said that when he read this report, he did two things. First, he called his wife and told her to go to the supermarket and buy their entire supply of the artificial sweetener. Then he called the press and announced the ban.

While on my cardiology rotation, I attended a seminar in which a visiting professor described increased heart risk from the use of certain modified fats in food. Immediately after the seminar, there was a line eight deep of residents and staff waiting to use the two landline phones in the department. Everyone panicked. They had to call their family immediately to tell them to stop using the modified fat. They had been eating it for years, but the information could not wait until that evening. Before the days of cellphones.

We Don't Know What We Don't Know

I recall discussions and teaching about Parkinson's disease and duodenal ulcers while in medical school and resident training. There was strong opinion that Parkinson's disease was a secondary effect of the flu epidemic of 1917. We were taught that everyone who had Parkinson's had had the flu in 1917. We were taught that Parkinson's disease would become rare in the future. We now know that this "knowledge" was nonsense.

We were also taught that ulcers mainly occurred in Type A, passive aggressive personalities. I recall standing outside of a patient's room while on rounds. We listened to him scream on the phone at an employee of his about how awful it was to be cooped up in the hospital with an ulcer. We then entered the room. The patient smiled and greeted us warmly. Our attending later explained how this patient's behavior was typical for an ulcer patient. We now know that ulcers result from a bacterial infection.

We so often hear the trite, but wise, saying uttered, "We don't know what we don't know." This statement is, of course, true. Equally important is the fact that we don't know which parts of "what we really think we know" are false. Herd mentality enters here. It is difficult to change our beliefs when we believe them strongly.

Medicare and the Law of Unintended Consequences

I want to briefly discuss the "law of unintended consequences" with respect to governmental regulation. The Medicare law was passed in 1965. According to the law, the government paid for hospital tests ordered on inpatients, but did not pay for tests ordered on outpatients. As a result, doctors admitted patients to the hospital, ordered the tests, then discharged the patients. Thus, the number of unnecessary hospital admissions soared. All paid for by taxpayers, that is, by you and me. There was no control over hospital admissions. That has now changed. Now, Medicare will pay for post-hospitalization rehabilitation if a patient has been admitted as an inpatient for more than three days. Many patients who are ready for rehab before three days has passed are kept in the hospital until the three-day period has elapsed. Then they are transferred to rehab, paid for by Medicare. Thus, extra days of hospitalization are paid for by Medicare.

I have recently read of another unintended consequence issue resulting from government regulation and oversight. Hospitals are carefully monitored for incidents of falls causing injury to inpatients. Hospitals in the category of highest incidence of falls are penalized financially. Correspondingly, nurses with the highest fall rate of their patients are also penalized. The result? Patients are not allowed out of bed! I have discussed previously the importance of moving fingers and shoulders. Movement is important for the health of the entire body. Elderly patients kept at bed rest rapidly decompensate, requiring prolonged rehabilitation. When my mother-in-law was hospitalized in her late 80s, the nurses would not allow her out of bed. They would not allow my wife, a trained physical therapist, to get her mother up and walk with her.

Thoughts Regarding Nursing Staffing in Hospitals

When I was in my training, nurses worked as a team. Each day when we residents came in to make rounds, the head nurse stopped what she was doing and walked with us on rounds. She knew all of the patients. Starting sometime in the late 1970s, I think, the structure of nursing care changed. The head nurses at many of the hospitals I worked at became administrators. They were forever at meetings and did not know the patients. The new system was called primary care nursing. Each nurse was assigned only a few patients. The thinking was that there would be a better patient-nurse relationship because the patient would see the same nurse every day.

When I was in practice in the 1980s, my partners and I noted that whenever we asked a nurse a question about a patient, we often received the reply, "I don't know. This is my first day taking care of this patient." For example, one day I rounded on a post-operative total hip replacement patient and found a wet betadine dressing on the wound. Worried that it was infected, I peeled down the dressing. The wound looked fine. The nurse in charge of my patient's care that morning said, "This is my first day taking care of the patient. I don't know." No nurse's notes from the previous day reflected who applied the wet betadine dressing or why this dressing was applied. No other nurse working on the floor that morning knew anything about my patient. None had taken care of her before. On any given morning, if I asked any nurse if she wanted to round with me, she laughed. None of the nurses then working had ever heard of such a thing.

After many similar episodes, I did a mini-survey of two of my hospitals. I asked 50 nurses how many days in a row they had been taking care of my patient I was rounding on. I also asked if they were full-time or part-time nurses. I found that a significant percentage of nurses were working part time. I found that slightly more than 50% of the time, it was a nurse's first day taking care of my patient. Thus, this method of structuring the nursing assignments actually resulted in reduced nurse-patient relationships.

When it is a nurse's first day taking care of a patient and when no other nurse on the floor knows the patient, there is poor follow up. If it is a nurse's first day taking care of a patient, there is no way that a nurse will be able to detect a subtle change in the patient. When there is a high percentage of part-time nurses, a team nursing approach will ensure that on any given day, there will be at least one nurse who was helping care for a patient the day before.

I brought my limited survey information to the head nurses of the two hospitals. I recommended they do larger surveys in their respective hospital. They were not interested. They were wedded to the concept of one nurse taking care of a few patients. During these same years, one of the hospitals I worked at continued the team nursing system. This hospital also employed older, more experienced nurses than the other two hospitals. The nursing care at that hospital was markedly superior. Let me emphasize: The difference in the quality of nursing care between these hospitals was due more to the "structure" of the nursing system than due to the individual nurses.

270

Airbags

Airbags in cars save countless lives. They also cause specific injuries themselves. I have read that the speed of the airbag at its initial deployment is nearly 200 miles per hour. Most of the injuries caused by airbags I have seen occurred in patients of short stature who sat close to the airbag. I have seen a number of unusual fractures and/or dislocations of fingers which occurred when the patient's hand was resting on the airbag cover when the airbag deployed. One patient saw a car closing at a high rate of speed in the rear-view mirror. He put up his hand in reflex as if to block the oncoming car. His car was hit and pushed into the car in front of him. The airbag deployed, pushing his arm forcefully upwards, severely injuring nerves in his shoulder area called a brachial plexus palsy. Permanent pain and weakness of the arm resulted.

When to Use a New Surgical Technique

As new procedures are developed in medicine and surgery, it is always difficult to know when to begin using a new procedure. There continues to be interest in a technique of minimal incision total hip replacement surgery. Using a minimal incision sounds so cool. I mean, really, if you had total hip surgery, wouldn't you like to have a smaller scar, with less pain and earlier discharge from the hospital? The possibilities for advertising and promotion are endless.

In the midst of the hoopla regarding this "new technique," an interesting paper was published from a large group of orthopedic surgeons in California. They reported on over 100 total hip replacements done the old way with the larger incision and over 100 total hip operations done the new way with the minimal incision. They found a significantly greater incidence of malposition of the prostheses in the group with the minimal incisions. Malposition means that the prosthesis was not placed in the optimal orientation. Malposition results in the total hip prosthesis not working as well and not lasting as long as it would if the position of the prosthesis was ideal. In addition, the incidence of malposition did not decrease with increasing experience with the minimal incision technique. The incidence of malposition of the total hip prosthesis did not appear to be a learning curve problem. It appeared to be a problem inherent with the technique. The incision was too small. Visibility was too limited. The surgeon could not see well enough to ensure correct alignment of the prosthesis. The authors of the article discouraged the use of the minimal incision for total hip surgery.

Treatment of Jehovah's Witness Patients

I have participated in the treatment of a few Jehovah's Witness patients over the years. Their religious tenets do not allow for the administration of blood or blood products. In an acute trauma situation with a conscious patient capable of making her wishes known, it is clear that these patients would rather die from blood loss than have a transfusion. I have never personally been involved in that situation. I have been involved in discussions with these patients regarding elective surgery. For minor surgery, there is no problem. The probability of needing blood transfusions is remote. For bigger operations like total joint replacements, the ethics are not clear. While many patients do not require blood transfusions, some do. Is it ethical for a surgeon to agree to perform an elective operation which might result in the death of a patient because of the inability to provide blood transfusions as treatment? I suppose each doctor has to decide for herself.

When I was in Boston in my orthopedic training, there was a "work around" that we sometimes used, with the patient's full knowledge and permission. We took the patient into the operation room, inserted a large bore needle into a large vein, allowed the patient's blood to drain out of the body into a blood bag by lowering the blood bag below the level of the patient. We replaced the lost blood volume with saline infusion. The key here is that we never turned a stopcock to disconnect the blood in the bag from the patient. This method the Jehovah's Witness patients allowed.

We then performed the surgery. Blood loss from the surgery was "diluted" blood, which had been diluted by the saline infused after the blood had been drained off. After the surgery was finished, the blood in the bags, which had been kept below the level of the patient, was then raised above the level of the

A Cornucopia of Vignettes

patient. The pressure of the elevated level caused the blood to flow back into the patient.

Incidence of Errors in Reading X-Rays

There is extensive literature examining and discussing the incidence of errors in reading X-rays, CT scans and MRIs. Chest X-rays were used for diagnosing tuberculosis prior to the 1970s. Small circular lesions in the lung, which are smaller than three centimeters, are called coin lesions. Coin lesions can be an early X-ray finding in lung cancer. The error rate in missing coin lesions in many studies easily exceeded ten percent. I was taught in my training to rotate every chest X-ray I was examining 90 degrees as part of my evaluation. Our brains are hardwired for recognizing patterns. Turning the X-ray 90 degrees eliminates the patterns we are used to seeing, like the shapes of the ribs, blood vessels and heart. This method of viewing chest X-rays allows circular shapes to pop into our consciousness. Most radiologists I have talked to were not taught this technique. Double independent reading of radiologic studies would cut down the error rate. To my knowledge, it is not done routinely for most radiologic studies.

When to Order a Diagnostic Test

Some problems are just really hard to diagnose. A pulmonologist referred me a patient with pain in the area of the lower ribs on the left side. The patient had had the rib pain for a few months. The pulmonologist had taken chest X-rays. They were normal. The physical examination was normal. I repeated the chest X-ray and took rib X-rays. All normal. I listened to the patient's chest. Normal. The patient's complaints seemed real. In desperation, I ordered a CT of the chest. It showed a small cancer hidden in the bottom of the lung far to the side. I called the pulmonologist with the finding.

For our own education, we reviewed all of the previous chest and rib X-rays. Even knowing where to look, we could not see the cancer. We took the X-rays and rib films to radiologists for review and none of us could see the cancer on any of the plain films. Why was I successful in making this patient's diagnosis?

I don't like to be stumped. I like to find answers. I listen to my patients. Perhaps I order more tests.

There is serious discussion in the medical community regarding possible harm to patients from ordering too many unnecessary diagnostic studies. There are risks from radiation from X-rays, bone scans and CT scans. There are risks from the additional studies performed to evaluate abnormal findings on the initial studies. Prior to my ordering the CT scan for this patient, it would have been easy to argue that this study was unnecessary, that it exposed the patient to too much X-ray. Clearly, it was "necessary" in this patient. It allowed the cancer to be detected sooner rather than later.

Earlier in my book, I discussed the question asked in my interview for general surgical internship at Mass General, "Can lung cancer ever present with pain as the first symptom?" This patient was a case of lung cancer presenting with pain as the initial symptom. Only one I ever saw. The cancer was at the edge of the lung and had spread into the space between the lung and the chest wall, which was the cause of the irritation and pain. I wonder if I had seen this patient before my interview whether my interview would have been better. Would my life have changed, for better or worse, by an internship at Mass General? So many "what ifs?" in life.

When Abortions Were Illegal

In the late 1960s and early 1970s abortions were severely restricted in Massachusetts. I was taught that the only legal reason for an abortion was psychiatric. For some of the years during my training, two abortions were performed each Friday at Peter Bent Brigham Hospital. Two women in the first trimester of pregnancy were admitted to the hospital and seen by two psychiatrists. Each psychiatrist wrote an opinion that the patient was now normal but would have serious psychiatric issues if the pregnancy was continued. Such were the machinations necessary to subvert restrictive regulations.

Many abortions were performed illegally outside of hospitals, so-called kitchen table abortions, often, I was told, performed with bent coat hangers.

The ends of coat hangers are sharp, making it easy to perforate the uterus during the procedure. When the uterus is perforated, infection can enter the pelvis and abdomen causing death or sterility.

When the government makes something illegal, it makes it dangerous and/ or profitable. Both are serious and unwanted civic outcomes. As a medical student, I volunteered at a free medical clinic in Cambridge. In the late 1960s, rich people who wanted abortions flew to Sweden for easy, safe abortions. Poor people did not have that option. The law of unintended consequences, sometimes stated as, "you can never do only one thing." Outlaw abortions? Doesn't impact the rich. They fly to Sweden. Impacts only the poor. They are at higher risk of death or sterility because they get the kitchen table abortions. As a medical student, I participated in the care of women who died from the complications of illegal abortions.

At the free medical clinic in Cambridge, I was told that there was an "underground railroad" to a "safe" abortionist. I was told at the clinic that if I saw someone who needed an abortion to give that patient a specific name. The name of the contact was a Catholic priest. Wow! Wonderful man. Holy man. A man with pity, truly caring for people who needed help. A man looking beyond doctrine to real need. A blessed man.

When considering the issue of unintended consequences, I think of the results to society from the criminalization of drugs. Certainly, legalizing drugs has its own serious consequences. The empowerment of drug gangs, which results from the criminalization of drugs, seems worse.

CHAPTER EIGHTEEN

The Importance of Making the Correct Diagnosis: Thinking Outside of the Cage (Box)

More vignettes. No obvious order. Watch the pinball of my memories bounce off the bumpers in my brain. Here are some more examples of when you have to think "outside the box" or "outside the cage" (I prefer cage) in medical practice, when you have to recognize that you have a patient with a problem which requires creative thinking.

A patient suffered an ankle fracture of the bones on each side of her ankle which were displaced. A displaced fracture of the bones on both sides of the ankle does not do well without surgery because it is difficult to manipulate the fragments into proper position and then hold them in the correct position. More than difficult, it is usually impossible. This patient's legs were covered with innumerable scratches and scabs of different ages. She had a problem called neurotic dermatitis. She was continually scratching her legs to the point of drawing blood. Her legs were covered with multiple open contaminated sores in different stages of healing.

Operating on his ankle immediately was inadvisable. The probability of deep infection following open surgery was high due to the colonization of all of the open sores with bacteria.

There is a technique for trying to manipulate the bone fragments into place which was called Quigley traction in Boston at that time. A long stocking (the material is called stockinette) is placed up the leg to the upper thigh, with the patient lying on his back. The leg is then crossed, like when you are sitting cross-legged. The end of the stockinette is kept long and tied to an IV pole so that the ankle is suspended in the air with pressure of the stockinette holding the ankle internally rotated and inverted. Quigley traction frequently reduces the displaced ankle fracture fragments into proper position without other specific manipulation. A cast is then applied while the leg is hanging in this position.

I placed the leg in Quigley traction and applied a long leg cast. I planned to keep the cast on for two weeks. The cast would prevent further scratching and would allow all of the sores to heal. I planned on removing the cast and proceeding to surgery after the two-week period of skin healing. I and the patient had unexpected good luck. The fracture remained in good position and healed in good position in the cast. I never had to operate.

I had a patient with a similar fracture of the bones on both sides of the ankle. She weighed 360 pounds and was five foot four inches tall. The distal fracture fragments were quite small, less than half an inch in size on each side of the ankle. The size of the leg was too big for any cast to hold the fracture fragments in any position which would approach satisfactory. Surgery would not work because any fixation would not be strong due to the small size of the distal fracture fragments. In addition, any surgical fixation could not be protected by a cast due to the size and shape of the patient's leg. Closed manipulation and casting as discussed above would not work for the reasons given above. What to do?

There are techniques of external fixation in which pins are placed into the bones with a long end sticking out of the skin. I have discussed techniques of external fixation previously for treatment of wrist fractures and for treatment of the segmental femoral fracture. I chose to manipulate the fracture fragments into position and hold them in position using pins into bones of the feet and pins into bones of the lower legs. I then locked everything in position with an external fixator. Given the size of the patient and the difficult nature of the fracture, she did surprisingly well. I had never seen external fixation used for a similar ankle fracture before. Proper treatment required creative thinking.

More on thinking outside of the cage. I operated on a workers' compensation patient with a torn meniscus in her knee. The operation was "routine." I was able to quickly and easily remove the torn portion of the meniscus. She was young. Normally after routine arthroscopic surgery, patients improve rapidly and often return to work in three weeks for non-strenuous work and six weeks for strenuous work. My patient did not move her knee post-op. The therapists were unable to get her to move her knee. It was not clear if she had a psychological block or was attempting to obtain more money from the workers' compensation insurance company. What to do?

At three weeks post-op, with essentially no knee motion, I took the patient back to the operating room and manipulated the knee under general anesthesia. The motion obtained with manipulation under general anesthesia prevents scarring and permanent contracture from the scarring. Knee manipulation after surgery is something I occasionally do after total knee replacements but never after knee arthroscopy. After the manipulation, the knee is taped in a flexed position until after the patient is fully awake. That way the patient sees the knee in a flexed position and mentally "understands" that it will flex.

This particular patient did not move her knee after the manipulation despite intensive physical therapy. I took her back to the operating room a second time, three weeks after the first manipulation, for a second manipulation. She did not move her knee after the second manipulation. Three weeks later I took her back to the operating room for a third manipulation.

Finally, she moved her knee and her final result was excellent with full range of motion of her knee. Only time I ever used knee manipulation under general anesthesia following a routine knee arthroscopy. Only time I ever performed three consecutive knee manipulations on a patient. My treatment was creative "outside the cage" treatment that was necessary to obtain a good result in this specific patient.

What worked here? Clearly, I was confronted with an unusual patient. I was proactive in evaluating my patient's progress post-op. I recognized the problem early and was decisive in deciding to intervene in the post-op care early. If there is a need to manipulate a joint, it is better to do it early before maturation of scar occurs. There are surgeons who psychologically deny complications and avoid recognizing their complications. I am the opposite. I desperately want my patients to do well. Thus, I am always looking for problems and am proactive in evaluating and intervening when I find a patient is not doing as well as I expect them to do.

More on outside the cage thinking. Over the years I noted a number of female patients with chronic neck and/or shoulder pain who had negative imaging studies and who carried heavy purses. And I do mean heavy purses. I once weighed a patient's purse (with her permission) and the scale measured a little more than 30 pounds. The chronic neck and shoulder pain were the result of the chronic stress of carrying around a heavy purse. On a few occasions, with the patient's permission, I emptied their purse on the examining table to see what could be eliminated. On one occasion a patient in her late 30s was carrying a lifetime diary, which included multiple thick volumes. She also was carrying a lifetime address book three quarters of an inch thick. Also, in her purse were five lipsticks and five compacts. My treatment: for the diary, ditch the multiple volumes and switch to a new slim volume each year. For the address book, switch to a single sheet of paper. For the lipsticks and compacts: plan ahead and limit yourself to two a day. One for daytime and one for evening. Pain went away. Successful treatment here required observation of the heavy purse, looking for and assessing an unusual cause of symptoms and the willingness to confront the patient and counsel the patient. As I have stated before, often my best treatment is simple advice.

The most important part of treating a patient is getting the diagnosis right. If the doctor does not get the diagnosis right, the probability of the treatment being successful is small. A doctor has to be sufficiently knowledgeable of other fields to recognize that a patient referred to him for evaluation of a problem thought to be in that doctor's specialty may have a diagnosis in a different specialty. Again, I raise the question of how long should doctors' training last? There is much less cross-training today than there was in the past. Here are some examples of patients referred to an orthopedic surgeon who ultimately had a diagnosis in another field.

A patient is referred to the orthopedic surgeon by an internist with back pain. On careful questioning by the orthopedic surgeon, the back pain is found to be more in the lower chest and partly to the side. Listening with a stethoscope (yes, the orthopedic surgeon used a stethoscope), a rubbing sound is heard, which is the lung rubbing against the inside of the chest wall, which is not normal. Further workup discloses a pulmonary embolism (blood clot that has travelled to the lung), not an orthopedic problem. The internist initially resisted the orthopedic surgeon's recommendation for a lung scan. Pulmonary embolism is a serious life-threatening problem which requires immediate treatment.

Another patient is referred by an internist to an orthopedic surgeon with back pain. Careful workup, including palpation of the abdomen (yes, the orthopedic surgeon palpated the abdomen), discloses a large pulsatile mass in the abdomen. Further workup discloses a large dissecting abdominal aneurysm at risk of rupturing, requiring urgent surgery. Back pain can be a presenting symptom of abdominal aortic aneurysms, particularly when they are dissecting in the aortic wall and about to rupture. I assume the referring internist did not palpate the abdomen. Palpation of the abdomen should be part of every new patient low back pain exam.

Another patient with back pain is referred by an internist to an orthopedic surgeon. On questioning, the pain is more right-flank pain and not back pain. Physical examination of the abdomen discloses tenderness in the right upper quadrant of the abdomen. Ultrasound exam of the abdomen ordered by the orthopedic surgeon shows multiple large lymph nodes, with a final diagnosis of lymphoma, a type of cancer.

More on the importance of making the correct diagnosis. I have seen many patients for second opinions, whose correct diagnosis was missed. I am sure I have missed some myself that I don't know about. As stated before, the key, to me, is following a protocol that includes a thorough evaluation. It also requires knowledge of the many possibilities and a desperate desire to be right.

I was called to consult in the hospital on a middle-aged woman who complained of the rapid onset of weakness and the inability to flex her right hip associated with significant pain in the right hip and thigh area. She was unable to walk. I stopped by the nurses' station to look at her chart before seeing her. Her internist, a neurologist and a physiatrist were all sitting together discussing this patient. They did not have a diagnosis. On my exam, there was marked weakness of flexion of the right hip, preventing walking. Muscle strength in the rest of the body was normal examined in detail. I asked more questions. I obtained a past history of chickenpox. With a chaperone present, I examined the right upper thigh and pubic area. There was a linear distribution of a vesicle-like rash on the upper inner right thigh, consistent with shingles. After discussion with the patient, I walked out and described my findings and the diagnosis of shingles to the other three doctors. They all got up and rushed to the room to examine the rash. None of their physical examinations had included looking at the skin around the hip and groin area. Curiously, none of them congratulated me on making the diagnosis. Shingles often damages specific nerves and may cause paralysis of the involved nerves.

Why was I able to make that diagnosis when three other good doctors did not? Part of the explanation may go back to my previous discussion on the randomness of our training. Each of our experiences is wildly different. As a medical student, I participated in the evaluation of a patient with a paralyzed diaphragm on one side from shingles. The nerve which innervates the diaphragm on that side was not functioning, due to damage from the chickenpox virus. After a literature review, we found only five or six reports of similar findings reported in the world literature. The paralyzed diaphragm was significantly elevated on X-ray. This patient's diagnosis was sufficiently unusual that the possibility of unusual presentations of shingles was firmly implanted in my mind.

Additionally, when I was 50, I fell while skiing and tore the rotator cuff of my left shoulder. Within 30 minutes, the pain in my left shoulder became severe and weirdly unpleasant. I have suffered musculoskeletal injuries before. My pain was unlike any I had experienced previously. From my personal perspective, musculoskeletal pain is a pain my brain "understands." My new pain was a pain my brain could "not understand." I can't explain it any better than that. Seven days later, I developed a linear vesicular rash on the front of my left shoulder and upper arm, which made the diagnosis of shingles. I was left with some permanent, specific areas of muscle weakness and atrophy around my left shoulder and upper arm.

My personal experience with shingles further implanted the possibility of unusual presentations of shingles in my brain. I am actually the only "patient" I have ever seen with arm weakness from shingles. Unusual areas of weakness from shingles are rare. My personal experience with unusual presentations of shingles primed me for making this new patient's diagnosis. I was not necessarily a better doctor. Additionally, I clearly had a greater willingness and felt a greater need to obtain a chaperone and examine the skin in the hip and pubic area. This patient was the only patient I ever saw with leg weakness from shingles.

As a treating physician, you need to constantly look for the subtle unusual. I was performing a routine pre-op history and physical exam at Children's Hospital. The patient was a teenage boy with scoliosis, curvature of the spine. Scoliosis is more common in teenage girls, so a boy with scoliosis was a little unusual. Having examined him lying in bed, where I found him, I asked him to stand up for further exam. He got up quickly, but I sensed that he had used his arms more than typical as he sat up. I wasn't certain, I just had a sense that he moved oddly when sitting up from a lying down position. I asked him to lie back down. I then asked him to sit up without using his arms. He could not. I informed the attending orthopedic surgeon. Surgery was cancelled. Further workup with electromyographic studies confirmed a mild form of muscular dystrophy. The subtle weakness was not previously identified by the attending pediatric orthopedic surgeon nor by the patient's pediatrician. Muscle imbalance from his muscular dystrophy was the cause of his scoliosis. This case is an example where the "observation" part of the physical examination was critical to detecting the problem.

Some years ago, a young man came into my office complaining of bilateral shoulder pain. There was no history of injury. I asked him to lift his arms as part of his shoulder exam. He had full active range of motion of his shoulders. However, he seemed in an odd way to throw his arms up to get them started. I wasn't certain but his method of raising his arms seemed a little "off." Further careful exam showed atrophy of his shoulder muscles. Electrodiagnostic studies showed a muscular dystrophy which just affects the proximal arm muscles called fascio scapular humeral dystrophy. Again, the "observation" part of the physical exam was key.

I have previously discussed the necessity for asking patients the right questions and the importance of making the correct diagnosis. Here is another example. In my practice of orthopedic surgery, many patients come into my office with complaints of chronic neck and shoulder pain. X-rays are normal. MRIs of the neck are normal. Sometimes, but not always, I can feel tight muscles running along the side of the neck and/or down the mid-back and/or out to the shoulders. The workup is negative for any clear anatomic cause of the pain. One of the questions I often ask these patients is: "When you write with a pen or pencil, do you hold it loosely, or do you hold it with a tight 'death' grip?" Often, these patients answer my question, "Yes, I hold it with a tight 'death' grip."

I find the answer to this question helpful. It allows me to sort out a group of patients who are chronically anxious, tense and tight. Medicine and surgery are not indicated for these patients. Instead, I sit down and discuss lifestyle changes. I start out explaining that what I am about to discuss is easy to talk about, hard to achieve, but worth trying to achieve. I discuss breathing exercises for relaxation. I discuss relaxation exercises in which the patient goes through an inventory of their body. For example, tighten your right shoulder. Relax your right shoulder. Tighten your right upper arm. Relax your right upper arm. Tighten your right forearm. Relax your right forearm. Go through your entire body, until you have relaxed each part and kept it relaxed. Then continue sitting or lying down for 15 minutes, consciously remaining relaxed. Do this series of relaxation exercises four times a day. I also discuss simple meditation types of exercises for relaxation.

Other advice includes: Go to bed half an hour earlier than you usually do. Wake up half an hour earlier than you usually do. Make sure with the extra time that you get ready for work in a slower more relaxed way. Leave for work at least 15 minutes earlier than usual, so that you are not rushed and tense, trying to get to work on time. If you get to work early, sit in your car, in a bathroom or in a quiet place and do relaxation exercises with the extra time. Lifestyle change is easy to talk about and hard to do. You have to really want to do it. You have to plan it.

This lifestyle change can make a world of difference for tense, anxious patients with chronic neck and shoulder pain. I also encourage these patients to try to work at a 90% or 95% pace; not a 100% or 105% pace while at work. Slowing down just a little helps these patients keep their tension tamped down. This lifestyle change often helps chronic pain issues related to chronic anxiety and tension. Another situation in which my "best" treatment is often just advice.

More about asking the right questions and the importance of making the correct diagnosis. Here are some examples of evaluations of patients with chronic pain. As a hand surgeon I frequently evaluate patients with chronic forearm pain. Some years ago, I was evaluating a 35-year-old woman with bilateral chronic forearm pain. Her exam was normal. No tenderness. The location of her pain was diffuse, not specific, not localized. There are two types of pain systems in your body. The superficial pain system is essentially just the skin's pain system. It has the characteristics of being acute or sharp in nature and precisely localized. Think about the last time you were bitten by a mosquito. You knew exactly where the mosquito was biting you and could slap it. The same with a papercut. You know exactly where you've been cut.

The deep pain system has the characteristics of being diffuse, achy and poorly localized. Deep pain often radiates away from its origin. Think about the last time you had a stomachache. Where was it located? It was sort of all over your abdomen. You did not know where the pain was coming from. You could not pinpoint its origin. Hip pain can radiate down the thigh towards the knee. Shoulder pain can radiate down the arm towards the elbow. Patients with carpal tunnel syndrome may have discomfort which radiates up to the shoulder and rarely to the neck or upper back.

The fact that my patient's pain in the forearm was poorly localized did not mean that she was a poor historian. It simply meant that it was a deep pain, which I would expect to be poorly localized and difficult to describe. I have discussed previously how important it is to ask the right questions or to keep asking questions until you find the right question, which will give you the right answer. Chronic pain can come from overuse. It can be overuse over a long period of time. It can also be overuse over a shorter period of time. I asked her in general terms to tell me what she was doing with her arms. How was she using her forearms?

After persistent questioning, she finally told me that she was carrying her plastic grocery bags on her forearms. Montgomery County, Maryland passed a new "bag law" in 2011. This "bag law" was enacted a few months before the new patient came to my office with her chronic forearm pain complaints. The government of Montgomery County, Maryland, began charging a tax of five cents per bag, regardless of whether it was paper or plastic. One result of this new law was that in grocery stores, bags were packed full, not partially full. It did not matter whether you were buying bags or you brought your own. The average bag was now much heavier than before.

My patient told me that she found that the bags were too heavy to carry with her hands. So, she was putting the thin plastic handles of the plastic grocery bags on her forearms and was carrying several bags at a time on each forearm with her forearms parallel to the ground. The pressure from the thin plastic handles was bruising the muscles and irritating the nerves in her forearms. Once I figured out the "diagnosis," I advised her to stop carrying bags on her forearms. Her pain went away.

All my years of training, all my surgical skills, all my experience: If I don't ask the right questions, if I don't make the correct diagnosis, and therefore don't tell her to stop that activity, the patient won't get better. Her "diagnosis" was a new one. Shall I call it, "Montgomery County, Maryland 2011 shopping bag law forearm pain syndrome?" Another situation in which my best treatment is often just advice.

Another example. Twenty-year-old college junior comes in complaining of pain on the outside of her right foot. Physical exam normal. X-rays normal. No history of excessive running or walking. More questions. What do you do with your foot in your daily life? Answer: finally. She sits for hours talking to friends on a hard floor cross-legged with the right foot underneath. Treatment: Stop doing that! Pain goes away.

Another example. Forty-four-year-old typist with chronic neck pain. X-rays typical for her age. MRI unremarkable. Again, questions. "How do you use your neck?" type of questions. She types from handwritten pages. She places the handwritten pages to her far right, so that her neck is rotated completely to the right. You ask, "Why does she do that?" I don't know. But, she does. After enough questioning, I elicit this important information. I suggest that she move the paper she is reading from her far right to the front. She follows my advice. Her pain goes away. Again, she doesn't need surgery. She doesn't need medicine. She doesn't need therapy. She simply needs an accurate diagnosis and advice regarding lifestyle change.

Another patient with recent onset of knee pain. X-rays show early arthritis of her knee. Why did it start hurting now? Further questioning discloses a recent job change in which she now is running up and down stairs many times a day. My expert treatment? I advised her to use the elevator. Her pain decreased to the point that she did not require interventional treatment at that time.

When a new patient comes into my office complaining of pain, I always ask myself these silent questions: Why are you coming into my office now? Why not last year? Why not next year? What has happened that you are coming in now? I find that enunciating these questions silently to myself helps me in my history taking.

Another patient. Myself. I have been jogging for exercise since my first year in medical school. Years later, I suddenly began to have foot pain after running for 20 minutes or more. I tried treating my pain with cushion inserts in my running shoes. If anything, I was worse. My symptoms continued for three or four months. Finally, I guess, I started asking myself more detailed questions. Specifically, I asked myself, "What changed three to four months ago?" I then realized or remembered I had purchased new running shoes. My shoes were too tight. The tightness was subtle. There was no problem walking. However, when you run, your feet swell a little bit. The swelling inside of my shoe was causing increased pressure on my feet, which was interfering with the blood flow to my feet. The decreased blood flow was causing the aching. Again, you have to ask the right questions. I threw away the running shoes and bought wider running shoes. Problem solved. I like running shoes that come in widths and get them wider than the shoe salesperson wants to sell.

An acquaintance of mine came into my office complaining of the recent onset of low back pain. A medical student was shadowing me. I was trying to teach the medical student the importance of questioning for new activity or excessive activity. For 20 minutes, the patient denied any new or excessive activity. Just as I was giving up on successfully teaching my point, my wife, working with me as hand therapist, saw the patient through a briefly opened door. My wife asked my patient why she was here. The patient replied without pause, "I must have thrown my back out moving all those chairs at the PTA meeting."

Why do I relate this story? If I fail to elicit the history of the moving of the chairs, it won't really influence treatment. I find this story evocative of the difficulty we doctors have in obtaining accurate information from patients. There are patients who ramble and are unable to tell a coherent story. There are patients who don't listen to the question but wait for a pause to tell you whatever is on their mind. Here was a situation where it was clear to the patient that I was spending extra time to teach the medical student. I was still unable to elicit an accurate history. Then, a question from a third party and out comes the accurate history.

Another vignette. Sometimes the right questions are embarrassing questions. Often doctors hesitate to ask embarrassing questions. Years ago. Federal judge. Now deceased. Developed a painful, swollen wrist. He consulted three rheumatologists (medical arthritis doctors) over the course of a year as his wrist joint steadily worsened. On sequential X-rays, the wrist joint space gradually disappeared. No accurate diagnosis. No successful treatment.

Finally, he consulted rheumatologist number four. Rheumatologist number four took a sexual history. Because he was a federal judge, none of the previous doctors had done so. On questioning by the fourth rheumatologist the judge freely admitted seeing prostitutes on a weekly basis. The fourth doctor made the diagnosis of chronic gonorrheal infection of the wrist joint. The gonorrheal infection was not properly treated for a year because of the initial doctors' reluctance to ask the right questions. I saw this patient on one occasion, after the diagnosis had been made, for advice regarding treatment for the destroyed wrist.

Another vignette regarding both observation and asking the right questions. A man came to my office complaining of a sprained ankle, which was not healing. He had sprained his ankle four weeks earlier and consulted another orthopedic surgeon. At a three-week follow up visit with the other orthopedic surgeon, his pain was worse. By the patient's history, the other orthopedic surgeon yanked on the patient's ankle and accused him of being lazy and not wanting to work.

I looked at his ankle as we talked. I noted that the swelling was globular. It looked more like swelling from inflammation, possibly from infection, rather than from a four-week-old sprain. From my observation, gonorrheal infection of the ankle joint was immediately high on my mental differential diagnosis list. I let him finish talking. Then. My first question. "Have you had unprotected intercourse in the past four months?" His answer. "Yes." My second question. "Heterosexual or homosexual?" At that time homosexuals were at much higher risk of HIV or AIDS. His reply. "Homosexual." Gonorrhea can lie dormant without symptoms for months. He had an acute gonorrheal infection in his ankle. I treated him with ankle arthroscopic surgery to wash out his ankle joint and antibiotics. Unfortunately, unknown to him, he was HIV positive, which I also diagnosed. He was in a long-term relationship but did not know that his partner was not faithful. Here is another example where the "observation" part of the examination allowed me to quickly make the diagnosis. Here is also another example of the need to be willing to ask embarrassing questions.

Over the years I have seen other gonorrheal infections in the wrist, knee and ankle joints. I have also seen three women in their late 20s or early 30s complaining of the spontaneous onset of unilateral hip pain. On exam there was pain on rotation of the hip. Each patient gave a history of unprotected intercourse within the previous four months. It is hard to obtain fluid for study from a hip joint. All three improved with antibiotics, which covered gonorrhea. I cannot prove these patients had gonorrheal infections of the hip, but I suspect it. Having seen the federal judge patient early in my career, any patient of mine with a swollen, warm or painful joint got detailed questioning regarding sexual exposure. I talk so often about the randomness of medical and surgical training. The experience of seeing the federal judge patient, whose diagnosis was missed by three excellent doctors for a year, was sufficient to convince me that I never wanted to miss the diagnosis of gonorrheal arthritis. It pushed me past concerns regarding asking embarrassing questions. I also note that on a few occasions in my career, patients with an area of chronic musculoskeletal pain have seen that pain disappear following a course of antibiotics administered for another reason. It may have been coincidence but is also possible that the course of antibiotics cured some unrecognized and unknown infection.

It is important to constantly look for unexpected problems. Looking for unexpected problems is part of the "observation" side of the practice of medicine and surgery. One morning while making rounds in one of the hospitals I used to work in, I overheard one nurse say to another, "We have another infected total joint." Intrigued, I asked for more information. I asked how many total joints she estimated they did each year and was told 75. I then asked how many infected total joints she thought they had seen the previous 12 months and was told six or seven. This estimate of an eight to nine per cent infection rate for total joint replacements was astounding. I wrote a letter to the infection control committee recommending that they investigate the infection rate in total joints. I received a letter in response stating that the hospital did not have an infection problem.

I then went to the hospital record room and asked for the statistics of the number of total joint surgeries and the number of infected total joint surgeries for the previous 12 months, something the infection control committee should have done but did not bother to do. The actual numbers matched the nurse's estimate. I forwarded these statistics to the infection control committee. Then and only then the hospital responded. They brought in outside consultants. The source of the infections was never determined. The high infection rate lasted two years and finally disappeared.

Another decision-making situation. I was referred an 88-year-old woman for a total hip replacement because she had severe difficulty walking. She could not walk across a room without stopping. X-rays showed severe arthritis of her hip. Hip arthritis can cause severe pain, frequently limits motion of the hip and can severely limit walking distance. However, it rarely limits walking to less than 20 feet. Severe limitation of walking distance, which resolves in five to ten minutes, and then allows a patient to walk a similar short distance is called claudication. The two most common causes of claudication are poor blood supply to the muscles of the legs and narrowing of the spinal canal, which restricts blood supply to the nerves in the spinal canal. This problem is called lumbar spinal stenosis. My patient had good pulses in her feet, indicating good blood supply to the legs. An MRI of the lumbar spine showed severe spinal stenosis, that is, severe narrowing of the bony canal in the lower back. I felt this patient had two separate severe problems, spinal stenosis and hip arthritis. I felt that the spinal stenosis problem was causing her more trouble than the hip arthritis. Here is another example of the need to constantly look for more than one diagnosis when evaluating a patient.

I recommended surgery to open up the spinal canal first, followed by a total hip replacement six months later. She did well with both operations. I know she lived at least until age 94, since I saw her then for another problem. Her internist was outraged that I did not immediately do the operation he had referred the patient for. His attitude seemed to be that I should be a technician and follow his orders. I was not supposed to think. I never saw another referral from him. I felt that my role was to evaluate the patient; diagnose the problem or problems; then recommend a strategy to solve the problems. This, I did successfully.

When I was in the army, I had a patient who was recovering from a fractured tibia (lower leg bone). The fracture healed uneventfully. Months went by and I could not convince him to stop using a cane. Finally, one day I happened to see him in the parking lot of the army hospital. We stopped and chatted. While chatting with him, I asked to look at his cane. After we were done chatting, I walked off with his cane. He did not ask for another and finally began walking well without it. I don't think I would have dared to do that in private practice. I was young. In retrospect, I am surprised at my audacious "treatment." Who would think that "stealing" a patient's cane would be "appropriate" treatment? However, it worked! Again, thinking out of the cage.

As a patient, you, the reader, need to be an educated consumer. You need to read up on your symptoms, read up on your diagnosis. Decide: "Do you think you doctor's diagnosis is correct?" Question everything! When your doctor prescribes medicine ask about side effects. My personal experience is that my doctors tend to skip glibly over the side effects of medicines. I mentioned before having had muscle aches for two years all over my body that finally went away after I stopped a blood pressure medication. My wife read about the muscle aches being a possible side effect of the blood pressure medication I was taking. My doctor did not pick this up.

I have been on another medication which made me emotionally labile and depressed. The prescribing doctor did not warn me of the possible side effects. I only realized what had happened when I went off the medicine for other reasons. Even I as a doctor, aware of the possible side effects of medicines, did not understand at the time it was happening what was going on. Be aware. Your doctor can put you on another medicine to treat a side effect of a prior medicine. Sometimes the best "treatment" is to go off all of the medications you can safely go off of and see what your baseline is. Do not go off all of your medications without your physician's knowledge.

PART FOUR

Beyond the Memoir

A Discussion of Some Common and Rare Diagnoses

Part Four moves beyond my memoir as such. I have had ten years of medical and surgical training with four years of medical school, two years of general surgical training, three years of orthopedic surgical training and one year of hand surgery training. I have had nearly 40 years of medical and surgical practice experience if you include my 37 ½ years of orthopedic and hand surgical practice, two years of orthopedic practice in the US Army and the emergency room moonlighting practice I did during my medical and surgical training, my service in the army and the one year I spent in a research lab. During the year I spent in the research lab, I worked in suburban emergency rooms every fifth night for a 12-hour shift including weeknights and weekends.

I have approached my training and my practice experience with an inquiring mind, trying to figure out "What works?" and equally important "What isn't working?" I have constantly asked myself which things that work I should keep doing. I have also kept asking myself which things aren't working that need to change. As discussed previously I am constantly trying to figure out and fight herd mentality when it is inaccurate and interferes with successful diagnosis and treatment.

In the chapters that follow, I discuss my approach, my thoughts and my ideas about a number of diagnoses. First, I discuss the anatomy, the physiology, the diagnosis and the treatment of some common diagnoses. I write both for non-medical and medical readers. Later I discuss some rare interesting diagnoses. Internists, general practitioners, emergency room physicians, orthopedic surgeons and hand surgeons will eventually see many of these rare diagnoses if they practice long enough. The question is, "Will they recognize them when they see them?" I hope that by reading these chapters they will be more likely to make the correct diagnosis.

CHAPTER NINETEEN

Discussion of Common Diagnoses and Their Treatment

- Carpal Tunnel Syndrome
- Recurrent Carpal Tunnel Syndrome
- Cubital Tunnel Syndrome
- Heat Exhaustion; Heat Stroke
- Fibromyalgia
- Non-Displaced and Minimally Displaced Fractures: Distal Radius, Phalanges
- Sprains
- Frozen Shoulder

Carpal Tunnel Syndrome

At the level of the heel of the hand, the bones of the wrist create a valley surrounded on three sides by bone. A layer of tough tissue crosses over the top of the wrist "valley" creating a tunnel which is called the carpal tunnel. Carpal is a medical term for wrist. So carpal tunnel quite simply means wrist tunnel. Nine tendons and one large nerve pass through the carpal tunnel, extending from the forearm into the hand and fingers. Mild swelling of the tissues within the carpal tunnel increases the pressure inside of the tunnel, which interferes with the flow of blood to the nerve. Decreased flow of blood to the median nerve causes decreased function of the nerve. Early in the development of carpal tunnel syndrome the decreased function may be temporary and reversible. Late or severe and the decreased function becomes permanent. Medicines and injections do not provide a long-term cure.

Carpal tunnel syndrome is a common problem. One of my mentor hand surgeons used to joke that everybody has carpal tunnel syndrome. They just aren't all symptomatic yet. Classic carpal tunnel syndrome presents with numbness and tingling of the thumb, index and middle fingers. The "classic symptoms" probably only occur 30 per cent of the time. Carpal tunnel syndrome may present with diffuse aching in the hand, wrist, forearm, upper arm and/or neck and mid-back. Common symptoms also include a sense of clumsiness, easy fatiguing of the hand, dropping things and awakening at night with pain and/or numbness and tingling in the hand.

As with all patients, I take a detailed history and ask a lot of questions. My physical examination includes testing for light touch sensation. Specific diagnostic tests include the Tinel's sign test, the median nerve compression test, the Phalen's test and a test for the strength of the muscle that elevates the thumb out of the palm, the abductor pollicis brevis. The Tinel's test involves light tapping on the nerve looking for increased sensitivity of the nerve causing numbness and tingling radiating to the fingers. The median nerve compression test involves gentle pressure on the nerve looking for similar increased sensitivity of the nerve. The Phalen's test involves gently placing the wrist in a fully flexed position, again looking for increased sensitivity of the nerve. The muscle test looks for weakness of this one specific muscle which gets its nerve supply from the median nerve.

The tests enumerated above are at best somewhat helpful. I have seen patients with severe changes on electrical studies whose clinical tests were all normal. Positive clinical tests for carpal tunnel syndrome are suggestive of carpal tunnel syndrome but not definitive.

After the evaluation discussed above, my approach to the evaluation and treatment of patients with suspected carpal tunnel syndrome includes electrodiagnostic tests including measurements of the nerve conduction velocities and measurements of the spontaneous electrical activity of certain muscles called electromyography. While these electrodiagnostic tests are not considered mandatory in the evaluation of suspected carpal tunnel syndrome, I use these tests for two reasons: first, as an attempt to confirm the diagnosis with abnormal test results; second, as a method of measuring the severity of the carpal tunnel syndrome.

Patients with suspected carpal tunnel syndrome can be categorized into separate groups. There is a group with clear cut classic carpal tunnel syndrome symptoms, positive clinical tests and unequivocal abnormal electrodiagnostic studies. For all of these patients I recommend carpal tunnel release surgery. My reasoning: the probability of the accuracy of the diagnosis is high and the abnormal electrodiagnostic studies demonstrate significant ongoing damage to the nerve. Without surgery, the probability of continued worsening is high. The purpose of the surgery is to keep the problem from worsening and to obtain as much improvement as possible. The more severe the electrical studies, the less likely a patient will obtain full recovery due to the fact that permanent damage to the nerve has already occurred.

There is a group with classic abnormal carpal tunnel symptoms and physical findings with normal electrodiagnostic studies. Due to the "classic" nature of the symptoms and the physical findings, the probability of the accuracy of the diagnosis is still high. The normal electrodiagnostic studies suggest that no serious damage to the nerve had yet occurred. For these patients I offer the carpal tunnel release surgery but I tell them it is not mandatory. I advise that surgery is available to them if their symptoms are bad enough. Only they, the patients, can determine how bad is bad enough. Given the classic symptoms and physical findings, most of these patients who choose surgery obtain good relief of symptoms from the surgery. For the patients who do not wish surgery, I recommend following them with repeat electrodiagnostic studies in six months. If the electrodiagnostic studies turn abnormal at follow-up, I recommend surgical release because there is now objective evidence of progressive injury to the median nerve.

There is a group of patients with "non-classic" symptoms and physical findings and normal electrodiagnostic studies for whom I suspect the diagnosis of carpal tunnel syndrome. I am not certain of the diagnosis. If the diagnosis is carpal tunnel syndrome, it is mild without permanent damage to the nerve. For these patients, I do not offer surgery because the diagnosis is too uncertain. I recommend a reevaluation and re-exam in my office and repeating the electrodiagnostic studies in six months if the symptoms persist. I also look carefully for another diagnosis which may explain the symptoms.

For all of my patients with possible carpal tunnel syndrome, I usually order the electrodiagnostic studies on both hands even if only one is symptomatic, in order to compare both sides. There is a group of patients who have abnormal electrodiagnostic studies on the asymptomatic side (that is, on the side with no symptoms). What to do with them? I recommend no specific follow up unless symptoms develop. I do not recommend surgery. Surgery might take an asymptomatic patient and cause the onset of symptoms. I am not aware of any studies which have followed this group of patients long term, which informs us regarding best treatment. Such a study is needed. Obviously, a hand with no symptoms and normal electrodiagnostic studies does not have carpal tunnel syndrome.

There is a wide difference of opinion in the medical community regarding when carpal tunnel surgery is indicated. Overall, I tend to be more conservative with respect to advising surgical versus conservative (i.e., non-operative) treatment for most problems. When it comes to carpal tunnel syndrome, I find myself more on the aggressive side.

All of the neurologists I know treat their patients with carpal tunnel syndrome non-operatively as long as possible. When a neurologist refers a patient to me for carpal release surgery, it always seems like the patient has had symptoms for at least ten years or already has severe electrodiagnostic changes. The patient always has decreased sensation (i.e., decreased ability to feel), severe decreased function on electrical tests (EMGs) and marked muscle atrophy of the muscle pad at the base of the thumb. While these patients often get relief of discomfort after my carpal tunnel release surgery, they usually have only partial improvement of their strength or feeling because of permanent damage to the nerve due to years of pressure on the nerve. The neurologists then say that the surgery doesn't work. My results with surgery on my own patients are superior because I operate on patients much earlier, before there is significant permanent damage to the nerve. Here is another situation in which the physician you are referred to will determine which treatment you are offered. The subspecialty of the physician you are referred to will determine the treatment you are offered.

Which technique should you use for carpal tunnel release? A relatively recent technique for performing carpal tunnel release is the percutaneous carpal tunnel release. Advantages for this technique are described as a smaller scar and perhaps a one-week earlier return to work. Let's look at these advantages. Look at the next 20 people you see. How many of their palms do you see? None. You don't typically see people's palms unless they are begging in the old fashioned way. So, a scar in a palm is not a cosmetic problem. In addition, we expect to see lines in palms. So, even if you "see" a line on a palm, your brain will not highlight it as abnormal. Thus, you won't "see" it.

Returning to work a week earlier is, admittedly, a small advantage. Operating with the percutaneous technique, the visibility is limited. There are a number of reports in the academic literature of a small incidence of cutting the major nerve to the hand, the median nerve, of 1 in 100 or 1 in 200. Cutting the median nerve is a life-altering, life-ruining event. I have treated, in my career, two patients whose median nerves were cut during endoscopic carpal tunnel release surgeries by other surgeons.

When new technologies evolve, when do you stick with the tried and true? When do you switch to the "new?" The new can be cooler and sexier and sell well. No easy answers. If I am getting good results with an old, tried and true operation, I will stick with it, unless the new is really demonstrably better. Personally, my results with open carpal tunnel release were so good, I never tried the percutaneous.

One of the cut median nerves I repaired as a treating physician was the plaintiff of a potential malpractice lawsuit. I spoke to the attorneys of both sides regarding the objective surgical findings I saw during my surgery to repair the nerve. I knew from talking with operating room nurses at the hospital at which this surgeon worked that the surgeon who had cut the nerve was continuing to perform the same operation. Bad judgement of one specific surgeon. He had a major complication. He actually did not even recognize the complication. I diagnosed the cut nerve when the patient came to me for a second opinion. The original orthopedic surgeon was continuing to use the same technique which had resulted in a serious complication. There seems to be no way our society is able to prevent poor judgement of physicians. From my perspective, the use of this technique is a triumph of technique over reason. One cut median nerve is one too many. Many hand surgeons will disagree with me because they like the new technique.

During the course of my career, I performed more than 1500 open carpal tunnel release surgeries. My patients suffered few complications. I recall one superficial infection, which resolved easily. One other patient developed unusual, extensive scarring and snapping of tendons within the carpal canal, which resolved following surgery to remove the unusual scar formation. No patient of mine suffered a nerve injury. Only two patients developed recurrent symptoms and worsening of EMG findings years later.

Recurrent Carpal Tunnel Syndrome

Carpal tunnel syndrome occurs commonly. Carpal tunnel release surgery is utilized frequently. Some patients develop recurrence of carpal tunnel syndrome symptoms following carpal tunnel release surgery. Hand surgery courses often cover the treatment of recurrent carpal tunnel syndrome. What follows is a discussion of my personal experience treating patients with recurrent carpal tunnel syndrome.

During the course of my career, I saw between 20 and 25 patients with "recurrent" carpal tunnel syndrome, who had previously been operated on by other surgeons. All but one of them had undergone open carpal tunnel release operations with short proximal incisions. For all of these patients electrodiagnostic studies showed worsening of the electrical activity of the carpal tunnel nerve following the initial surgery. Post-operative MRIs of the wrist showed persistence of the distal end of the carpal ligament at the level of the hook of the hamate in all but one of these patients. The persistence of the carpal ligament was something I had to look for myself on the MRIs. None of the radiologists who read the MRIs initially mentioned that in their reports. They were not looking for that. When I pointed out the residual carpal ligament, all of the radiologists agreed with my finding. In short, all of these patients except one had incomplete initial releases. Their recurrent symptoms were the result of an initial incomplete carpal tunnel release surgery rather than recurrence of carpal tunnel syndrome following a complete release. All improved after repeat exploration and full release of the carpal canal.

There were three patients, two of whom were mine and the one mentioned above, who had recurrence of carpal tunnel symptoms and worse electrical studies years after the initial surgery in the presence of a previous complete release. I operated on two of these three patients. In these two patients, I found constrictive scarring around the nerve and released the scar. These two did well after that surgery.

Thus, my personal experience with "recurrent" carpal tunnel syndrome is that most are actually incomplete first operations. Workup of a patient with possible recurrent carpal tunnel syndrome should include an MRI of the wrist with a careful look for a portion of unreleased carpal ligament at the level of the hook of the hamate.

Surgical Approach to Open Carpal Tunnel Release

There are two approaches to performing the open carpal tunnel release surgery. The most common one I have seen involves opening the wrist proximally and then gradually moving towards the fingers. This technique results in a visible scar on the forearm proximal to the wrist flexion crease. The other approach, which I prefer, is to open the palm distal to the carpal canal and then dissect carefully toward the forearm.

What is the difference between a good surgeon and an average surgeon? The good surgeon has fewer complications. The good surgeon knows how to stay out of trouble. One way of staying out of trouble is knowing the anatomic variants that may occur in the area you are operating in. There is a small nerve branch (motor branch) from the median nerve which gives nerve power to a muscle (abductor pollicis brevis) at the base of the thumb. The nerve usually comes off the median nerve on the thumb side of the median nerve near the base of the thumb. Normally this small nerve is not at significant risk during carpal tunnel release surgery. Rarely, the motor branch nerve arises further distal than usual on the little finger side of the median nerve and crosses the line of a carpal tunnel release surgical incision. I was always slow and careful looking for this variant. I found it three times in my career. Two of the times, the adductor pollicis muscle crossed the center of the palm further distal than usual. The abnormal extent of muscle seemed to be a warning of this possible variant.

I once saw an 88-year-old woman with symptomatic carpal tunnel syndrome and abnormal electrical studies. I only perform carpal tunnel release surgery on elderly patients under local anesthesia to eliminate any possibility of mental confusion following anesthesia. My patient declined surgery due to her age. She returned to my office six years later at age 94. The symptoms from the carpal tunnel syndrome at that time were so bad that she was unable to get a decent night's sleep. I operated under local anesthesia to release her carpal tunnel. She had dramatic relief of symptoms. She told me that she regretted not having had the surgery six years earlier. Age should not necessarily be a contraindication to carpal tunnel release surgery.

Cubital Tunnel Syndrome

Another nerve in the arm which travels through a tunnel and may undergo compression and irritation within that tunnel is the ulnar nerve, which travels through a tunnel just behind the prominence of bone on the little finger side of the elbow. In medical parlance, the word for elbow is cubitus or cubital if used as an adjective. Pressure on the ulnar nerve at the elbow is called cubital tunnel syndrome.

Patients with cubital tunnel syndrome often come to my office complaining of medial elbow pain, numbness and tingling, often in the ring and little finger and/or weakness of grip. Rarely, a patient will present with curvature of the ring and little finger, called an ulnar claw hand. As part of my history taking, I want to determine if the patient's elbow or forearm discomfort is more on the lateral side of the elbow or more on the medial side. Given the extent of rotation of the arm at the shoulder and the rotation of the forearm, it is often hard to tell if a patient's pain at the elbow is on the medial or lateral side. I ask patients to rotate their forearm so that their palm is facing up. Then I point to the medial and lateral sides of the elbow and ask which side hurts more, which minimizes confusion in determining where the discomfort is greatest.

In the absence of a history of trauma, pain on the lateral side of the elbow is most commonly lateral epicondylitis, also called tennis elbow. In my practice, less than one per cent of my patients played tennis on a daily basis. Pain on the medial side is most commonly cubital tunnel syndrome. Medial epicondylitis, sometimes called golfers' elbow, is less common.

Further history taking. I ask these patients if they rest on their elbows a lot. Many say, "Yes." I then ask about sleeping position. Sleeping on your stomach with your arms over your head puts direct pressure on the ulnar nerve in the cubital tunnel. Sleeping on your side with the elbows bent, the fetal position, kinks the cubital tunnel and puts pressure on the nerve. Sleeping on your side with the downside elbow bent and raised above the head both kinks the tunnel and puts direct pressure on the nerve. Most patients with cubital tunnel syndrome say yes to at least one of these questions. One patient was a college cheerleader. More than 100 times she climbed up a pyramid of male cheerleaders on their hands and knees. She then did a back flip off of the top of the pyramid and was caught by another cheerleader. Each time she performed this maneuver, she received a hard blow to the inside of her elbow as she was caught.

She presented with an ulnar claw hand, an unusual repetitive injury which I elicited in taking her history. This was an unusual case of cubital tunnel syndrome.

Evaluating my cubital tunnel syndrome patients with electromyography, I found only about 1 in 20 showed sufficiently severe damage to the nerve that surgical release was indicated. For the other 95%, my treatment included advice and night splinting. It is important to change the sleeping position, if possible, to sleeping on the side with the arms relatively straight. There are cubital tunnel splints which can be worn at night which keep the elbow straight. For patients who cannot afford a splint, a tube of stiff cloth can be sewn or safety pinned to suffice. I recommend using the splint for four to six months until the sleeping position habit changes. Changing habits like your sleeping position is hard.

I also recommend that the patients stop resting on their elbow. Some patients find the habit too ingrained and are unable to stop. I tell these patients to take a jack from a set of children's jacks and tape it to the posterior medial side of the elbow. That way, every time the patient goes to rest on that elbow there is immediate negative feedback. A small pebble can serve the same purpose as the jack. For patients who cannot stop sleeping on their stomach, tape a jack to their breastbone (sternum) before bed each night. Works like a charm in preventing stomach sleeping.

I attended a hand surgery meeting which emphasized different techniques for performing cubital tunnel surgery on the elbow. There are five accepted operations for cubital tunnel syndrome. The first is simple release of the tunnel. Few surgeons use this technique. The nerve remains tensioned behind the bony bump on the medial elbow, the medial epicondyle. The most common operation used is the subcutaneous anterior transposition of the ulnar nerve. The entrapped nerve is freed from its tunnel and then brought anterior to the medial epicondyle. It is held in place with a subcutaneous suture. I never liked this procedure since it involves stripping blood supply from a long segment of the nerve. It also appears to have a risk of kinking at the level of the subcutaneous suture.

The third operation involves opening the tunnel and then shaving down the medial epicondyle (the bony bump on the inside of the elbow). I use this operation. It does not involve stripping blood supply from the nerve. I am not certain I obtain better results with it than with the subcutaneous anterior transposition, but certainly as good. The fourth operation involves significant stripping of the muscle in the proximal forearm and placing the nerve deep in the forearm. I don't know anyone who uses this technique routinely, since it involves extensive surgical dissection. The fifth is a newer small incision type of technique which seems to me to be little more than the tunnel opening operation.

If you need surgery for severe cubital tunnel syndrome, you will find that you are again in a situation in which the surgeon you choose will determine the operation you are offered. While I was at an elbow surgery course, I was talking with one of the instructors about which operation he used for normal, uncomplicated cubital tunnel syndrome. He was using the subcutaneous anterior transposition operation but was unhappy with his results. I told him about my experience with the shaving down the medial epicondyle operation. He said he thought he would try it. Again, in a situation in which there is more than one operation used, no one operation has clearly proved superior.

Heat Exhaustion; Heat Stroke

During the Vietnam War, the United States still had a draft for the military. The management of the draft was grossly unfair. If you were in school, you received a deferment from the draft. If you were not in school, you were subject to the draft. When I entered Yale in the Fall of 1963, there were rigid rules of behavior in place. Yale was all male at that time. If you were caught with a girl in your dorm room after midnight, you were expelled. Period. End of discussion. Rapidly, the administration realized that any student expelled could be immediately drafted. If drafted; sent to Vietnam; if sent to Vietnam; real risk of death or serious injury. Visit the Vietnam Memorial in Washington. Examine all of the names on that somber black wall. The risk was real and unfair! Overnight, there was no student behavior which would lead to expulsion. All of the rules disappeared. They were unenforceable.

One hundred percent of medical school graduates were drafted. All! The military needed all of the graduating doctors. I was 4F due to decreased hearing in one ear. I was not eligible for the regular draft. After graduating from medical school, I was eligible for the medical draft and was drafted. The government had a plan called the Berry Plan. You could go into the military as a GMO, that is, a General Medical Officer, or you could defer your entry into the military until you finished your advanced training and then go in. I elected to use the Berry Plan. By the time I entered the army in 1977, after my orthopedic residency, President Carter had already pardoned the draft evaders, who had fled to Canada.

We, Berry Plan doctors, entering the army after our advanced medical or surgical training, were given a three-week course for our basic training at Fort Sam Houston, near San Antonio, Texas. We had 30 hours of lecture on chemical, biological and nuclear warfare to provide us with knowledge about these subjects not covered in medical school. I also remember lectures on heat exhaustion and heat stroke, topics which were not well covered in medical school. We were taught that sufficient intake of water will prevent heat exhaustion and heat stroke. We were shown pictures of the Israeli army maneuvering in the desert. We were told that the soldiers of each small unit of the Israeli army wheeled a tank of water with them into the desert. We were told that it was a court martial offense for a supervising officer if one of his soldiers got heat exhaustion or heat stroke.

Information about the prevention of heat exhaustion and heat stroke unfortunately is not well known or accepted by everyone in the civilian sector. A football player at the University of Maryland died in the Fall of 2018 from heat stroke. There seemed to be a sense that if you were man enough or strong enough, you could "muscle" through without water. No! No! No! No! No! If you supervise children or adults in hot weather, you should enforce and require water breaks. Enforcing water breaks is the policy of the Israeli army. If you are an athlete or someone else under supervision, do not allow anyone to prevent you from frequent water breaks during hot weather. If anyone attempts to limit your water intake, quit. Immediately. Note to coaches: Please read and reread this paragraph!

One last note: I wish to emphasize the importance of establishing a water discipline to ensure adequate intake of water. You may reach the stage of heat exhaustion or heat stroke without feeling thirsty. If you are in a hot environment and begin to feel faint, lightheaded or ill, you may be approaching a state of serious dehydration without feeling thirsty. Drink a lot immediately. I developed dehydration while on a compass course at Fort Sam Houston. I began to feel faint and lightheaded but not thirsty. Recognizing that I was severely dehydrated, I immediately drank two full canteens of water. Within 20 minutes I felt fine.

Fibromyalgia

There are many patients who carry the diagnosis of fibromyalgia. Over the course of my career, I found many patients who were given the diagnosis of fibromyalgia too freely. I recall one 82-year-old woman who was involved in a motor vehicle accident three years prior to my seeing her. She developed severe pain in her right shoulder, right hip and right knee. Her doctors diagnosed fibromyalgia and stated that the pain in these three joints and her fibromyalgia was caused by the accident. No diagnostic X-ray was ever taken of these three joints following the accident. I saw her as part of the evaluation for the accident. I obtained X-rays of the right shoulder, right hip and right knee. All three joints had severe bone-on-bone degenerative osteoarthritis. This patient had a degenerative condition not related to the accident. She did not have fibromyalgia. The diagnosis of fibromyalgia was incorrect.

Fibromyalgia is one of those diagnoses for which, as of this writing, there is no blood test or imaging test, which gives a definitive yes or no answer to the question, "Is the diagnosis fibromyalgia?" I have seen numerous patients who have come to me with the diagnosis of fibromyalgia who, on careful workup, have a different diagnosis or different diagnoses. I can think of several patients with aching in their necks, shoulders, arms and mid-back who had severe degenerative disc disease in their cervical spines on MRI who initially came to me with a diagnosis of fibromyalgia. I think the diagnosis of fibromyalgia is given too easily. Other possible causes of a patient's symptoms should be thoroughly evaluated. If a doctor gives you a diagnosis of fibromyalgia, seek other opinions.

Non-Displaced and Minimally Displaced Fractures: Distal Radius, Phalanges

Long bones are covered by a tough tissue called periosteum. The only parts of long bones not covered by periosteum are the gliding surfaces of joints and attachments of ligaments. A fracture of a long bone in which the bone fragments are significantly displaced includes tearing of the periosteum. Thus, significantly displaced fractures are more likely to be unstable after the displaced fracture fragments have been manipulated back into their proper position. In a non-displaced or minimally displaced fracture, much of the periosteum remains intact. The portion of the periosteum which remains intact lends stability to the fracture; that is, the fracture is unlikely to slip or shift further out of position. Thus, non-displaced or minimally displaced fractures do not require rigid immobilization in order to prevent further displacement.

Unfortunately, many non-displaced or minimally displaced fractures are treated with rigid immobilization with a cast or splint. As I have stated before, joints and tendons like to move and glide. Uninjured joints and tendons become stiff if immobilized for days to weeks. Some of the stiffness many of you feel in the morning is the subtle onset of stiffness from the brief immobility of your sleep time. Imagine how stiff you would be if you slept for three or six weeks.

I have seen many patients whose non-displaced wrist fractures were treated with a rigid cast for six weeks. These patients came to me for a second opinion due to their post-treatment stiff wrist, hand and/or fingers. I have seen many patients with stiff fingers whose non-displaced fracture of a finger bone (phalanx) was treated for three to six weeks in a rigid splint. These "bad" outcomes resulted from the overtreatment of their injuries.

For non-displaced and minimally displaced fractures, I treat all with removable splints and early active motion and exercises. If patient is anxious and demonstrates a reluctance to move, I immediately send them for hand therapy with Lynne. I recall only two patients who displaced their non-displaced fractures during treatment in removable splits. One fell down the stairs while drunk, not wearing his splint. The other was wearing a plaster forearm splint. She was involved in a motor vehicle accident severe enough to break the plaster splint and displace the fracture.

Sprains

A ligament is a segment of tough, flexible soft tissue which crosses joints and connects to the bone on either side of the joint. Along with the shape of the joint surfaces, a ligament limits the direction and extent of motion of a joint. If a joint is stressed beyond the limits of its normal motion, then the restraining and controlling ligaments may tear, which is called a sprain. There are essentially three levels of severity of sprains. The most severe is complete rupture of the ligament. The middle level is partial tearing with some stretching of the ligament, which lengthens it. The third is a less severe, partial tearing of the ligament. The length of the ligament is unchanged. There may be swelling, tenderness, pain and bruising following a sprain.

Following a sprain (i.e., following an injury which tears a ligament), the degree of pain experienced does not correlate well with the degree of injury. In fact, a complete tear of a ligament may have little pain. With an intact but torn ligament, any motion of the joint will pull on the torn ligament and cause pain. If the ligament is completely torn, motion of the joint may move the torn ligament ends apart, but because the ligament is completely torn, there is no tension on the torn ligament, which would cause pain.

Thus, the complete tearing of a ligament of the knee often causes surprisingly less pain than a partial tear of the same ligament. The second joint down from the tip of the thumb is called the first metacarpal phalangeal joint. It is the joint between the first metacarpal bone and the proximal phalanx of the thumb.

Sufficient outward pressure on the thumb may cause tearing of the ligament on the little finger side of this joint, which is called a Gamekeepers' Thumb. Scottish gamekeepers used to break the necks of rabbits by hitting the rabbits' necks with their hand between the thumb and index finger. It became a known occupational injury for Scottish gamekeepers due to the frequent use of their hands in this manner. Today, tearing of this ligament is a common sports injury.

When the Gamekeeper's Thumb ligament is completely torn, there is less pain than "expected" because of the complete tear. This injury requires surgical repair. It does not heal on its own. An unstable thumb resulting from an untreated Gamekeepers' Thumb prevents tight gripping or pinching using the thumb. This injury is frequently missed by emergency room physicians and primary care physicians. If stability of the joint is not specifically tested for in a precise manner, the instability will be overlooked. When seen late, this instability requires a different operation than would be needed if seen early.

I often evaluated patients with acute sprains of this joint who had distinct instability on examination. When I operated on these patients, I found that about ten percent of the patients with an "acute" sprain actually had an acute "minor" sprain on top of an "old" severe injury. In these patients, the ends of the completely torn ligament were covered in smooth old scar. Thus, for every patient I operated on for an "acute" sprain, I told them before surgery, that it might be old and that I might have to do the different operation appropriate for the "old" injury.

Frozen Shoulder

Stiffness or decreased range of motion of the shoulder joint is a common problem often seen by primary care physicians, internists, orthopedic surgeons and hand surgeons. This diagnosis is frequently missed by treating physicians because the patient does not complain about it and the examining physician does not specifically examine for it. I have discussed previously about the need for a physician to utilize a specific examination protocol in order to avoid missing diagnoses. As a hand surgeon, when I begin my physical examination of a patient with a hand complaint, I ask a new patient to raise his hand over his head. If he is able to do this, then the shoulder motion is probably satisfactory. If he is unable to elevate his hand over his head, then my "hand" examination switches to a shoulder examination first.

Anything that causes pain in the shoulder, arm or hand may cause a patient to stop using or moving their shoulder. The shoulder then rapidly becomes stiff. In order for a shoulder to move through a full range of motion, many tissue surfaces glide across each other. Within a period of days or weeks of immobility, these surfaces begin to stick to each other, limiting motion of the shoulder. Previously I noted that fingers like to move. This is also true of shoulders and every other joint. Lack of motion is "harmful." Following any injury to the arm or hand, the treating physician should be proactive about testing for limited shoulder motion and proactive about encouraging shoulder motion to prevent the development of a frozen shoulder. Shoulder motion should be evaluated at every follow-up appointment.

CHAPTER TWENTY

Unusual and Rare Diagnoses and Their Treatment

- Atypical Mycobacterial and Fungal Infections
- An Unexpected Death
- Handcuff Neuropathy
- Chronic Exertional Compartment Syndrome
- Glomus Tumor
- Septic Arthritis of the Acromioclavicular Joint
- Meningococcal Septicemia and Septic Arthritis
- Arcane Niches of Medical Lore
- Painful Pisiform Syndrome
- Kienbock's Disease: Proximal Row Carpectomy

In this chapter I discuss some unusual and rare diagnoses that I find fascinating.

Atypical Mycobacterial and Fungal Infections

I have discussed before the need to constantly look for the rare and unusual. During my career as a hand surgeon, I have seen a multitude of patients complaining of painless lumps in their hands or fingers. Most are benign, but not all. I have seen six patients whose masses were irregular in shape and felt woody and densely spongey to palpation. This type of mass is caused by either a slow-growing fungal infection or a slow-growing second cousin to the tuberculosis bacteria, called atypical mycobacterium. Most of these patients gave a history of a scrape or puncture wound in a saltwater marine or freshwater environment. Treatment consists of surgical removal of the bulk of the infected tissue, then appropriate antifungal or anti-tuberculosis antibiotics. The key to treatment is the recognition of the possibility of fungal or atypical mycobacterial infection prior to surgery. That way, special cultures for fungus and atypical mycobacterium can be planted at the time of surgery. Ordinary bacterial cultures will not give positive results for these infections. These organisms need special culture mediums, and the culture plates need to be kept for up to six weeks in an incubator due to the slow rate of growth of these organisms.

An Unexpected Death

Sometimes bad things happen to patients and you cannot figure out what went wrong. In my training, we had a patient scheduled for an upper abdominal operation. He received a shot of 50 mg of Demerol into the buttock muscle on the ward before surgery for sedation. This is a medium dose of this medicine. In those days 100 mg was used for severe pain. This patient came to the operating suite heavily sedated, almost unconscious. We noted this at the time. He went through the operation with only nitrous oxide, truly minimal anesthesia. He did not require stronger anesthetics. No one had ever seen this reaction to Demerol before. No one had seen a patient go through this type of operation with so little anesthesia before. I was on call the first night after his surgery. This patient required no pain medication for the entire first night after surgery. After an upper abdominal operation, essentially everybody needs strong pain medicine.

On rounds the next morning, the patient told the chief resident that he was having some pain and asked for pain medicine. The chief resident ordered 50 mg of Demerol. This was a low to medium dose. I spoke up, expressing concern and detailed the previous day's events. The chief resident listened and changed the order to a 25 mg intramuscular shot of Demerol. This is a really low dose. The head nurse administered the shot. The patient arrested 15 minutes later and was not successfully resuscitated. Was this an idiosyncratic reaction to Demerol, which I have never seen before or since? Was there adulteration in the medicine? I don't know. I do know that the head nurse was a fantastic nurse who I worked with intensely for two years. I "know" this was not a medication error.

Handcuff Neuropathy

This next case falls under the category of "be polite to police officers." A "patient to be" of mine was speeding on an expressway when pulled over by a state patrol officer. Words were exchanged. Not a good idea. Always better to de-escalate conflicts. My "patient to be" tore up the ticket. Whereupon, my "patient to be" was placed in handcuffs. Not only handcuffs, but tight handcuffs. Not only tight handcuffs. but tight handcuffs for hours. This put pressure on multiple nerves and caused permanent damage to multiple nerves requiring nerve release surgery. This is called handcuff neuropathy. You can look it up.

More on the issue of de-escalation. In any confrontation situation, it is important to keep your anger under control. You want to defuse the other person's anger, if possible. In any interaction with a police officer, it is important to try to defuse the situation. You may be angry or scared because of the interaction with the police officer. Forget for a minute, the emotions you are feeling. Think for a moment what the police officer is feeling. In the first two months of 2019, my online search lists 21-work related police officer deaths. This averages one every three days. Be aware. Even in a routine traffic stop, the officer is thinking about these statistics. He or she is wondering if this interaction is going to be fatal for him or her. Even if he does not show it, this police officer is anxious and nervous. Thus, your ideal behavior should be trying to calm the officer down and assure him or her that this interaction will go smoothly. Show your hands and palms to demonstrate that you do not have a weapon. Do not approach the officer quickly. If you are asked for identification, tell the officer that you are about to reach into your pocket or purse to get your wallet. Then move slowly.

Chronic Exertional Compartment Syndrome

I have had three teenagers in my practice over the years with the following similar histories. Sitting around they are totally normal. If they try to run, after 15 to 20 minutes, their lower legs begin to ache and hurt. They have to stop running. After a while they feel better. They can then run a similar distance. Examination is totally, utterly, completely normal.

There is an uncommon syndrome called chronic exertional compartment syndrome. Normally, the muscles in the calf are surrounded by a sleeve of firm tough tissue. It seems in these patients, there is an imbalance in the size of the muscle and the size of the sleeve. When muscles are exercised, they swell. If the compartment is too tight, then the swelling of the muscle causes increased pressure inside the muscle compartment. The increased pressure interferes with circulation of blood inside the muscle compartment. The decrease in blood flow to the muscles causes an increase in lactic acid, which results in increased pain and difficulty using the muscles. The patient has to stop running. Many of these patients go undiagnosed and are criticized as "wusses" because they are "unwilling" to run far.

One of the patients I operated on had been seen at two medical centers and both parents were physicians. For reasons best known to them, they elected to have me treat their child. The key to treatment is, as I discuss so frequently, listening to the patient, believing the patient, asking the right questions and making the right diagnosis. If you don't make the correct diagnosis: surprise, surprise! You won't get the patient better. Sometimes increased compartment pressures can be measured before and after exercise. With the correct diagnosis, in the operating room, a small incision is made in the upper anterolateral lower leg. A surgical scissors may be used to slice open the tough sleeve of tissue which surrounds the muscle compartment. Takes less than 20 minutes. Full recovery. "Easy" operation. "Hard" diagnosis.

Note to coaches, physical education teachers and pediatricians: If you see a child struggling to run distance, do not berate him as a wuss. Consider this diagnosis and refer him for evaluation of this possibility. Pediatricians: Put the question, "Do you have trouble running long distance?" into your yearly evaluation of teenagers. The typical delay from onset of symptoms to diagnosis is almost two years. Children who struggle to run distance may have other issues, including congenital heart problems, asthma, congenital small lungs or poor nutrition.

Glomus Tumor

Another syndrome. Another more or less easy operation, yet difficult diagnosis. First, let me discuss in broad strokes the difference between benign tumors and malignant tumors or cancers. Cancers are growths of cells which are wildly out of control. They often spread to multiple parts of the body. Benign tumors are slow-growing masses of tissue. They have "controlled" growth. One way I understand benign tumors is the following. During our growth as an embryo and later, there are constant chemical signals to various cells and groups of cells. Some of these signals may contain chemical instructions to start growing, continue growing, stop growing or even die. When joints are formed in the developing embryo, certain cells are signaled to die in the area where a joint space forms. In the development of benign tumors, I think that certain cells or groups of cells fail to receive a signal to stop growing or they lose the ability to receive or understand the signal to stop growing. So, they keep growing in a slow "controlled" fashion.

There is an anatomic structure near the skin called a glomus body. The glomus body is thought to play a role in temperature regulation by shunting blood flow. Glomus bodies are most common in the fingertips. Benign tumors of the glomus body, called glomus tumors, are rare and usually occur in the fingertips, often under the nail bed. The characteristic presentation of a patient with a glomus tumor is the complaint of disturbing pain in a fingertip with a totally normal physical examination. In reported series of patients with glomus tumors, the average patient has seen multiple physicians without a correct diagnosis. The average patient with a glomus tumor has had pain for seven years before diagnosis is made. If the average length of time from onset of pain to diagnosis is seven years, this means half have gone undiagnosed for longer than that. A few patients recognize that their symptoms are exacerbated by exposure of the finger to cold.

In my practice, I have seen seven patients with glomus tumors whom I diagnosed on their first visit to me. If I have missed others, I am unaware of it. When I learned about this diagnosis in my training, I found it fascinating. I was always on the lookout for patients with this problem. The first step in diagnosing a glomus tumor is to be thinking about it and looking for it. A few of these patients had a bluish spot under the fingernail. Transillumination of the end of the finger helped in the diagnosis of others. I saw a one to two-millimeter grayish spot on transillumination. Other patients had point tenderness to pressure from the tip of a pen without other abnormality on physical exam. Looking for temperature sensitivity by placing an ice cube on the area of point tenderness helped in only a few cases. In the case of the bluish discoloration or the spot seen on transillumination, the diagnosis is much easier. Sometimes, point tenderness was the only confirmatory finding. If you press with the tip of a pen, the tender area will only be a few millimeters wide.

The surgery is simple, as I say, for an arguable definition of simple. For a glomus tumor of the nail bed, with local anesthesia, under a ten-power operating microscope, cut a 5x5 millimeter square with a tiny, sharp blade, just through the nail. Lift off the small square of nail. Make a similar cut through the nail bed on three sides of the square. Lift up the flap of the nail bed tissue with a tiny hook. Then, and only then, if your diagnosis is correct, you will see a small (few millimeter) translucent mass. Scoop out the mass with small ear curettes. Make sure all of the abnormal tissue is removed. Replace the nail bed tissue flap. You are done. As I said at the start: Operation "simple"; diagnosis difficult, unless the evaluating doctor is alert to the possibility of the diagnosis of glomus tumor.

Septic Arthritis of the Acromioclavicular Joint

Another rare and unusual diagnosis. Early one Sunday morning, a long-time patient of mine called me complaining of severe pain in his right shoulder. He had come to the hospital emergency room on Saturday evening complaining of right shoulder pain. The emergency room physician assumed bursitis and gave him a cortisone shot. The patient returned to the ER six hours later with increasingly severe pain. He was seen by a physician's assistant. Again, I write about the importance of protocols and the importance of following protocols. Protocol, at this hospital, required that all patients returning to the hospital emergency room be seen by a physician. Protocol was not followed. The physician's assistant who saw this patient assumed this patient was histrionic and summarily sent him out. The patient called me a few hours later, desperate because of the severity of his pain. As I stated above, I knew this patient. I knew this patient was "real." I knew this patient was not histrionic. I told him to come directly back to the ER. I drove in to meet him.

As I have discussed previously, when I examine a patient, I do not randomly touch the patient. I systematically palpate specific structures, in a specific order, looking for specific areas of tenderness. As part of my examination, as part of my protocol for examining the shoulder, I pushed on the joint between the collarbone and the bone that forms the rest of the shoulder (acromioclavicular joint). Chandelier sign! What is a chandelier sign? Tenderness to palpation which is so severe that the patient rises off the table and metaphorically hits the chandelier. I diagnosed an acute bacterial infection in the acromioclavicular joint and called the operating room to schedule urgent surgery. An acute bacterial infection is the most likely cause of pain in a joint which is that severe. Gout and pseudogout can also cause severe joint pain. The emergency room physician told me that if my diagnosis was correct, he would give me a six pack of beer. At operation, there was indeed a bacterial infection in that joint. Really rare. I only ever saw one infection in that joint. Never did get that six pack of beer. Still waiting. Don't blame the ER doc for missing it. I talk a lot about protocols.

A careful shoulder exam that specifically examined and palpated each structure sequentially might have allowed an earlier diagnosis. It is hard to make a rare diagnosis early. It is much easier when you are the third doc.

Meningococcal Septicemia and Septic Arthritis

Another time I was called to the ER in the evening to see a patient with a swollen, painful, warm wrist. I was told the patient had a temperature of 103 degrees F. I reached the ER within 20 minutes. While standing at the bedside evaluating the patient and his wrist, I watched a knee joint and an ankle joint swell up over the next half hour. The patient rapidly became increasingly seriously ill. Eventually, the patient was diagnosed with septicemia (infection in the bloodstream) with meningococcus, the bacteria which causes meningitis. The wrist was seriously infected and needed arthroscopy to wash out the joint. The patient was deemed too ill to be taken to the operating room. So, we came to him. Operating personnel and equipment came to the ICU and set up for surgery. Under local anesthesia, I operated to wash out the joint in the ICU. Once again, thinking outside of the cage.

Arcane Niches of Medical Lore

The medical world is filled with savants who specialize in and research in small, arcane niches of medical lore. One example is the book *Borderlands of the Normal and Early Pathologic in Skeletal Roentgenology*, 11th edition, by Kohler and Zimmer, translated and edited by Stefan Wilk, 1968. There are other books like it, but this was a classic when I was in my training. The authors of the many past editions spent entire lifetimes collecting the oddities of X-ray findings and sorting out the variants of normal anatomy seen on X-ray and where these variants intersected with the abnormal.

This stuff is often of only arcane interest but can be useful. Some years ago, I inherited patients after one of my partners retired. My retiring partner had treated a patient who had suffered a wrist fracture in an automobile accident. On the acute X-ray of the wrist, there was an obvious indentation in the distal end of the radius consistent with a non-displaced fracture, which had entered the joint. My partner treated this patient in a cast for six weeks. Four months later, my partner ordered an MRI of the wrist, because of continuing wrist pain. About a year later, after my partner had retired, I received a letter from the patient's attorney asking me to testify in the third-party liability case related to the accident.

In preparing for my testimony, I reviewed the patient's records in detail. I noted that the MRI did not show any altered signal consistent with a four-month-old healed fracture. MRI findings after a fracture will last for at least several years. I double checked that the MRI was of this patient. With an MRI showing no increased signal, there was no way this patient had had a fracture at the time of the accident. Trying to explain the indentation in the distal end of the radius, I opened my personal copy of "Borderlands" and perused the section on the distal radius.

When babies are born, much of their skeleton is cartilage rather than bone. As children grow, the cartilage in their bones is replaced by bone in a progressive fashion. At specific areas inside of the cartilage, blood vessels grow in and a focus of bone formation begins. The focus of bone formation then spreads until all of the cartilage is converted to bone. Normally, there are two foci of initial bone formation in the distal radius that eventually merge smoothly. Rarely, the two foci of bone formation do not fully merge and leave a small divot at the articular surface more to the little finger side of the distal radius. There was a picture in "Borderlands" which exactly matched this patient's X-ray finding. I concluded that there had not been a fracture but this subtle abnormality, which looked like a fracture. I called the attorney and told him that my partner's diagnosis had been incorrect. There was no fracture. Settle the case. The book is a treasure trove of oddities like that.

Sir Sydney Sunderland published a book, *Nerves and Nerve Injuries.* The second edition was published in 1978. In his research, he dissected hundreds of cadaver arms in extensive and exquisite detail. In his book he details for each nerve when different branches leave the nerve to enter a specific muscle. For a given nerve, he will say that a certain branch comes off, for example, 3–5 cm after a specific structure 23% of the time, 5–7 cm 39% of the time, etc. Or he might say that a specific muscle is innervated by Nerve A 96% of the time and by Nerve B 4% of the time. This information is useful, especially when trying to figure out a diagnosis that may not be clear.

For example, there is a nerve in the forearm called the anterior interosseous nerve. This nerve innervates muscles deep in the forearm, specifically the muscles that cause the tips of the thumb and index finger to flex. If this nerve loses function due to pressure on it, the only physical findings may be weakness or loss of function of the tips of the thumb and index finger. That is the clinical presentation most of the time. Rarely, the anterior interosseous nerve only innervates the muscle that flexes the tip of the thumb. If a patient comes in complaining of the inability to flex the tip of the thumb as the only complaint, there are two possibilities: The spontaneous rupture of the tendon to the tip of the thumb, which may occur in patients with severe rheumatoid arthritis, and the rare case of compression of the anterior interosseous nerve, which is only innervating the muscle which bends the tip of the thumb. Knowledge of this possibility can prevent a hand surgeon from operating for a ruptured tendon when the tendon is actually intact.

Painful Pisiform Syndrome

The fields of medicine and surgery are filled with arcane oddities. A good physician will constantly be on the lookout for them. I have already discussed a number of them. Here is another. If you palpate the heel of your hand in line with the little finger, you will feel a bony prominence which is a small wrist bone called the pisiform. While this bone is described as one of the eight small bones which form the wrist joint, actually this bone is not part of the wrist joint. It is inserted in the middle of a tendon which crosses the wrist, similar to the patella or kneecap, which is, in essence, inserted into the quadriceps tendon. The patella serves to displace the quadriceps tendon away from the axis of rotation, which increases the power of the quadriceps muscle in straightening the knee joint. The undersurface of the patella glides against the distal end of the femur, smoothing the glide of the contraction of the quadriceps muscle. The pisiform bone serves a similar function in moving the tendon (flexor carpi ulnaris) away from the axis of rotation of the wrist and in smoothing the glide of the tendon during movement of the wrist joint.

Occasionally, patients complain of pain in this region. They are tender to direct palpation of the pisiform. The rest of their physical examination is normal. X-rays and MRIs are normal. Some of them may have early arthritis of the underlying joint, but this often cannot be imaged. When rest, anti-inflammatory medication and time do not solve the problem, the pisiform bone can be excised. I have done this operation five or six times with happy patients post-op. On a few other occasions, patients' MRIs showed benign fluid-filled cysts called ganglions involving the joint under the pisiform. Excision of the pisiform and the underlying ganglion provided relief of pain. This is another situation in which a failure to perform a thorough examination protocol of the hand and wrist, one which omits palpation of the pisiform, will fail to elicit this diagnosis.

Kienbocks Disease: Proximal Row Carpectomy

The wrist joint consists of two rows of small bones held together by numerous ligaments. One of the bones in the first row is box-like in shape and is called the lunate. For reasons not entirely clear, this bone occasionally loses its blood supply. This occurs more often in men than in women. It occurs more often between the ages of 20 and 40 and occurs approximately 1 in 10,000 people. When the bone dies from the loss of blood supply, it gradually collapses. Living bone continually remodels and responds actively to stress. Dead bone is unable to respond to stress and eventually breaks and collapses from material fatigue, similar to metal fatigue I have discussed earlier. The uneven surfaces of the collapsed bone cause serious pain and stiffness in the wrist.

Revascularization is sometimes attempted for early cases which have not collapsed. For later cases the collapsed bone has to be removed. Then the question occurs, "What do I do next?" There is a long history of trying to replace the collapsed bone with an artificial bone. Generally, the results are not good. The stability of a normal wrist joint comes from the attachments of the many supporting ligaments. The artificial bones do not have attachments to the ligaments and often displace out of position. Another treatment involves trying to fuse some of the remaining wrist bones together for stability. The abnormal stresses which result from this partial wrist fusion often cause degenerative arthritis at the neighboring joints. Fusing all of the wrist bones together may relieve a patient's pain; however, the lack of motion at the wrist is a significant handicap to patients. The simple task of wiping your bottom after going to the bathroom actually requires about 30 degrees of flexion at the wrist. Thus, a full wrist fusion is only used as a last resort salvage procedure.

In 1939, a surgeon in London tried removing the first row of bones of the wrist (proximal row carpectomy) in a patient for treatment of failure to heal a fracture of a different bone, the scaphoid. Removing an entire row of bones from the wrist seems bizarre. Seriously, the procedure sounds absurd. I remain amazed at how often intuitive, *a priori* reasoning fails when trying to decide what works and what will not work in medicine. Somehow this surgeon was on to something. The results of this procedure are remarkable. I performed this procedure about 20 times in my career without a single unhappy patient. The results last. None of my patients returned later due to increasing wrist pain and stiffness.

I once saw a patient with a severe lymphangitis infection of his arm. Some years earlier he had previously had a proximal row carpectomy which had not done well. He had a low level of persistent pain. An MRI scan showed increased fluid within the proximal row carpectomy joint space. Concerned that he had a septic arthritis in the joint space, I operated by arthroscopy to examine this "artificial" joint. There was no infection in the joint. However, the lining of the joint was severely inflamed. I cleaned out the inflamed tissue using the wrist arthroscope. His wrist pain went away. I cured the arm infection with antibiotics. If I had seen this patient without the infection, I do not think I would have reached the point of recommending arthroscopy of the proximal row carpectomy joint. I cured his chronic wrist pain by serendipity because of my assumption that this joint was also infected.

CHAPTER TWENTY-ONE

Conclusion

I n my last six months of practice, I was called to the ER to see a new trauma patient. He was riding a bicycle downhill fast when a car suddenly pulled in front of him. He hit the car, went over the hood and landed on both of his hands. When I saw him in the ER, both of his wrists were severely deformed and swollen. Within an hour he developed numbness and tingling in both hands. When I entered the patient's cubicle in the ER, I was confronted with two terrified people: one, the patient; the other, his wife. I was able to reassure them that I could treat this problem although they should expect it to take about four months of treatment. I did not promise normal wrists. X-rays showed that both wrists were shattered into multiple fragments involving the joint surfaces.

I took the patient to the OR. Due to the severe fragmentation, I decided to try the 20 pounds of traction straight down, which I mentioned earlier in this book. With the traction and gentle manipulation of the fragments, I obtained satisfactory position of the fragments of both wrists. I then applied external fixators while the patient was in the vertical traction. After the application of the external fixator, I operated to perform an immediate carpal tunnel release on each wrist.

I arranged for this patient to be discharged from the hospital the next day and to come directly to my office to see Lynne in order to immediately begin early hand therapy. The patient came to his first visit with Lynne with marked anxiety. Lynne began therapy slowly in order to gain the patient's confidence.

The patient did remarkably well. The nerves recovered quickly and completely. He gained acceptable motion in both wrists and hands. With two useful hands, he was able to return to work.

All of my education, training and experience, which I have highlighted in this book, and all of Lynne's education, training and experience came together to obtain an excellent result for a potentially severely disabling injury. The training and experience Lynne and I have had, discussed and elaborated in this book allowed us to obtain such a good result in such a difficult situation.

As I have rambled on throughout this book, I have tried to give some sense of what the practice of medicine and surgery is like. The interaction with a patient can veer from the sublime to the ridiculous, from the heroic to the pathetic and from the mundane to the intellectually fascinating. There are times in athletics when time seems to slow; you are in a groove and your activity suddenly seems easier, more natural and more effective than usual. Similarly, there are times in medicine and surgery when everything seems to come together and click. Some of the "quick" diagnoses I made and discussed in this book were similar times. There are also the rare times you flub and miss. There are times when a complicated surgery seems to flow effortlessly and easily. Then there are the rare complications in which patients do poorly. All of these experiences were part of the practice of medicine and surgery I was fortunate to live through.

I have walked into an examination room and met a childhood friend of my sister from 40 years before. I have walked into an examination room and met a patient who had been a patient of my father, a pediatrician. Remember, my father was 45 years old when I was born. On multiple occasions I have walked into an examination area of an emergency room to see an absolutely terrified, injured patient and succeeded in calming him down, reassuring him and caring for him. I am proud of what I was able to accomplish.

The practice of medicine and surgery involves the heroic, such as I began this book with. It involves the grief stricken, such as I also discussed as part of my early training. It involves ethical challenges, which I have also discussed. The practice of medicine and surgery involves many good people trying as hard as they can to do as well as they can. And unfortunately, it involves others sliding by. Doctors are human like everybody else.

In the course of writing this manuscript I have ambled and traipsed through many a brambled garden in the unweeded recesses of my mind. I hope I have been able to transmit some of the wonder and awe I found in the practice of medicine and surgery. If you the reader are a potential patient, I hope I have served to educate you in the importance of being an involved and knowledge-able patient when, unfortunately, you are forced to act that role in your life. If you the reader are a medical student, resident in training or practicing physi-cian, I hope I have provided useful, practical tips and pearls. For both, I hope I have entertained and educated.